She's 4 feet, 8 inches of heartfelt ferocity, and nothing can stop this post-pubescent spitfire from claiming her fairytale—not jarring tragedy, not penile incompetence, not even the explosive demise of a new marriage. Not until Robyn finds her happily ever after...alone.

"It's a powerful glimpse into one woman's quest for happiness. Robyn will yank on your heartstrings one moment and then tickle your funny bone the next. Hang on for the ride!"
   --Alex J. Cavanaugh, Author of the best-selling Cassa series and Dragon of the Stars

"Woman on the Verge is clever, sarcastic, and darkly funny, but above that, it's heartfelt. It's a refreshingly honest look at the mythical fairytale romance, and if it doesn't tug on your heartstrings or make you laugh out loud then you clearly do not have a human soul."
   --Bryan Pedas, Blogger, A Beer For The Shower

"This story is fucking awesome!" and in reference to one particular scene, "I was so moved by her writing, I shared it with my husband. He was so deeply touched, he was unable to speak for a long time. He took what Robyn wrote to heart and made the changes that needed to be made...The transformation has been amazing."
   --Elsie Amata, Blogger, Mock Turtle Musings

Cover Photography by the fun-filled crew Roseville, CA.
Cover Graphic Design by the awesome artist, author, and friend, Bryan Pedas.

Author's Notes:

My memoir-ish novel includes overflowing cupfuls of honesty and scattered pinches of artistic liberty. It's 100% true and 100% creative. We'll call it *creative non-fiction.*

Nearly all characters' names and identifying facets were changed.

Identifying information regarding the male suitors and prospective suitors was altered or omitted. Any resemblance to actual men is either a mere coincidence, or due solely to the fact that people's idiosyncratic dating behaviors are more universal than we care to admit.

Finally, I do not recommend this book for:

1) Children
2) The Narrow-minded or
3) Martha Stewart

Dedication:

To the readers of my blog, Life by Chocolate, you have been unfaltering in your loyalty, caring, encouragement, hilarity, and playfulness. And so, my dear sillies, this one's for you. Lovingly.

Woman on the Verge of Paradise

Introduction: Paradise

"Mm, mm, this feels so good."

"You're delicious," he whispers. "I want to devour you tonight."

His brawny arms, luscious lips and tantalizing fingertips offer a bliss I've never known before. He's unbelievably attentive, passionate and incredibly hot. Plus he's mine, all mine, right now, completely naked and in bed with me.

"Mm, mm," I respond. "Yes, yes. I'm all yours."

"Are you sure you're ready, darling?"

God he's so caring, so sensitive and manly at the same time. "I'm sure. I want you. Take me all night long, baby."

He smooths his heated palm along my face, his eyes ecstatically beaming. Our hearts race with excited passion. He pauses to reach towards the nightstand, Trojans in plain sight.

—*happens every time.*

My body jolts. My eyelids shoot open. "Damn radio alarm!"

—*dream is never mine.*

Pushing myself up to sitting position, I bemoan, "Can't even get lucky in my dreams."

I sigh heavily, regrettably, then pull up the hem of my lengthy pink and white Hello Kitty pajama shirt to sneak a peek. My granny panties, still on.

—*Yet I yearn so much, to awaken to your touch.*

"He was such a good one too." I draw out a long, hard breath mixed with sexual repression and hatred for mornings.

4

"Refocus," I tell myself.

I turn to study the numbers on the face of my radio alarm clock: 7:34.

My next sigh is loud enough to awake the neighbors.

I gaze longingly at my bed sheets.

"He's gone." It's been so long since I've had sex, I realize.

"Seems like eighty-five years," I state with lackadaisical factuality.

My head plops back onto my pillow. My arm extends itself alongside my body, grazing the comforter, carefully, hopefully, as if intent on finding a part of the man, at least his penis, thereby proving it wasn't a dream. And I could get lucky after all.

—everything I see. Still, you don't belong to me.

"Shut the fuck up!"

My body undergoes the physical challenges of pushing itself off the mattress and into a somewhat vertical frame. I haphazardly pull my dresser drawers out, one by one, plucking and tossing on garments that will undoubtedly clash in the daylight.

Trudging into the bathroom, I conduct my standard 4.75 second make-up job. Not to brag, but I could pass for someone who spends almost no time at all getting pretty.

Molecules of thought solidify, as I slog through the hallway.

"Food." I like food. "Must eat."

I find myself in the kitchen attempting to pour Kashi into a bowl, but realize I neglected to open the box. So I open the box.

Milk is needed. The microwave door swings open, seemingly by my hand. Oops. "Note to self," I jest. "This, self, is microwave, not fridge. Try again."

I find the refrigerator now, in the same spot it's always been. A carton of vanilla soy milk beckons.

I manage to prepare, then quickly eat, breakfast.

As I place my bowl in the sink, I realize I hadn't tasted my food. It's probably for the best, I think. I don't like that healthy shit anyway.

The hallway seems so long this morning. I'm still tired, not one of those God awful annoying chipper morning people like Kelly Ripa. Were I married to her fine looking husband, I would be, but only if she was out of the picture. Damn chipper bitch.

I step towards my bed and reach for the radio alarm. Now, Charlene's ballad, "I've Never Been to Me" resonates.

I pause, after shutting it off.

Great song, I think, sincerely. We're always searching outside of ourselves. Beauty's inside. I grin, confident to tackle a new day.

My purse rests at the foot of my bed, and I wrap my hand around its handle.

Seconds later, I'm at the front door.

It's always a bit tricky to get out without Mojo zipping by me and running away. He's an indoor cat; we'd like to keep it that way. Mojo darts towards me. I slither out abruptly and shut the door behind, before that rascal could cut loose.

The crisp morning air sends an awakening chill to my eardrums, as if to shout loud and clear: "It was only a dream, girlfriend!" I know. I know.

Ah, but he was so sexy and so caring and so naked and so in bed with me and so on the verge of devouring every last inch of me. I snort out a sharp whiff of disappointment, while turning my keys to lock the dead-bolt.

I proceed to hop down the driveway to the mailbox, a daily ritual since I moved here nearly a year ago.

It's one thing I love about suburbia: the free-standing mailboxes with little red arms that you push up when you want a pick-up. If only it were so easy to get a man or a first class delivery from one of those hot UPS drivers in tight brown shorts.

No such luck today, but I'm excited to find a piece of mail personally addressed to me. Dawn's handwriting and return address cross the face of the small but bulgy envelope. I'm always nervous when I hear from Dawn. We love each other quietly, almost secretly. We've had our sisterly ups and downs, yet the downs have taken us to dark, intense places that neither of us really understands or wants to understand.

I anxiously open the envelope to find a note, along with a delicate gold chain strung through the loop of a heart-shaped pendant. The heart is embellished by a Jewish star; atop the star, the small Hebrew letters, *chet* and *yud*, which together spell "chai" meaning "life."[1]

I secure the necklace in my fist, as I read Dawn's note:

December 24, 2011

Hey Robyn ~ I've been meaning to mail this to you for a long time. This necklace is Mom's and I never wear it. I thought you'd like it. Have a great 2012!!!
Love,
Dawn

My eyes transfix on "chai." The word's sameness with the spelling of English "chai" doesn't escape me, especially because I'm bound for a chocolate chai tea frost at Tea Fusion this morning.

I unclasp the chain and wrap the necklace around my neck, then fasten it. I press the charm lightly against my neckline. A piece of Mom on me now, I gaze nostalgically at the houses across the street.

This residential niche of Northern California reminds me of West 84th Place, where I grew up. An image of our old house greets me, its sky blue exterior, accented with navy blue; silvery-black numbers "8, 4, 2, 9" that Dawn had painted in ceramics class at Orville Wright Junior High School, aligned vertically along the front door frame.

Now, as if I'd just unlocked that door, I'm welcomed by a surge of memories.

Chapter One: Happiness

Have you ever noticed that catastrophic events tend to occur on otherwise mundane days?

It was just another weekend morning in the spring of 1975. I'd cleaned off a bowl of Lucky Charms, set it in the kitchen sink alongside a greasy gunk-filled black frying pan.

Ten minutes earlier, my rambunctious brothers had darted out the front door to toss a baseball.

The house was quiet, save for Sunday morning cartoon murmurs emitted from the monstrous Zenith—the family room's main draw.

Everything was fine so far. Perfectly boring. Within seconds, though, completely unaware, I'd receive the news.

Dawn spun from the living room into the kitchen, when she closed in on me.

"Robyn, Mommy told me how babies are made. Wanna know?" Dawn allowed no time for response.

A fragile nine year old, I planned to avoid boys forever. Until I married one. And after that too. But I'd be way older then, like 19. In this moment, I wasn't at all curious about boys or babies or anything else except stepping back into the family room to watch Josie and the Pussy Cats.

Yet Dawn commanded vast wisdom and authority. My big sister, the first of four, was a 10 year old! So as she stood inches from me on the blue and white speckled kitchen tiles, I couldn't help but pay attention.

Dawn scrunched up her face in preparation. She inhaled quickly, decisively. Next, the news poured out in a tone overflowing with equal measures of disgust and glory. "The man puts his penis in the woman's va-gi-na." As she infused enthusiastic emphasis on each syllable of "va-gi-na," Dawn's eyebrows shot up and down her forehead.

I froze, flustered, mortified, determined to shake off this horrifyingly disturbing news-bite.

Dawn's talk was an anomaly. Usually, a loud silence choked our home with messages of shame about our bodies and sexuality. Sex was never to be discussed, talked about, or, God forbid, delighted in.

Once I failed to wear panties under my blue cotton dress before a routine doctor's visit. This still perplexes me. How could Mom and I forget? Did I want to go au natural? Was Mom trying to save time? Too scattered by four young kids at home?

I was four then, second in line. Like many pieces of my childhood, this incident will never make sense. Dr. Glickman held a cold stethoscope to my petite chest. He checked my leg reflexes and couldn't help but notice my lack of panties. Mom hadn't reacted nor offered any explanation for this.

Even before child abuse mandates were in full-swing, the doctor handled the situation as gracefully but responsibly as possible. He very gently touched his thumb to my vaginal lips, took a quick peek inside (checking for bleeding or redness, anything unusual), released his hand and resumed a friendly, professional demeanor.

Meanwhile, Mom's face had turned pink.

At home, when the entire family gazed at the TV screen, Mom announced "Dr. Glickman was very thorough with Robyn today. He even" —she giggled— "checked her private girl parts." Dad chuckled. The rest of us fell silent.

Having worked in social services for a couple of decades now, I've seen the devastating effects of sexual and physical abuse. It's shockingly pervasive, numbers of incomprehensible incidents ever on the rise.

If my parents were sexually or physically abused as kids, and we're not sure, they refrained from passing down these patterns. I'm very lucky and grateful for this.

Emotional abuse and neglect, though, pose dangers of going unnoticed, even and especially by their victims.

In lieu of no visible scars, and having grown up in a White middle class, highly respected and well educated family, I neither recognized nor acknowledged that I navigated a chronic slathering of this throughout my childhood. Not until adulthood would I even consider the possibility.

After classes at Westrey Swim School, when I was maybe seven, our whole family paraded into Sizzler for dinner. I donned my red Kentwood Elementary sweat shirt, which fit like a dress, over my bathing suit.

"Miss Kentwood," teased a stranger, a tall man dressed in jeans and a mustard yellow t-shirt. With arms outstretched, he came at me. I

11

didn't know him. What's going on? It happened so fast. I was suddenly up in the air, above his head, and then back down. Thankfully, he let me go.

I turned towards Mom and Dad, yards away now, having procured a table for the family. I walked as fast as I could towards them.

Dawn looked at me, concerned. "Mom and Dad, did you see that man pick up Robyn?"

They guffawed and elbow-nudged each other. "Yeah we saw it." Mom said. "We think he was trying to see if she was wearing anything under her sweatshirt." Mom and Dad looked at each other, like two kids trying to refrain from bursting into uproarious laughter.

I sat despondent. Nobody noticed. Well, maybe Dawn did.

I ate only a few nibbles of fries.

The late bloomer that I was—and still am. I'm still waiting to bloom—I didn't start my period until age 17. When I called Mom and asked that she bring home tampons that day, she agreed. But Mom came home with a large box of Stayfree Maxi Pads instead.

"Robyn, you need to use pads," Mom instructed. "Tampons cause Toxic Shock Syndrome and can kill you."

That was it for my sex education from the parental unit: Beware of killer tampons.

When Jonathan, the youngest and most charming of the foursome, got his first call from a girl, Adrienne, he wasn't a baby. He was fifteen. Yet Mom remarked that Adrienne was "slutty." Though

Mom so rarely used that kind of language, she proceeded to emphasize that "Girls shouldn't call boys. If they do, they're too aggressive."

All told, if I'd ever have sex, and I likely would *not* ever have sex, I'd wait until marriage. I guess it would be okay then. I guess my parents had sex sometimes. I didn't know, didn't want to think about it.

I only knew that sexual intimacy scared the hell out of me. It's bad and shameful. So I'd learned.

Thus my plan for celibacy guarded my dread of boys and later, men; lust, passion, sex—that surreal, glamorous, devious world others appeared to revel in with glowing ease and confidence. I'd stay away, possibly forever. At least for now.

God, how annoying Jan Brady was! That hyper-dramatic, whiny, agonizing second daughter inspired me to be like Marcia, and not like her. I failed miserably. Dawn played Marcia. As much as I hate admitting it, I played Jan, and I played her well.

Jealous of my big sister's popularity with boys, I despised my freckly face, and had many an imaginary overnight with George Glass.

I lounged in front of the TV one Sunday afternoon, in my early teens, when my brothers' pal Kevin dropped by. The three of them invaded our den. Glenn-David and Kevin settled into either side of me on the black vinyl couch, and Jonathan approached the gargantuan Zenith.

Flipping the channels casually while staring at the screen, he informed me, "We're going to watch the game now."

I snapped in a fury: "You can't do that! I was watching, you BRATS! That's not fair!"

My blood vessels seething, I stomped off towards my bedroom.

"Daang, she needs to get laid!" Kevin remarked.

"I heard that!" I shouted from the hallway, maintaining an enraged demeanor while laughing inside. I reveled in the concept of me as a sexual being, and especially in the knowing that Kevin identified me as such.

"Daang, she has ears like a bat," he added, a bit softer this time.

I shrieked, "Heard that too!" They guffawed, but abruptly silenced themselves, fearfully.

Kevin was just one of many neighborhood kids who gravitated to our house after school and on weekends. He impressed with blue eyes, blond hair, and a surfer's laid back confidence. I'd hoped that someday he'd offer to relieve me of my frustrations, but he never would. I suppose some things stand the test of time: guys hate drama.

Westchester, a middle-class, suburban district of Los Angeles, housed our endearing clan. We were the family whose kids always got good grades, were kind and thoughtful, and didn't mess with drugs or anything even questionably illegal. In our most rebellious state, we could be witnessed after 8:00pm tossing rolls of toilet paper into the neighbors' trees, giggling hysterically, and charging home—panicked that we'd be caught and thrown in jail. Plus, it was bedtime.

In our defense, we hadn't initiated the ritual. Rhonda, the coolest parent on the block, took charge. She even provided all the toilet paper. "Please don't squeeze the Charmin," Rhonda laughed, while doling out rolls of toilet paper.

Rhonda coached me in proper toilet paper launching strategy, pointing at high branches and stepping forward with her right foot in synchronicity with a thrusting arm motion.

"Like this, Rhonda?" I inquired anxiously, flinging my arm back, then raising it with gusto towards the rim of the Smiths' avocado tree. I watched the roll drop clumsily at my feet.

Though I never got beyond adding splashes of tissue to the neighbors' front lawns, those moments were glorious. After-all, rarely did an Engel skirt the line of defiance.

Rather, we'd be seen making pledges at Indian Guides or Girl Scout meetings. Dad was Red Fox, Glenn-David, Sly Owl; and Jonathan, Running Bull. Dawn was in Juniors, Troop 54, and I was a Brownie in Troop 12. The boys excelled in baseball and basketball, football, weightlifting, any and all athletics they took on.

After school and on weekends, our house was the place to be. "So I can play here?" little Jimmy Mendezo asked daily, following a polite knock at the door. He was soon joined by Victor, Daniel, and the Coulter brothers.

Meanwhile, Dawn and I chatted, played board games, or baked lemon squares with the sister-duo who lived across the street, Carrie and Camila.

When Mom bought brownie mix home from the store, as she often did, I readily whipped up a batch.

Jonathan got on the phone to tell his friends, "Come over. Robyn made brownies." Within minutes, the den was filled with boys and brownie crumbs. Thanks to Mom, Betty Crocker, and my instinctive fear of burning precious chocolate, I was a hit amongst the boys.

My parents appeared the idyllic, gracious couple too. Mom reigned as the local chapter president of Woman's American ORT[2] and dad passed drugs to the community; a charming, always humorous pharmacist at Thrifty Drugstore.

"Your dad's so nice," my friends often said. To his credit —Dad created the lyrics and sang with the most gumption—we adopted a family song:

We are the Engel family, yes sirree.
We are the Engel fam-i-lee, ee ee.
We run along, sing our song, play all day, the Engel way
Yes sirree, yes sirree yes sirree ee, ee ee!

Packed in our 1968 red and white striped Rebel station wagon, we proudly belted out this hymn when headed for McDonalds; Yosemite; and our biggest family excursion, a 1980 road trip to Canada to see Mom's home country.

My admiration for Mom grew as I learned more about her. She earned her degree in Home Economics from the University of

Alberta, having graduated top in her class. Her family lost Grandpa Isaac to a heart attack when Mom was only eighteen.

At 27, she moved on her own from Alberta, Canada to Los Angeles, California. Though she'd accepted a job as Head Dietician at Cedar Sinai Medical Center, Mom's primary goal was to find a husband and start a family.

As her 28th birthday loomed, Mom and Dad went on a double date–with other people. They hit it off, ditched their dates, and married three weeks later.

"How could you get married so fast?" Dawn asked Dad one day.

Without hesitation, he responded, "When you care about someone, you know right away."

It sounded lovely. As adults, though, Dawn and I finally calculated the number of months between Mom and Dad's wedding date and Dawn's birth. No matter how we do the math, we arrive at the number eight. Dawn was not born premature, we'd been told. But to this day, we prefer to scoff at basic mathematics in favor of insisting that Mom was ever wholesome.

When the three Engel girls journeyed to Broadway Department store on Sepulveda Boulevard one weekend morning, Dawn asked, "Mom, what first attracted you to Dad?"

I listened intently, too shy to ask these pointed questions but anxious to hear the response.

"Well," Mom started. She stopped to think. And think. It seemed a fair amount of time elapsed before she answered, "he was handsome and…generous."

"Really? Dad used to be generous?" Dawn asked.

"Well," Mom chimed, "yes, he was generous on our first date."

The three of us chuckled in an "I shouldn't be laughing but it's funny" way.

Actually, Mom realized her dreams. On a fast track to family, she readily secured a smart, nice-looking, fairly ambitious husband. She'd dreamt of birthing four kids—two girls and two boys. Within six years, we dutifully provided that exact combination: Dawn and then me, Glenn-David (They couldn't decide between the names Glenn and David, so they went with both) and Jonathan.

Raising four kids wasn't enough for Mom, though. In her late 30's, she enrolled in law school at Inglewood's Northrop University. Every afternoon, I watched her grab a bright yellow highlighter, Number Two pencil, pastel bed-sheet, and hefty Law Journal or two. Mom slipped into the backyard, sprawled out under the apricot tree, and studied for hours.

Inside, we chucked Swanson's TV dinners into our new microwave. It all seemed so effortless—both the nuking and mom's law school undertaking.

"Don't stand too close to the microwave when you're using it, kids." Dad instructed. "It might cause brain damage. Essentially, we don't know. It's a new invention, and not enough research has been done."

While Dad impressed with four-syllable words like "essentially," I figured the benefits far outweighed prospective brain damage. So I'd pull a black vinyl kitchen chair over to the microwave, toss in a

Swanson's TV dinner, and spy through the microwave door of the Amana Radar Range, gawking at how the once small brownie expanded rapidly to ten or fifteen times its original size.

"What a deal!" I'd boast, when it was done. "Look," I'd show my siblings. "I get this huuuge brownie!"

They weren't impressed. "Gross! Those things taste gnarly," Dawn sneered. She was right. It was usually burnt and tasted gnarly. But I still loved those ginormous brownies. [I suppose I've always focused on quantity versus quality of chocolate.]

That Radar Range freed Mom to pour more time into her studies. It worked, though I'm sure she'd have done well regardless. Mom routinely and quietly mentioned having scored second in class on the latest exam. We didn't know the man who edged her out each time, but we loathed the guy.

One day months after graduating, Mom chatted by phone with her girlfriend from law school. "Oh shit!" she shouted.

It was a good "Oh shit!" a happy "Oh shit!", and the only time I ever heard Mom emit an "Oh shit!" She had just learned she'd passed the State Bar, as had her friend —both on their first attempts.

Shortly thereafter, Mom opened a small law office in a popular, trendy locale, walking distance from Hermosa Beach. We were all so proud.

From my young, naïve perspective, Mom and Dad had the perfect marriage. They shared a quick kiss and "I love you" before parting ways each morning. They seemed to have an easy way with each other. Dad threw Mom a big surprise party when she passed the bar with a cake that read "For Edith, the best, Bar none!"

I remember talking with a neighbor about the outbreak of divorces on our street.

"My parents are never going to divorce," I happily boasted.

Happiness: an elusive and illusory key to survival.

I can't forget one painful night. I lay in bed listening to each stride of Dad's black patent leather shoes as they met the wood paneled floor. He trekked through the boys' room next door, making the nightly goodnight kiss rounds. I heard him walk over to Jonathan's bed in the far corner, and then to Glenn-David's bed, closer to my wall.

Next, Dad's shoes entered our bedroom. He approached Dawn's bed and kissed her cheek. I kept my eyes closed, pretending to sleep while awaiting my goodnight kiss.

Time froze.

Dad's footsteps grew faint.

I waited and waited, but he'd left the room and didn't return.

That was one of many nights in which I clung to the fairytale. My sweet, handsome prince loved me forever and without condition. Snuggling my big brown cushy teddy-bear was the only way I could calm myself enough to rest, if not sleep. My bear, my prince, saw me through.

The next morning, I awoke to a slicing pain and the reality that Dad had skipped me when making a round of goodnight kisses.

I had to do something. I couldn't talk to him. All I could think to do was enlist Dawn, my protective big sister, to communicate with him for me. "Ask Dad why he didn't kiss me goodnight," I urged. She agreed to play intermediary.

Dawn left the room and returned shortly thereafter with a report. "He said 'number one, she was asleep and number two, she doesn't like to be kissed.'" More confused by his explanation, I was also more certain that he hated me.

When Mom got wind of the situation, she brought Dad into my room. One by one, my parents said they loved me. But Dad's stance was robotic. He embarked on a monologue.

For starters, he sighed heavily. "I love you but I work very hard every day, only to come home to you not saying 'hello' or asking how my day was. And there's a sink full of dishes and trash that wasn't taken out to the curb. That's what I come home to every single day."

He sighed heavily again. "With four active children, honey, it's not easy for me to remember who's who and what's what."

I looked at Mom. She looked at Dad, contemplating whether or not he'd finished. She nodded, as if he'd done his part.

Dad sighed heavily again before asking, "Do you understand?"

Of course not. Harmful parenting makes no sense. In that moment, though, I nodded in affirmation. What alternatives did I have? I didn't want to hear anything else about my contributions to Dad's miserable existence. Heavy, heavy sigh. And another. Yet once more.

Time and again, Mom escorted Dad to me to affirm that he loved me, and to make sure that I understood his frustrations.

As they departed my room after the apology regarding Dad's failure to kiss me goodnight, Mom turned back towards me and said, in a warm calm voice, "Everything's going to be alright, Robyn. You're going to be fine."

School provided a safe haven, but only inside the classroom. My peers adored me. I voluntarily tutored them in Math and English, and I helped them with their multiplication tables. Teachers dubbed me their "littlest angel."

I didn't know I was very different, or different at all, from the other kids. I initially learned this at Kentwood Elementary School.

Recess and lunch times were the worst. At the bell's blasting, I ran onto Kentwood Elementary's endless black-top, classmates scurrying to their favorite spots for vicious games of dodge ball, sock ball or—the one I hated most—Red Rover.

Ridicule began when I wandered aimlessly in search of a playmate. They slapped my head and brushed by with "How's the weather down there?" and "Get out of the way, you shrimp!"

With hundreds of kids running wild, the two Yard Monitors attempted to patrol the entire area by blowing into fat, shiny, silver whistles every few seconds. They either never witnessed the mockery, or were concerned with bigger problems of the day, like kids bringing Skittles, Pop Rocks, or Coca Cola to school. (How times have changed.)

I grew accustomed to the teasing, and hadn't told anyone about it. Nor did anyone, including my parents, ever initiate a conversation about being "different." So I didn't know any better than to take the mistreatment, attempt to ignore it, and feel like garbage.

April 24, 1979: Dear Diary, Here I am 12 going on 13 in June. I wish I was pretty and also at least 4 ft. 10. Right now all my measurements are excact. I wear a seven in clothes. I fit size 1 in shoes. I am 50 lbs. and 4 ft. tall. Everyone in school seems to have a boyfriend or girlfriend. I can't imagine ever going on a date & doubt if I'll ever get married! Who would marry me? Why did God make me the one to be so small and to be called names every single solitary day? I DON'T KNOW! I JUST DON'T KNOW!

In retrospect, I wish I'd shown those bullies the weather *down there*, with their faces flat against the hot asphalt following a swift, brash kick to each kneecap.

Teachers and friends, though, would placate me with the saying, "Good things come in small packages." That statement was somewhat consoling.

However, many years later, when I began dating and getting sexually intimate with men, I'd learn that small packages are not necessarily good.

Fortunately, friendships always came easy.

I stood by a blue-gray door that would open to my first day of Mrs. Matsuda's ninth grade Geometry class at Orville Wright Junior High School. Two of us arrived ten minutes early and planted ourselves in standing position, clinging to our three-ring binders. The other girl looked timid, so I broke the ice.

"Hi. I'm Robyn."

"I'm Susan," she smiled sweetly. "It's nice to meet you."

"It's nice to meet you too." I'd never seen her before. "Are you from Westchester, Susan?"

"No," she responded, with a slight guffaw. "Farther away. Actually, my family recently moved here from the Philippines."

"Wow. That's hard. Well, welcome."

Clearly grateful to make a new friend, Susan said, "Thank you."

When Mrs. Matsuda opened the door, Susan and I deliberately sat next to each other, as we would in every class we'd share for the remainder of our school days.

It wasn't long before Susan began to split her attention between me and Mike. I was happy for Susan, though. Unlike the other blond cuties, Mike was a nice, quiet, non-surfer, smart one.

She described a moment of their first date, "We sat outside on the front porch talking, Robyn. He took off his jacket and put it around me, because it was getting cold."

My eyes widened. "That's sooo romantic, Susan."

Thereafter, I pined for a guy who would take off his jacket for me.

Still, I could never relate to boys in a way that felt anything but weird. I was usually too shy to talk or even say "hi" to them. On occasion, though, a (very) random guy paid attention to me.

There was Robbie, for example, who used to visit the library every week when I did Library Service as an elective at Orville Wright.

24

Robbie was a lanky kid who donned thick-framed glasses, resembling a White Steve Urkel. He sauntered in whenever I managed the front desk. It was Robbie's "free period," or so he told me.

I had no interest in Robbie, but I liked the attention. When I told Susan about him, she suggested I give Robbie a chance. "Robyn, he really likes you. He seems like a nice guy," she goaded.

Easy for you to say, I thought. You got one who doesn't pull his pants up above his belly button.

One day Robbie leaned in really close, reading the title of a book I was stamping (this was back in the day when we stamped a book's due date on the front inside cover), and "accidentally" touched his hand to mine.

"Wow, your skin is really soft, Robyn," he told me.

Robbie's gentle touch felt sweet, as did the compliment. "Thanks," I said softly, slightly blushing.

"Robyn?"

"Yeah?" I hid my giddiness, awaiting the question. Was he going to ask for a date? Tell me he'd been in love with me since he first set eyes on me? Ask me the all-important question of the day: "Will you go with me?"[3]

Robbie quickly turned his head from side to side, as if to assure nobody was around.

I scanned our immediate vicinity too. Nobody else was nearby. It was just me and Robbie. Robbie and Robyn, all alone at the front desk of Orville Wright Junior High School's library. Nobody else existed in the world.

Robbie dropped his head closer, preparing to ask the question. I could almost envision butterflies fluttering joyously around my heart.

"Robyn," he said with pause. "Do you have fifty cents I can borrow for a soda? I'll pay you back next week."

And so it went. My spectacularly unromantic romantic life.

My open-hearted, tenacious, klutzy quest for love, passion, and self-worth.

My story: the anti-fairytale.

Chapter Two: Crushing

Why we women flatter ourselves by pining for "the one that got away," I don't know. Did it ever occur to us that perhaps he got away because he wanted to get away—far, far away, where we couldn't possibly find him? Or because he's a scumbag cheat who hooks-up and gets away, time and again? Or because he never noticed us in the first place, in which case he couldn't possibly be the one that got away? Or, um, because he's married? If he's gonna cheat on his wife, he's gonna cheat on you, girlfriends. You're not *that* special.

Though I'm much more cynical than romantic, I tend to believe that he'll stick around if he wants to.

While I don't buy into the whole "one that got away" thing, I do miss Joseph. And I can't help but wonder if he was my last good chance for happiness. Maybe I just wasn't yet ready for what he had to offer.

Joseph's love for me revealed a sweet purity I'd never before experienced. Delicate dimples marked either side of his bright, sincere smile. I adored his bold blue-green eyes too. Moreover, Joseph embodied an attractive albeit idiosyncratic mixture of clumsy and generous. He bore chocolate brown greased-back hair, imitation Lacrosse shirts and pants that flooded[4] to expose his skimpy ankles.

I remember every moment of that slice of third grade. Mrs. Siegal had instructed the entire class to play hand ball, as our end-of-the-day Physical Education.

"Tap, tap, tap!" Cindy blared, flinging her hair back for added authoritarian impact. The first to the handball court set the rules, a ritual initiated by the tapping of one's fist on the horizontal line spanning the court wall. Cindy was always first to tap. "No waterfalls except on second serve. You can't do savesies but you can do double-bouncies but only on the first serve. And it's outta bounds if it hits the line but only if you're not the server. And no take-overs!"

Whatever. I didn't care. She'd change the rules every two minutes to suit her needs anyhow.

I hated Cindy.

October 17, 1974: There are some mean people in my class like, a girl named Cindy well, at recess when I play tetherball even If I'm the first one there she says "You can't play, there are too many people" just to get me away from the area. Maybe someday if I get famous someone will read this diary. But not until then! People in my class say I'm babyed because I'm so small. I don't think that's true. Sometimes I want to be someone else like Leanna or Erin. Life would be easier.

I stood watching the ball bounce off the black asphalt, then off of the pale peach wall. Then the blacktop. Then the wall. Over and over.

My turn came. Butterflies swarmed my system, when I realized I'd play against Joseph. I approached him. Joseph smiled and handed me the big red ball. I grinned flirtatiously, blood cells delivering a waterfall of blush to my face. I then became aware that everyone was watching.

I gave that rubber ball my most meek gesture, barely touching it with my right knuckle such that it would take approximately twelve bounces before hitting the wall. Next I scrambled to the end of the line and studied my brown buckle shoes.

Back in the classroom, Mrs. Siegal announced art time. "Draw whatever you feel like drawing." Still overcome by an unfamiliar thrill, I decided to, I don't know, draw a horse. No, a house. Maybe a boat. A flower would be pretty. Oh, I'd just made a spiral design to keep myself busy. My heart kept racing.

Giggling and snickering consumed the back of the classroom. Something major had captured their interest.

"Robyn, dear, come on over here," Mrs. Siegal said.

Gulp. What's going on? I walked to the back of the classroom, where my teacher sat holding a picture to her chest, her face gushing with exciting news. Joseph stood next to her and donned a very proud smile.

"Look what Joseph drew." Mrs. Siegal flipped the paper over to display Joseph's artwork.

I studied the picture, a crayon drawing of me in the blue and green checkered dress I was wearing, with my yellow socks, brown buckle shoes, and spirals of curly brown hair. A big red u-shaped curve centered my face. My nose, a black *L*. My eyes, cobalt blue, and my eyelashes, long and pretty. Above me, huge letters spelled out: "I Love Rodyn."

I stood frozen—scared, overwhelmed, unworthy.

"I feel sick," I told Mom the next morning. "I think I need to stay home from school today."

"Okay, honey."

Wait, how could it be so easy? You didn't feel my forehead, shove a thermometer under my tongue, ask what's wrong or spoil me with tapioca pudding? A bit disappointed and highly remorseful, I kept quiet while viewing a day's worth of television.

Upon returning to Room 8, the flame between me and Joseph extinguished. I eyed my shoes whenever he strolled by. As far as I can remember, we never talked again; I'm not sure if we'd ever spoken in the first place. Nobody else breathed a word about our short and sweet love.

It's as if it never happened.

In Junior High, I fixated on Daniel. His dirty-blonde curly hair and fair skin contrasted harmoniously with his dark brown eyes. Daniel was a girl's fantasy: intelligent, compassionate, smart, and friendly. He always toted a womanly harem, charming them during lunch on the quad, encircled by them in class, and carrying their books to the bus when school commenced. Such a gentleman.

They say "When it's right, you just know it." So I figured, I knew it. Daniel was the one for me. We'd met in eighth grade Honors English. I'd planted myself kitty-corner to him, and looked his way throughout most of the year before Daniel dropped his pen and it rolled to my feet.

I handed it over, nervously. He said "thank you." It was fate.

May 9, 1979: I'm sort of high right now, Diary, because I talked to Daniel today – I think he likes me at least a little. I really like him. We said hi to each other. I want things to work out nice and smoothly. The ice is broken now! But what if I don't see him next year??? And what if he falls in love with someone else?? I'm going to – maybe—ask him to sign my yearbook and write something nice in his. I think about him all the time."

May 17, 1979: As for Daniel, forget it. It's so stupid of me. I don't know. I'll fall in love, someday when I don't expect to (like 50 years from now).

June 4, 1979: Daniel wrote in my yearbook: "It's been nice knowing you. I'm sure I'll see you sometime in the near future." He was sad to write it, I'm sure.

June 12, 1979: We talked for a while. I'm really crazy about him. I feel as if my dreams of being with him are closer to reality than ever before.

June 13, 1979: It's funny what a shithead I've been to even think for a minute that Daniel would like me. He's been really cold to me and didn't even say 'hi' once this week. NEVER EVER again will I ever start to care about someone.

    I didn't see or ponder Daniel much the following years. I'd notice him here and there during high school, and we'd say "hi." I was no longer fixated, though. I rarely saw him and needed a new focus.

    I recently learned that Daniel's been in a long-term relationship. My crush was moot, because I'd never have the one thing he found in a life-partner. In fact, I've been seeking it too: a penis.

    I wish Daniel well. He's a good one.

Brad shined with charisma and all things good. He harbored a quiet confidence, the kind of *still waters* persona I admired. Suave and debonair, Brad typically appeared deep in thought. He was the handsome, dark complexioned, intellectual type who reclined at his desk, resting chin on palm whilst appearing to strategize a plan for world peace.

In actuality, Brad was more likely thinking, "Yowzah! That's one gnarly-ass booger in my nostril!" He didn't seem the type to shelter huge boogers, though. Brad's nose, like his face, was exquisitely sculpted – not too big, not too small. Everything about him appeared just right.

Brad and I engaged in actual discourse too, helping each other with Calculus and Physics problems.

Susan and Mike, still "going together," supported my crush too. Sometimes, during lunch time in the quad, they drew me and Brad over to swap answers on our physics homework. That was fun: talking energy, fusion and atomic charge with my dream guy.

My years at Westchester High had progressed swimmingly until the most dreadful of all dreadful high school events, the prom, hovered overhead. Bids went on sale, $60 for one or $120 for two tickets. The boys played nonchalant, while the girls gossiped like a drunken Martha Stewart at a doily convention.

May 4, 1984: I've felt like crying all week, Di. It just hurts so fuckin much whenever people start talking about the prom. I feel like shit because nobody wants to take me and I don't know how I'll survive these next 2 weeks until it's over. You know what else? I found out that Brad doesn't have a date YET. He's the only guy that I'd love to go with and wish to death he'd ask me. But Denise plans on asking him. She's such a slut and she always gets her guy. Damnit! I want to pick up the phone and call him. But I could never do that. I'd better face the fact that no guy would want to take someone so short to the prom. But Brad – I wish you'd ask me!!! I could die I want to go with him so badly. I hate having these dreams. I could probably make it come true, but I don't know. I just want to be asked.

Incapable of comprehending why the high school years, billed as excitingly promising, were so laden with ugly crap, courage propelled me to make my life better.

I'd seen Dawn go to dances like Winter Wonderland and the prom. Jonathan was going to parties. Glenn-David and I were both too shy, and lacking in confidence, to enter that terrain.

I wanted love and romance and all that to finally begin. Actually, I didn't. I still wasn't ready. Regardless, I didn't want to miss the all-important senior prom. That would be humiliating.

So I viewed my right hand in slow motion, shaking uncontrollably. I witnessed the index finger gently compress each numbered square on the receiver, one by one, until the seventh was pushed. As my heart readied to leave my body, I experienced lengthy oxygenated inhalations but couldn't exhale.

Ring. Ring. "Hello."

"Hi Brad?"

"Yes."

"This is Robyn."

"Hi."

"Hi...Um, I was wondering if you're going to the prom?"

"No, I'm not going."

"Oh"…audible silence for about a year…"okaybye." Click.

I cried loud and hard and for hours.

Then I called Susan.

"I asked Brad to the prom and"—sniffling—"he said 'no', Susan."

"Oh, Rob. I'm sorry, but it's his loss. Hey, you deserve better."

"But he's, he's pretty good," I argued. "And now I'm not going to the prom! It's my loss too."

She sighed. "I'm sorry, Rob. You'll be okay."

At school, I learned through the grapevine that Denise, class hussy, had also asked Brad to the prom. I never even saw that slut talk to him, much less share physics notes. It seemed he'd decided not to go at all, because he didn't want to go with her. I guess Brad did the noble thing, though he shattered my heart in the process.

May 23, 1984: He said "no." He'd already made up his mind not to go before I called. I think he's a jerk now. He's not even going at all. He's told everyone that Denise asked him to go. Of course, they're glad he rejected that slut. In physics the guy next to me asked Brad 'Who did you reject?' He didn't even answer. You can imagine that I felt a bit uncomfortable. I wanted to scream 'HE REJECTED ME!'

Ultimately prom night was mundane. I watched television and turned in early. All that hype and nobody at school appeared to mutter a word about it.

How quickly the monumental becomes the petty. If only today's youth understood this.

We live so many lifetimes in one lifetime. Dreams shift, reality transforms, and emotional resiliency sees us through.

The true misfits are the ones who don't think they are.

Twenty years later, I scoured the L.A. Airport Hilton for Brad—to no avail. He must have bypassed the reunion hoopla. Denise made her presence known, though. True to form, she honed in on her prey: a decent looking but tacky albeit innocent and fairly nice alum. I can't say Denise exhibits poor taste; she targeted me.

During Marvin Gaye's Sexual Healing, I found myself on the dance floor, a fingertip's distance from Denise.

"Hey Robyn, it's so totally cool to see you!" Denise spun in slow circles around me, her long stringy red hair whipping my face as her arms swirled meditatively overhead in Hare-Krishna like fashion. The music continued, and suggested we get down tonight.

"You too Denise."

"Do this now." Denise propped her chest out, shifted her buttocks back and glided towards me. Next she launched a series of pelvic thrusts over my left, then right leg. I slowly stepped back, held a smile and initiated full-throttle gyrations in hopes nobody was watching.

"Woohoo! Let it loose, girlfriend!"

I attempted to embrace the moment and all, but the damn song wouldn't end.

"Say let's exchange numbers. I'll teach you some more dance moves."

Sultry lyrics countered my mood.

"Sure." I flashed a wide grin, wondering at what point in the past two decades Denise had turned hippie-Hare-exotic-dancer. Then again, I thought, a little experimentation might be fun, but with someone who's not…weird.

As Marvin sang about masturbation, I decided it best to relinquish my twenty year old grudge. Second, I'd get the hell away from her.

Denise kept twirling, when I made a beeline for the bar.

Karina, a former classmate, and her husband downed martinis as I arrived.

"Ooh baby," Karina's husband joshed. "I was getting all hot and sweaty watching you two go at it on the dance floor."

Crap!

I turned to the bartender, "Make mine a screaming orgasm."

Chapter Three: Groundbreaking News

"Yes! Yes! Yes!" I cheered, jumping up and down whilst attempting airborne scissor kicks. I fell on my butt, one leg stretched out in front of me, the other twisted awkwardly behind my torso. Truthfully, I ached, but I didn't care. I had the letter, and I continued to hold tight to it. It christened me a UCLA Bruin.

Next steps: (1) Move out

          (2) Find Prince Charming at UCLA, and

          (3) Live happily ever after. The end.

Mom was on-edge at the time and snapped at me sporadically. I imagine it was a difficult time for her. Mom saw herself in me, I'd later learn. I'm told I was her favorite. An inextricably deep, silent bond connected us.

I can't imagine how I'd have survived Dad's temperament without her. I'm sure Mom did much, by her mere presence, to allay Dad's demons too.

With my one calming force unraveling now, I couldn't plan an escape fast enough.

The dorm room lottery had showcased promise, and a winning ticket arrived that spring.

April 21, 1984: I GOT INTO THE DORMS, DIARY! I'm so extremely glad. It's going to be fantastic (I hope). I can't believe that I'm a college girl who'll be getting away from home next year. It's mind boggling. Mom thinks that I'm an ungrateful bitch. She just yelled at me, only because I locked my bedroom door while she's cleaning up. Taking all the crap possible from this family only makes me want to get the hell out of here!

On a mild mid-September day, I stuffed boxes and suitcases into the rear of our new Buick station wagon. With Dad at the wheel and Mom by his side, we traversed the 405-North destined for my new residence 12 miles away: UCLA's Sproul Hall.

Fighting back ecstasy, Dad rapidly helped me unload.

Fighting back tears, Mom said "goodbye."

And so with "Erotic City" blasting the halls; my best friend Susan and I sharing a shoe-box size living space; navigating a spectacular campus in order to locate lecture halls wherein I'd learn yet again about the Oedipus complex—to which Psychology professors seemed perversely attached; and loads of breath-taking guys speckled across the scene; I relished in the first six weeks of college life.

I made good friends too.

Kathryn's door was open as I walked by towards the shared restroom. She sat on the edge of her bed, holding a Ziploc bag that appeared to be filled with a brown-green mixture of dirt or something. She heard me, looked up, and her warm, friendly smile invited introduction.

"Hi, I'm Robyn."

"Hi, Robyn." She stood and walked to me for a handshake. "Nice to meet you. I'm Kathryn. Do you want some pot? I was just gonna have a smoke."

Oh my God. Play it cool, I told myself. She seems sweet.

"No thank you. Not right now. Maybe later." As in never.

Kathryn giggled. "It's okay. No worries. So where are you from?"

I could tell that Kathryn could tell that her offer shocked me. But she wanted to chat anyway.

We instantly engaged in girlie blather. She was also from Los Angeles—Carson, she said. Her parents still lived there. Kathryn was "sorta seeing someone, but he's being a butthead." We giggled.

I told her I had no boyfriend but was hoping to change that. "There are so many cuties around here."

"Oh, I know. I'm like, 'Okay, um, what did I come here for? Damn I guess I should crack open a book once in a while.'"

"Seriously. Well, I gotta go pee," I told her. "I've been holding it in." I started doing the potty dance, and we both chuckled. "Don't make me laugh, Kathryn. It'll come out on your carpet."

"Alright, Robyn. You go do your thing. Let's meet up and go for dinner."

"Sounds like a plan. I'll drop by around 6pm. You go smoke." I added, trying to sound cool.

Kathryn giggled, this time with slight embarrassment. "Nah, I was just bored."

The glorious kaleidoscope of my life seemed too good to be true.

I'd decided to skip the Halloween dance in favor of studying. Nothing would offset my obsessive need to get A's. Well, almost nothing.

The phone rang at 9:03pm. Susan was busily sorting M&M's and Sweet Tarts, so I took the call.

"Your mother is seriously ill," Dad said. His voice cracked while Dad relayed Mom's phone-number at the hospital.

Numb and scared, I moved to the bathroom and felt tears stream down my face.

Twenty or so minutes later, I returned to the room to tell Susan.

"That was my Dad who called, Susan. My Mom's really sick." I blew out a breath. "I feel guilty. I haven't been home for a long time. I never even told her I love her."

Susan pushed aside a pile of candy wrappers to offer focused consolation, "I'm sure she'll be okay, Rob."

"I don't know, Susan. My Dad sounded tearful. It's bad. I just know it."

The night passed and I skipped morning classes to call Mom.

"How much do you know?" was Mom's only question. She didn't want me to know, as if I'd never find out.

I lied. "Just that you're in the hospital." Dad hadn't told me Mom had cancer, and it was terminal, but I knew. I knew I was losing her, losing the air I breathed, the ground I stood on. Losing my footing. My calm.

"Anyhow, I'll be fine," she said. I heard a speck of doubt. "I love you very much."

My demeanor softened, "I love you too, Mom."

Tears spilled out again as I clicked the receiver.

The rest of my college education would progress and freeze, like a surreal paradox: a loving, hateful vivid blur. I'd struggle to reconcile my dark, frozen insides with a glaring, spinning world. For the most part, I skillfully spun along and excelled academically and socially— except in terms of boys. That arena would never quite gel for me.

It was more than enough to deal with Mom's illness, determined to also get A's and make the most of volunteer opportunities. I'd keep men at a safe distance. Who'd want to date me in this condition, anyway? So I'd convinced myself.

A day or two after learning of Mom's illness, another unexpected phone-call interrupted my studies. It was a guy. He sounded serious.

"Hi. This is Bob. I'm conducting a research study on the orgasm. It will only take a minute. You're a student, right?"

"Yes."

"Your age, major, and year in school, please?"

"Eighteen, Psychology, freshman."

"Have you ever had an orgasm?"

My face flushed and heart rate sped. "No I don't think, no."

"Hmm, really? On a scale of 1 to 5, 1 being 'not at all interested,' and 5 being 'extremely interested', how interested are you in having an orgasm, say, if you could have one right now?"

I heard they're good, I thought. "Five."

"You sound REALLY interested. Is that right?"

Crap. I quelled my enthusiasm. "Maybe, yeah."

"So why haven't you had an orgasm?"

I was quick to defend my innocence. "I've been dealing with other things, like my mom's dying of cancer."

"Oh. Thank you for your time."

"Okay bye." Wait. Don't go!

Click.

Honestly, he sounded like a researcher, and I believed he was. I still think he was conducting a clinical study. But I'm naïve. Had he known who he was calling, and that I could use some stress relief? Had I missed a groundbreaking opportunity? Did I turn him off by telling him that my Mom was dying of cancer? I can see how that might have killed the mood. I'll never know for sure.

That weekend, our family went to Kaiser, West LA, to visit Mom. Every person wearing a white jacket in that drab, cold facility turned their backs on me and my siblings, literally. We were losing our Mom, yet nobody said as much as "hello." They had more important things to attend to.

Thinking about it now, I'm struck by the hypocrisy of the Hippocratic Oath. I'd like to believe that the healthcare profession has grown with respectfulness and compassion since the 1980s. While I know a good number of compassionate nurses and doctors, I remain skeptical about the integrity of the greater field. Hell, let's be real. It's getting worse by the millisecond.

That day, one doctor stopped to talk to Dad briefly. I overheard a few words: "started in the colon," "aggressive," and "chemotherapy immediately."

We entered Mom's room as she lay in a hospital bed, her eyes closed, her face without color, and an I.V. stuck to her arm. She must have sensed our presence; Mom opened her eyes.

"We're all here," Dad and Dawn said.

"Everyone you love is here," I added.

"Why am I in so much pain?" Mom managed to ask amidst short, meager breaths.

I shifted to hide my face. The rest of them stood by stoically.

In the weeks and months to follow, we watched Mom shrivel down to an 80 pound skeleton fighting for each breath. A hospital bed overtook the family room. It would be Mom's cell for the next four and a half months.

As Sunday evenings approached, I escaped back to campus. I pushed even harder on my classes, on volunteer activities, and anything else I could control.

On weekends, I went home to watch Mom die. I trashed heaps of tissue and cursed incessantly, especially through writing, though the rest of the family appeared unaffected.

Dawn monopolized the phone lines for gossip sessions with her girlfriends. Glenn-David and Jonathan drew the neighborhood kids over for football, baseball and basketball games. Dad stayed busy with his job at Thrifty Drugs.

Everyone, except Mom and I, seemed fine. It made no sense.

Perhaps their abnormal normalcy afforded them the same type of solace I garnered from college life. There, life was not all about death.

43

I'd also contend with abnormal normalcy at UCLA, but with a more intriguing flavor.

One Psychology professor insisted that sibling incest is a healthy means of expression. Another, who taught Abnormal Psychology, had allegedly showered with and molested young boys. The day this scandal hit the Daily Bruin, the professor addressed our class by stating, merely, "I didn't do it." Next, a tall man with very broad shoulders escorted him out.

Where guys were concerned, I stayed in the crush zone or remained otherwise oblivious to their clumsy attempts at seduction.

Gil—a tall, dark, and mediocre looking freshman—lived two doors down. We quickly became close friends. During one of his visits to our room, with Susan away, he sputtered, "Robyn, if you ever need to, you know, come by at night, I'll leave my door open for you, you know, even if it's really late. Don't worry about the time. Just come by if, you know…I'll be waiting up for you."

I didn't understand at the time that he was making clumsy romantic advances. I was in such a vapid space.

There were others that amounted to, perhaps, missed opportunities.

Jake, for one, stared me down with his green-gray eyes during an all-hall meeting. Though yards away in a crowd of hundreds, he wouldn't take those dreamy eyes off of me. I felt as awkward as I did flattered. When the meeting adjourned, I nervously turned and left for our dorm room.

A month or so later, I trekked up Bruin walk, as Jake strolled down in my direction. He greeted me with a "Hi." I got anxious and said "Hi," I think, but I'm not sure my "Hi" was audible. And that was that, though I continued to have a crush on him for the remainder of the year.

There were many dances too. Once I danced with a guy from 8:30pm until 11:00pm. He seemed nice, a Political Science major, clean-cut and cordial. At the end of the night, he said "It'd be great to see you again." I said "Uh, yeah." He leaned in closer and asked, "What did you say?" Fumbling for the words I'd just spewed, I repeated myself, "uh I said 'yeah'." With a disappointed look, he replied "Well, take care."

One weekend, I drove straight to Bally's Health Club before going home. I had paid for membership, not to get fit, but to use the sauna and Jacuzzi.

That evening a few others lounged in the bubbling waters as I entered: a nicely tanned, burly blond man sitting alone, and two chipper females who conveniently left moments later.

Chad introduced himself and we discussed trivialities: the wondrous invention of the Jacuzzi, prime Southern California beaches for sunbathing, and the best food on the Santa Monica Boardwalk.

After a while, Chad prepared to excuse himself, saying he needed to get up extra early for work the next day. He closed with an offer. "If you ever want to see a movie or something, give me a call. You can't forget my number." Chad clued me in: "The letters spell 'free cat'."

I never did forget Chad's number (Note: I don't advise calling; his contact information may have changed since 1985.), but I skipped the free cat call.

He's too frat-boy-but-not-in-school-ish, I told myself, and—with self-effacing pathos—I redirected my energies to the home front.

In February of 1985, a wise, young hospice worker gathered my family in the living room. "It's very important to tell her whatever you still need to say, as hard as that may be," she advised. "There's little time left."

I moved in slow-motion through the living room, kitchen, and down one step into the family room. Mom lay awake in the hospital bed, as I knelt by her side. I took Mom's frail hand. We both held tight.

"Mom?"

"Hm, what?"

"Mom I'm sorry I wasn't such a good daughter."

"You always were…I understood everything."

"I love you Mom."

"I love you very much. You're a beautiful girl."

That was the first time anyone had called me "beautiful."

"You're a beautiful girl": Mom's last words to me. It was foreign to hear. I'd felt ugly all my life. I was sure I was ugly, not at all beautiful. More importantly, though, Mom didn't think that I was a bad daughter.

I kissed her hand and held it silently.

We never let go.

Mom was re-hospitalized and fell into a coma on March 19, 1985. Dad called at 8:25pm on March 20, 1985.

Dawn picked up the phone. "She what? She died? We love you. See you soon. B-bye."

Dawn relayed that Mom had opened her eyes, looked at Dad, and then closed her eyes for the final time.

I don't remember all the details but I remember waking up to the dilemma of what the hell to wear, and the grotesque absurdity of the fact that I worried about what the hell to wear to my Mother's funeral.

After-all, they'd be stealing glances of me to assure themselves I'd be fine. Then they could get on with their lives. I was supposed to wear black, though part of me wanted to rebel against it all. Black was too appropriately depressing. Nonetheless, I settled on a black and white shirt, black pants and gray shoes.

Over 300 people attended the service. My family sat in front, behind a translucent curtain. I scanned the crowd and saw aunts and uncles, cousins, synagogue members, and even teachers from Kentwood Elementary School. Mom and the Engels had left our mark on Westchester. Everybody knew and liked our family. Everyone who knew Mom loved her too. It was impossible not to.

After the service, we were chauffeured via limousine to the gravesite.

I remember a quick, fierce snip of the black ribbon pinned to my shirt, and thuds of stones that were cast onto Mom's coffin—a matter of Jewish protocol.

The "after-party" followed. Per tradition, family and friends visit the bereaved with food and drink, so that immediate family need not worry about such mundane matters during this time of intense grief. In our case, cousin Steve generously contributed food from his catering business. Other guests needed only show up and eat. And they did.

I was in a fog. People poured into our home with awkward beaming smiles and words of cheer. I hadn't spoken to most of them in years. I had no idea who some of them were. Others, I despised.

Yet they invaded the quiet that now defined our home. They focused excitedly on the fabulous growing display that forever altered our kitchen table: multi-flavored bagels, lox galore, bowls that were brightly decorated with tropical fruit, kosher pickles, and—for dessert—apple pie, pecan pie, and vanilla ice cream.

One by one, or two by two, they sauntered loudly through the front room and headed directly to the kitchen table. A few of them nodded as they passed through. Most, though, simply walked by.

All were dressed impeccably: the men in suits and ties, the women in dresses, nylons, and heels. Make-up had clearly been applied with great care.

They didn't even try to hide it. They rejoiced in seeing each other. They engaged in loud chatter about their recent vacation travels, their children's academic successes, and—above all—the glorious spread of food.

I ate nothing.

No one mentioned Mom. They smiled at Dad half-heartedly but resisted getting close. My sister and brothers were lost in the crowd. They played the game better. I refused to play.

Uncle Leo suddenly appeared distressed. Walking towards the front door, he turned to me and stated, "We have a problem. We're out of cups. Come with me to get some."

"No. I won't go," I responded in one breath that encapsulated my anger and indifference.

Instead, Dawn accompanied him on this all-important task. I'd later learn from Dawn that Uncle Leo complained to her about my resistance. In turn, Dawn informed him that my reaction was none of his business. "You're right," he'd told Dawn, but said nothing more to me.

Loud chatter and laughter continued, as I withdrew further from the table that had once been ours.

"We're back with the cups," Uncle Leo heroically announced shortly thereafter. Relieved guests expressed their gratitude.

I reminisced about Thanksgiving and Passover meals. Our family and Aunt Esther's gathered season after season, for predictably adequate meals that tasted heavenly: the appetizer, half of a grapefruit topped with a maraschino cherry; cheesy green-beans and mushrooms; green salad with Mom's homemade garlic dressing; a 12-pound turkey, nice and moist, with plenty for dark and light meat eaters; stove top stuffing; and a lemon Jell-O shaped like the star of David mixed with lots of cool-whip mixed in.

These intruders would surely have scoffed at those meals, but they meant family.

Mrs. Goldberg interrupted my memories with an austere expression, as though she was about to impart groundbreaking words of wisdom: "Robyn, just remember, tragedy brings a family closer together." I nodded lifelessly and walked away. You're full of shit, I thought.

As guests scurried away, I found myself in the family room with Dad. He sat on the black sofa, resigned, exhausted, in utter shock and despair. With all the sarcasm and of his depleted being, Dad muttered, "It's just like a party here, isn't it, Robyn? Bring out the dancing girls!"

Alas, I wasn't the only one who wanted them out. Not the only one who wanted to see a sparsely covered kitchen table with a few of Mom's special dishes, or with the festive Shabbat or Hanukah candle lights, or with nothing at all.

I wasn't the only one who would have preferred coming home from Mom's funeral to the lonely emptiness and quiet that was now ours and ours alone.

Dad and I sat in shared silence.

Chapter Four: Young Teachers, True Love

I never pondered whether or not I wanted to become a mom. It was a given. I've always had a much easier, more fun time with little versus big people.

Unlike adults, youngsters don't tend to knead their insecurities into rancid globs of putrid slime. Nor do kids viciously project these rancid globs at their closest targets only to label said targets an appalling mess. Instead, children love with unquestioning hearts.

It's no surprise, then, that I both found and placed myself amid kids throughout my otherwise despairing college years.

"Rob," Susan entered our dorm room and interrupted my studies, "I just started volunteering at the Med Center. Kathryn told me about it. You should join us."

The thought of entering a sterile, depressing hospital ward again didn't attract me. "I don't know, Susan...Well" —I thought for a moment— "could I work with kids?"

"Yeah. Just tell them you want to volunteer in Pediatrics." Susan pulled a business card out of her pocket. "Here's Jane's contact info. She's the volunteer coordinator. Give her a call."

A glamorous brunette, who looked like a Mary Kay model, walked along the drab corridor towards me. She reached out her had in businesslike manner. "I'm Jane," she said.

"I'm Robyn. Nice to meet you."

"You too." Jane looked at her watch, distracted. "Well your application looked good. I'll talk through some protocol with you before you leave today. I thought I'd introduce you to someone right now."

"Sure."

"Let's go this way." She gestured back down the corridor. Jane's heels click-clacked against the slick floor tiles as we traversed the long walkway, and I learned a few things about my soon-to-be patient.

"Brianne's four. She has leukemia. She's been in and out of the hospital eight times in the last year and a half." Jane made this statement matter-of-factly. She quieted as we neared an open door.

Jane held a hand up, signaling me to stay there. "I'll make sure she's good with company."

She disappeared. I heard whispering. Why would someone like Jane work here and not in Hollywood? I wondered. She's an odd fit.

"Okay," Jane startled me. "Go on in and I'll follow up with you later." Without allowing response, she briskly headed for the nurses' station.

Trying not to overwhelm Brianne, I entered quietly, slipping by an empty bed to my left. Beyond it, a small girl popped her head up. She flashed a smile so glowingly, it seemed Brianne hadn't seen another human in months.

"Hi Brianne. I'm Robyn."

"Hi," she blurted, scooting into a sitting position.

Brianne's eyes struck me – the same deep blue as Mom's, and with beautiful long, dark lashes. She otherwise lacked color. Brianne bore only a bit of peach fuzz on her head; her body, pale and depleted; and her life, dependent upon an I.V. stuck into her right hand.

"It's great to meet you sweetie," I smiled. "How are you?"

She pasted a half-smile-half-frown on her face. "So-so," Brianne replied, adult-like. "Can we play?" Her mood lifted.

"Sure! What would you like to play?"

Brianne's shoulders shot up and down, her mood shifting to sad again. "Do you know how much more I have to stay in here?"

"Oh, sweetie, I wish I knew. I'm sorry, but" —I spontaneously assumed a low-pitched, manly voice—"I'm Doctor Seussapotamus," I said. "Now let's see, Miss Brianne." I pulled my glass frames up and rested the lenses on my head. "Wait a minute. Miss Brianne?" I turned around and pretended to be looking out the window. "Where'd you go? I can't see you." I turned around and stuck my hand into my front pants pocket, as if to look for her. "Brianne? Where are you?"

"I'm right here!" She laughed heartily.

"Oh," I said, setting my glasses back in place. "Oh, there you are! You must have been tricking me! Now, let's see." I got close to Brianne, as if to perform an inspection. "It looks like you have two arms and, yep, looks like you've got two feet too! And there's a pretty face on your neck." She chortled energetically. "So I promise you, Miss Brianne, you are going to be alright. It might take a much longer time than we want it to. Those cancer cells are meanie booger monsters, aren't they?"

She nodded in affirmation, still giggling.

"Well we're gonna get rid of all of those meanie booger monsters. So can I give you a shot with magic medicine in it?"

Her eyebrows lifted, and she looked a bit scared. "Will it hurt?"

"No, Miss Brianne. It'll be a super-fast one, and it will help us beat up the meanie booger monsters. Okay?"

"'Kay!"

I pointed my index finger and touched it momentarily to her forearm. "See that was it. Now you're going to be alright. The meanie booger monster cells are going to go away, slower than we want them to. But they're going to leave. I promise."

We continued in this manner.

Time dashed away. I looked at my watch and realized Jane was likely waiting for me. "Oh my golly Missy," I said, "I wish Doctor Seussapotamus didn't have to leave. But I'm afraid it's time."

I switched back to my regular voice and guffawed lovingly. "It was really fun meeting you, Brianne. I'm sorry that I have to leave now. But I'll be back next Tuesday. Okay?"

Her face grew heavy.

"I'm sorry, sweetie. I'll miss you. Can I give you a hug?"

Brianne readily accepted and conferred a loving hug.

"I'll miss you, honey. I'll be back soon."

"'Kay. I'm gonna miss you too."

I shifted to walk away.

"Can you leave the door open?" Brianne asked. It struck me how terribly lonely she was.

"Sure, honey. You take care, okay? I'll see you soon."

I remember all of the campus buildings appearing gray inside, even the ones with red brick exteriors. This couldn't have been the actual case. It's interesting how memories mix with emotions to form the vivid but imaginary photographs our brains keep stored for years or a lifetime.

As far as I can recall, I sat on a gray chair in a little gray room.

"What's your reason for this request?" The academic counselor's thick black glass frames shifted closer to the tip of her narrow, pointy nose.

Tall walls closed in on me, as I coerced words to travel out of my facial orifice: "My Mom died of cancer."

She remained stone-faced.

"It's kind of hard to study sometimes." I watched her eyebrow to the right stretch upwards, as her brow to the left slanted towards her nose.

Breathe, I told myself, interlocking my fingers. Keep breathing.

She raised a hand to her glass frames, lifted them an inch or two, then rested them on the bridge of her nose," while maintaining a focus on my Petition.

It's one damn class, I thought. But this would put me under the minimum required 12 units per quarter, and thus necessitated a plethora of hurdles.

As if struck by a profound inquiry, she abruptly grabbed her glass frames and pulled them down onto her dark oak desktop.

"So what's different now?" She sounded dumbfounded. "I mean, what's different at home?" She pressed. "Do you have more chores to do?"

Chores? Are you fuckin kidding me? I lost my one and only source of unconditional love and you ask about household chores! Sure, lady, you're the expert. Yep, Mama, God bless her, was up at 4am, before the rooster crowed. By the time the Olesons opened the General Store, Mama had milked all the cows and collected dozens of eggs. Then she hand-washed our school clothes and spun wool for hours to make us new outfits. Ma even got down on her hands and knees to scrub the floors clean every day, just the way Pa liked it.

And when wildflowers were in season, Mama collected them in bunches and bunches. She gave some to the Reverend Alden, Mr. Edwards, and Doc Baker. Yeah, it takes a lot of time to fill Ma's shoes, and she made those herself too. I dunno how to make shoes. I can barely tie my Nikes.

The counselor starred at me, irritated, as if attuned to my sarcastic litany. "Um, yeah, I have a lot of chores I guess."

It seems I responded correctly. She penned her signature on the Petition, handed me the form without a word, and signaled the next student in line to approach her.

After my next visit to Brianne, I wrote:

May 28, 1985: For a while when I stroked her back, I thought: Here I am with this little doll who has a lot of love but is suffering – her insides are eating her away. I'm healthy, able to comfort her. I

56

closed my eyes momentarily, then opened them to look down at my body – my two legs, me standing upright, strong, and secure. I really do have a lot to work with. When our time was up, Brianne made everything wonderful by saying, "Come here, I want to give you a BIG HUG." So I held her and thanked her.

Unfortunately, classes also beckoned my attention. I really hated History, and I hated the fact that I had to take a History course if I planned to graduate. Which I did. It perplexed me that, while my friends in the computer sciences breezed through school without learning to write a proper essay, or even paragraph, I had to be versed on countless historical minutiae, all of which seemed extremely irrelevant to my life.

When exposed to historical facts, my mind still latches onto petty details like why anyone would label a war "civil" or that "Napoleon" sounds like a dessert and now I really crave a sundae drenched in hot fudge with peppermint chocolate chip ice-cream, three fancy swirls of whipped cream and a maraschino cherry atop, hold the nuts.

Luckily I happened to sit next to Eric —a History buff—on the first day of class sophomore year. Eric, I'd learn, was on UCLA's gymnastics team. He'd practiced with Mitch Gaylord, even, the first American gymnast to score a perfect 10. Eric was cute like Mitch, too, a bit less striking. He had dark brown hair and a subtle, well-trimmed goatee. When he mentioned that he volunteered with the Special Olympics, I knew Eric was a good one. And I wanted to marry him.

It became routine for Eric and I to save each other a seat, depending upon who got to class first.

When our midterm was returned, Eric spied my perfect score. "Look at you, smarty pants!" He nudged me jokingly. "All that doodling I've seen you doing during lectures too!" I smiled humbly, pretending that I hadn't noticed his B-. Maybe he needs individual tutoring, I thought. I'm too shy. I don't know if he likes me. God, I like him.

We exited the lecture hall. "See ya," Eric and I chimed in unison, before heading in opposite directions.

I'd become so immediately and strongly attached to Brianne that I thought about her between classes. Once, I visited unannounced. I was scheduled to see her the next day, but found myself with a free hour and knew she'd be happy to see me.

June 3, 1985: Today I saw Brianne again. She's so cute! First thing she said was "It's been a long day since I saw you." I told her "Yeah, it's been almost a week. I missed you." She gave me a big hug. Our visit was short, because she was drowsy. But I'm glad to have seen her today.

"Robyn, we need to talk," Jane looked distressed. "Come with me." She guided me towards a small office room and sat me down for a talk.

Am I in trouble? What did I do wrong? I had no idea. I'd just come back to see Brianne today – my regularly scheduled time.

"I heard that you were here yesterday." Her tone was accusatory.

I got nervous and nodded, though she didn't ask any questions.

"We cannot allow any volunteers to visit the patients except during their scheduled shifts because…" Jane stifled some apparently highly secretive information…"it just can't happen. I thought I made that clear."

Look, Witch Mary Kay, I said in my head, you failed to make anything *clear*, except that you're *clearly* in the wrong line of work. My friends who volunteer stop by impromptu to see their patients also. They've never been disciplined for it. What's the problem? Brianne has nobody else to talk to. *Clearly* you don't get it!"

Jane stood up, finished with her scolding.

Enough of the bullshit, I thought, as I headed for Brianne's room.

"Hey," Brianne popped up. "I'm waiting for you!"

I gave her a hug. Brianne displayed a playful, spry mood, more hopeful than ever. "My Daddy sent me a card." She pointed at a Get Well card resting on the table between beds.

"How nice of your Daddy. I'm sure he loves and misses you."

"Yeah, he does," she smiled.

I thought it odd that I hadn't seen any visitors, and I had no idea about her family situation. Why would her Dad send a card and not visit? At any rate, I'm glad it cheered her.

Leaving Brianne was always hard, for both of us.

"I'll see you soon, sweetie. Take care."

"Okay," she said, as we hugged "goodbye."

I wished I was a natural smarty-pants, like Eric thought I was, and like my sister Dawn seemed to be. But I needed to work really hard to get A's. Or so I believed. I believed I needed to sacrifice meals and sleep, and I needed to study and re-study and re-study the same materials that I already knew very well and could practically recite in my sleep. If I didn't give it my all and then some, I'd fail and be a failure.

"Come and have dinner with us," Kathryn would say. "No, I can't. I have to study. I can't fail this test." She tried to convince me otherwise, to no avail.

It was ridiculous. I was ridiculous. Yet growing up, my grades were the only thing I had control over. I knew that if I studied hard, I would excel in school. This meant to me that I was at least somewhat smart, but not nearly as smart as people who didn't need to study as hard but still got A's. The fact that I didn't always get A's proved to me that I didn't have natural intellect. I constantly berated myself in this manner, flaunting unreasonable superhero expectations. It's not smart. It's ludicrous, really.

Upon my next visit to see Brianne, I arrived to an empty bed. Jane found me and explained that Brianne had stabilized, might or might not return to the unit, and we'd keep good thoughts for her. Jane imparted a half-grin, turned around and walked back down the hall. She snapped her head back and said to me, "Oh, go ahead and see if Hannah wants a visitor." Jane pointed towards an open door across from Brianne's.

I went home instead, fighting tears with each step I took up Bruin Walk.

"To think, she's only 4," I wrote, "and won't ever be able to see dreams come true. I miss her already. Damn cancer's taken too much from me!"

I never returned to the UCLA Medical Center.

Home meant different things throughout college. My living venues offered variety. After Sproul Hall residency, I lived at home, in apartments on streets with names like Stoner Avenue —Susan suggested we give the street name a French twist and call it "Stahn-e'", and home again.

Life there was miserable. I recall long, slow walks to catch the bus at 85th and Sepulveda Boulevard, as I trudged a massive, lonesome pain.

Somehow I was certain that I was the sole carrier of all the earth's pain. Nobody could or would ever understand me. Nobody could or would ever love me, well, except Mom and Brianne. And who'd be next to love me and die? I was certain Brianne would die soon; this was a given, in my mind.

Step by slow, heavy step, I glanced at the houses along 84th Place sandwiched between Kentwood and Alverstone Avenues. One by one, each neatly squared house broke through the blur of my tears. Every one bore paint that was several shades lighter than its trim and shingles. I saw sky blues and azure blues, beiges and light browns, pinks and magentas. The houses also boasted perfectly trimmed bushes that spanned the front porches to the driveways on either side.

All of those people living in those damn houses lived normal, happy lives. I was certain of this. I was the pariah – the one and only one devastated in a way that nobody could or would ever understand.

The best way to escape my pain was to keep busy, and to keep kids in my life.

The children's program that stole my heart with the strongest grip was Project Mac. We'd trekked to Mac Laren Children's Center in El Monte every week under the guise of bringing fun-filled activities to abused children. Truth was, we went for their smiles, hugs and love.

One incident stands out in my memory bank.

We'd just arrived. I walked through the halls and saw a young girl laying face-down on her bed, staring at the walls, hopelessness overtaking the room. I assumed she was new to Mac Laren; I hadn't seen her before.

I approached, rested my palm softly on her back and said nothing. She cried until she was done, ten minutes or so later. The young girl, maybe 9 or 10 years old, lifted herself, stood up, gave me a kiss on the cheek, and said "Thank you."

How can children who've never really been loved have so much of it to give?

Family continued onward, as if not shaken. Dad was actively dating. Dawn and Jonathan proceeded to socialize and get together with friends regularly. Once in a while, though, I caught glimpses of

Glenn-David entering a cocoon. He'd sink into my spot on the black sofa, looking somber. I guessed he missed Mom too, but I didn't say anything. Neither did he.

I loathed my brother's heightened insecurities and remarkably bleak void of self-confidence. Glenn-David was too much like me, so I either fought with or ignored him. Nobody else seemed attentive to my brother's sadness; it surely wasn't worthy of concern. No, I was the only troubled Engel. I believed it too.

In actuality, Glenn-David de-compensated to a realm too dismal for this book. I've placed that story on the shelf for a treatise of its own. Anything short of that doesn't feel right.

In attempts to fill the otherwise empty summers, I participated in UCLA's Unicamp. As a matter of protocol, I needed to adopt a camp name. Susan suggested "Pebbles." I loved it until I kept meeting Pebbles after Pebbles through camp activities; there were five others in the summer of 1987.

Based on camp names alone, Boulder and I were drawn to each other. He'd routinely put his arm around me and tell me, in a soft spoken but definitive manner, how much he missed me. Yet only a few hours had lapsed since we'd last seen each other in the dining hall.

Even now, I'm not sure if his affection meant anything, or if it was just part of the big love fest that defined, and still defines, nearly every group of camp counselors everywhere in the world. At any rate, I couldn't stop thinking about Boulder and experienced a strange, sick mushy alien force taking over my being. I figured I was falling in love.

It's appropriate, I suppose, that I married at this time. The camp carnival included a wedding booth. While I wished for Boulder to propose, the offer came in a much smaller, sweeter package.

I don't even remember when or how I'd met Christopher. But he asked, "Pebbles will you marry me?" and I accepted. In response, Christopher's face beamed with a spectacular mixture of the pristine vigor of Buckwheat and the polite charm of Opie. In retrospect, I never had it so good.

The young minister, a Counselor in Training, handed me a lovely blue and yellow tissue paper bouquet. "Pebbles and Christopher, do you promise to always be woodsy friends?" he asked.

"Yes," I said, as Christopher said "Yeah."

"Very good. I now announce you boy and wife. You may hug the bride," he added.

My new husband and I exchanged a hug, happily. I readily relinquished my bouquet to Raindrop and Lightning Bolt. Christopher ran off to join the potato-sack races. I walked briskly to catch up with Boulder by the face painting.

As the carnival wrapped up, Boulder rendered a memorable embrace. His fingers massaged my back tenderly, all over, and for a nice long time.

July 21, 1987: I'm a little crazy lately. I never stop thinking about Boulder. At the end of the camp carnival he gave me the longest, warmest, most wonderful hug a girl could ever get.

Eric had urged me to take another History class with him again, so I did. When I spotted him in the crowded lecture hall on the first day, he greeted me with, "I was looking for you and saved you a seat." I was thrilled but played it casual.

Before and after lectures, we talked about our lives—nothing too deep, always fun. This one was definitely promising, I thought, until he dropped the bomb one day after I asked about his weekend.

"It was kind of weird," he said. "This girl I'm kind of seeing called me her boyfriend and I said 'I didn't know I was your boyfriend.'"

I think I heard my heart crumble.

October 17, 1987: My dream guy fuckin told me he has a girlfriend. I told myself, "Don't show any emotion – just get through this half hour and who gives a shit?" But two seconds later he asked me, "For the second time I'm asking you, are you going to take any History classes with me next quarter?" Why the fuck does he want me to take a class with him? Fuck that! I don't just want to be friends with him. Being the dummy I am, I asked him, "What am I supposed to take?" and wrote down the two classes he's taking - some Byzantine or Colonial Aboriginal Circa AD ergo 727 bullshit. Crap, what does this mean? If he likes me, he wouldn't have said he has a girlfriend. If he doesn't like me, he wouldn't keep asking me to take classes with him. Why play with my mind this way?

Boulder and I gravitated to each other during a Unicamp winter party. We hadn't seen or talked to each other in months.

"How've you been?" he asked.

"I'm good, and you?"

"Doing fine. Getting ready for Christmas. I love this time of year. Don't you?"

"Well, not that much. I don't celebrate Christmas, so it's—"

"How could you not celebrate Christmas? Oh are you one of those Jews?"

I couldn't believe his reaction. "Yes, I'm one of those Jewish people, and I'm proud of it."

"No, I mean, you don't believe in Jesus Christ?"

"It depends what you mean by 'believe in.'" I boiled inside. "I believe he was a generous man. He's not my God, but I want the same things he wanted for the world. In fact, he was Jewish."

Boulder looked bewildered. "I just never met one of you before."

Never met one of me? Dude, it's 1987, and we're in Los Angeles. You never met a Jew before? "We're good people. Most of us, at least," I giggled awkwardly.

We stood still, molecules of air thickening around us. I turned towards the kitchen. "Well, I'm going to go get a drink. See you later."

"Okay." Boulder walked over to Turtle and Lion. Jackass, I thought.

December 15, 1987: Dear Di, I'm embarrassed about all the room I wasted in you over something so stupid as infatuation; someone who didn't even care about me, at least not the way I wanted him to. He's a jerk, plain and simple! But I guess I do need to remember some of the special feelings if, for no other reason, because I had them.

At the end of our final volunteer visit in the summer of 1988, Mac Laren's staff gathered the kids to thank us. They handed me a plaque, imparted words of gratitude, and asked the kids if they had anything to say.

"That little lady is my favorite!" Scotty shouted, pointing at me.

I finished the History final. Eric was still taking the test. I took my time and rechecked my work, but he continued. We hadn't exchanged phone numbers. Damnit. I couldn't let him disappear from my life.

So I plopped down on a patch of lawn and waited. I had no idea what I'd say. I just needed to see Eric again.

The grass was damp, and time marched slowly.

My now former classmates started walking by in droves, but he wasn't among them.

I looked at my watch and waited some more, feelings of stupidity and disappointment growing by the second. After a solid half-hour, I sadly studied my blue Nikes as they met the cement walkway.

Eric must've gone out the door on the other side of the building.

I'd never see him again.

I was thrilled to have my hands on the graduation announcement. I placed it on the center of the kitchen table with a handwritten note:
"Dear Family,
It's here!! Save the date!!
Love, Robyn, almost a B.A.!"

Dad came in, while I sat with a book on the black leather couch. He stopped and saw my note. He breathed heavily in his way. "Robyn, it looks like I can't make it. I'm going to be in Europe. I didn't know you were going through ceremonies, because your sister didn't." Heavy sigh.

My heart quietly, privately burst into pieces. "Yeah," my voice dropped. "I'm graduating with honors. So I'm going through ceremonies."

"Sorry, baby. I've scheduled a Jewish Singles' European Tour. It's non-refundable."

"Okay." I walked past him to my bedroom to cry in private.

My Bruin days commenced on June 16, 1989. Bette Midler's "Wind Beneath My Wings" topped the charts that week, a spot dominated by Phil Collins' "Another Day in Paradise" for much of the year to that point. Popular graduate costumes included Batman, the Riddler, and the Energizer Bunny.

By my estimation at the time, I'd barely squeaked by. Now, though, I can't fathom how the hell I did it. In a class of over 4,000, I was 14th in line for the processional. (Order was based on credentials, not height.) I graduated with cum laude honors, community service honors and a Chancellor's Humanitarian Award.

Over 10,000 people sat slumped in the stands, subjected to speech after tedious speech, while we passed along free-for-all containers of Bartles and James, flasks of tequila, and a variety of unidentifiable elements. My fans included my siblings; Dawn's three closest girlfriends; Uncle Bill and Aunt Jean, who made appearances at all the important family events, didn't speak to me or each other, but imparted a quick kiss on my cheek when it was over; and our ever-supportive neighbors, Rhonda, Carrie and Camila.

My celebratory spirit was marred by the fact that I had no parents there. Mom's excuse (i.e., being dead) was valid and fairly full-proof. As for Dad, he'd left me a card and letter on the kitchen table, before catching his flight. He wrote that he was proud of me, added to a perplexing message: "It's my hope that you will start to treat others with the love that your Mother and I expressed to you, and that you will ultimately find a measure of the happiness that you've been rejecting over the years." I didn't, and still don't, understand the sentiment.

As the 1980s rolled into the 90s, I rested and floundered a bit, worked with kids and studied for the GRE's (graduate school entrance exams), dated and started anti-depressants. A planned one-year academic break became a two, then three year hiatus.

In 1991, I'd applied to two Graduate School Social Work programs, UCLA's and UC Berkeley's. Assuming I was a shoe-in for my alma-mater, I was shocked to receive a rejection letter from them, so shocked that I wrote to request an explanation. The dubious response stated, merely, that I didn't have what they were looking for.

Thankfully, UC Berkeley sent a more welcoming letter. I danced around with excitement, both about leaving LA and about acceptance to one of the world's most prestigious universities.

"You're moving to Northern California? You'll freeze your ass off up there," my friends said. I shopped for two more sweaters.

I needed one more kid-dose before the move. I thus joined Ronald McDonald's Camp Good Times. The children who'd arrive in a few hours, we learned, battled various forms of cancer but were healthy enough to fully participate in overnight camp. Many were returning campers surging with a year's worth of camp anticipation.

Only one cabin group needed a third counselor, the one with nine pre-teen girls. Lynn, Deb, and I exchanged fear-filled expressions upon learning we'd manage this extra special group.

"We can do it," I imparted encouragement. "I mean, it's only five days. We can do it, right?" We burst into laughter.

The buses arrived once we'd tossed our sleeping bags onto cabin 12's three upper bunks. Our campers scurried to meet us in front of the cabin, clenching backpacks and suitcases, pillows and teddy bears.

My co-counselors and I had decided to take turns reading each name on the roster, to greet our crew one-by-one and assist them with their belongings.

Deb welcomed Megan Jackson, then handed me the clipboard.

Goosebumps charged my system when I eyed the second name on the list: "Brianne" —my emotions escalated as I spoke each syllable— "Carlsen."

I looked up to re-meet Brianne's striking blue eyes, now a half-foot or so above mine. I dropped the clipboard, as we charged at each other for a long overdue hug.

Through that hug, Brianne replaced what cancer had so viciously stolen years earlier.

Chapter Five: Going Berzerkly

The Urban Dictionary defines "berzerk" as "something very exiciting or dramatic." I'd like to think that first "i" in "exiciting" was strategically placed to portray the random spontaneity inherent in going berzerk. Yet it more likely underscores a widespread condition plaguing even the most highly schooled urbanite: dullness of mind with measured weirdness.

"So you're going to Berzerkly?" Todd goaded.

My spinning brain failed to process his play on words. "Yeah, you'll have to come visit me sometime."

I wanted to give Todd one more chance. We'd worked together in the early 90s and stayed in touch sporadically.

A nice, attractive guy, Todd's cynical wit meshed well with my own. He'd asked for a date a few months earlier. Suppressing my excitement then, I casually agreed. The next day, though, Todd canceled in favor of an AC/DC concert with pals. I reaped an apology sans rain-check.

"You sure you're not mad?" he pried, half concerned, half relieved.

Get off the phone so I can go cry, jackass! "No, it's alright," I conveyed the sense of possessing a strong, independent, non-jaded and intact heart.

Now, a few years after he broke our date, I harbored an ounce of hope with a cupful of realism.

"Sure, yeah I'll go see you sometime," he said. I knew he wouldn't. "But Northern California, Robyn?" Todd joshed, "You'll freeze your ass off up there!"

"So I hear." I viciously shoved another raggedy sweatshirt into my suitcase, then politely ended the phone call.

Wait. I paused, "Berzerkly? What the hell am I getting myself into?"

But what could go wrong? I'd escape a scene that revolted me: gleaming Barbies and Kens with sprayed-on tans and blindingly bleached hair; smiles that lacked substance everywhere I turned; and the omnipresent race to be first – be it in line at a Starbuck's on Rodeo Drive or the restroom at Wendy's on Pico Boulevard. They zip around in their Mercedes', proudly displaying well-manicured middle fingers, in a war for prized parking at the local gym. Add to this my personal miseries, and I couldn't pack fast enough.

In August of 1992, Kathryn and Devon, who'd stayed friends since high school, assisted with an impressive car-cram. My wee 1989 rust-colored Ford Festiva would shelter a clumpy Panasonic TV that weighed approximately 203 pounds, decade-old Radio Shack boom-box, reliable Smith-Corona electric typewriter, books, photo albums, knickknacks, and meager wardrobe, with a solid inch of rearview vantage.

Kathryn and I shared a tight hug. "We'll be in touch, and you'll have to come visit me."

"Okay, girlie. You be good, but have some fun too."

"I will," I grinned.

As I shut the hatchback, Devon stepped back and glanced at me. "You've got that hopeful glow about you, Robyn. I give you thirteen

73

months to meet the man of your dreams. Thirteen months. He'll be one of those Northern California sensitive types too."

"Sounds good, Devon."

Until that day, I hated country music. Los Angelinos were supposed to. Over the next seven hours, though, I became one of its most enthused fans. Lacking a compact disc player, it was either that or the more grating dribble of static.

Billy Ray distracted me from the overwhelming scent of cow manure, as Highway 5 saw me through miles of nothingness peppered by towns like Gorman, which boasted one diner, one gas station and one nonfunctioning payphone —all seemingly connected as one in one little, conspicuous cluster by the freeway.

I eyed the speedometer. Crap. I should probably slow down. I didn't know the Festiva could get so close to race-car speed. "Lucky girl," I said aloud, when checking my rearview mirror for the police. Except for me and some truckers, it was a quiet day on the long stretch of road between Santa Monica and Oakland, California.

"You can tell your ma, I hate her damn coleslaw!" I belted, making up my own lyrics, windows wide open and the warm dry breeze lifting strands of hair as if to coordinate them in synchronicity with the music. "I cried an' cried! Nah, I done lied. I'm glad he died."

Three breaks and 350 miles later, I parked along Oakland's Lake Merritt. Diamond specks tickled the water's surface. A few drug stores, banks, semi-high rise buildings, and an Episcopal church eclipsed a peaceful backdrop. I sighed, relaxed, and assured: despite what I'd heard about Oakland, I'd be fine.

Next, I lugged my belongings through a four-story red-brick building, reminiscent of a 1950's Hitchcock film. The wrought iron overhang marked "Parkside Manor" in austere, black letters. Inside, marble floors, plush red carpeting, and an elevator accordion gate spotlighted its vintage appeal.

Alas, my quaint hard-wood floored studio apartment welcomed me home.

A week later, Devon decided to visit. I was surprised, but happily so. Though they'd been longstanding friends, and they even went to the high school prom together, Kathryn and Devon never had more than a friendly relationship.

"He's hot, and I tell him that all the time," she would say, "but there's not really anything there. He likes the bad girls," she said, unaffected.

Kathryn had suggested that Devon and I become a "thing."

"Oh yeah Kat, I'm such a bad girl I once wore short sleeves on a hot day." We cackled.

Truth be told, I liked the thought of me and Devon, but didn't want to make for weirdness with Kathryn. And he wasn't someone to get serious with. Devon didn't keep jobs or girlfriends. In fact, he didn't seem invested in much of anything. Besides, Devon had just prophesized my meeting someone else in thirteen months.

It seems odd, in retrospect, that I gave little thought to the seemingly clear fact that Devon would spend the night in my tiny studio apartment. I simply tossed a sleeping bag and pillow onto my brown sofa a few yards from my bed. Used to disappointment and ever naive, I didn't allow myself to fantasize about anything happening between us.

Moments after he arrived, Devon took a call. He was the first person I knew to carry a cell-phone. I wondered if it was related to drugs. I figured it must be. Why else would anyone own a cell-phone?

"Mm…no kidding!" He sounded concerned. "Where you at right now dude?"

He put his phone back into his jacket pocket and reported that his friend, Earl, had been in a car wreck. Though he wasn't badly hurt, and was home recovering, Devon needed to be with Earl; that's what best buddies do for each other. So he said.

"Do you want something to drink, at least, Devon? You just got here. I feel bad."

"No problem, Robyn. I'm good. I gotta be with my buddy."

Well so much for my first visitor – a man too. An attractive man, one willing to drive 350 miles to see me. And then turn around and drive 350 miles to leave me. What the hell?

Devon gave me a brief side-hug, grabbed his duffle bag and left to complete his 700 mile round trip in one day. I repressed my confused-disappointment, bundled up the sleeping back and shoved it back into the bottom of my closet.

I'd never see or hear from Devon again. Kathryn thought it was "damn weird" and, though she attempted to get an explanation from him, he only talked about Earl's car accident and how glad he was that everything was fine.

Devon would eventually move to Las Vegas. Kathryn lost contact with him altogether.

Meanwhile, Todd's phone calls continued for weeks. He missed me, it seemed. I was flattered, since he was the one initiating every phone call. We'd do a see-saw "You should visit" and "Yeah, I will some time" exchange every time we spoke.

Todd never committed to a plan. I thought to invite him to make the drive, come see my place and eye my raggedy brown cloth sleeping bag that would be his bed for the night, take a staged phone call, and then hit the road. But I didn't.

In fact, I didn't even notice that Todd's phone-calls petered out. My attention aimed elsewhere: the quintessential boy next door. Best yet, he lived next door.

With a grocery bag on hand, I'd trekked towards my door one Sunday afternoon. Alongside, a respectable young man in a beige sweatshirt and blue jeans, also toted groceries.

"Looks like we're neighbors," I said cheerfully. "I'm Robyn."

He stopped and placed his bags down. "I'm Noah, good to meet you." I encountered a warm, cordial palm against mine. "So, you here for school?"

"Yeah, I just moved from L.A. I'm starting tomorrow at the Graduate School of Social Welfare. What about you?"

"I'm from upstate New York, finishing med-school at UCSF. Couldn't afford to live in the city." He smirked with a hint of embarrassment. "But the East Bay's nice, slower-paced and all." Noah smiled and maneuvered his grocery bag, digging into his pocket for keys. "Well, really good to meet you. Guess I'll be seeing you."

"You too, great to meet you."

I closed the door and leaned against it with a hopeful grin.

Now, time to attend to scholarly endeavors. I quickly stored the food I'd bought, then moved a pack of new black Paper Mates into my bulging backpack. I set my alarm for 6:00am. No, I reasoned, 6:30. Well, 7's fine. In fact, I'll make it on time if I push it to 7:06. BART —Bay Area Rapid Transit— is only ten minutes from here if I power-walk. And it's a brief ride to campus. Plus I have faith in a subway system named after the most animated Simpson. (When sleep and/or avoiding reality is the goal, anything makes sense.)

The next morning, I meandered past majestic pine, gray ivy-tailored buildings, and a tranquil creek.

Upon entrance into Haviland Hall's Library, humility consumed me. Softly toned walls guarded countless books reaching for an elaborately detailed ceiling. Rows of shiny dark tabletops stretched across the room, each seating-space accompanied by a chair and golden desk lamp. I eased into a hard wooden seat, nervously propping my bag against the legs of my chair.

Rows of faces aligned the tabletops, mostly women and a few men, all stilled by silent reverence. The glowing lamp within reach tempted me to flick its switch to the tune of "Future's So Bright, I Gotta Wear Shades," just to shake things up. But I realized grand rhetoric had begun.

Someone official was saying we represented the crème de la crème, the chosen few who've already contributed greatly by helping the world's less fortunate, stuff like that.

Then Harry Specht, UC Berkeley's Social Welfare Department Dean since 1977, assumed center stage. Harry welcomed us in a voice effused with kind, sage-like wisdom. Wrinkled and frail, he looked about 120. Harry would see us in his class on social welfare foundations, the Dean proudly declared. There, Harry and I would become acquainted…

"You need to lower the self-esteem of abusive parents in order to get them to stop abusing their children," Specht asserted during one of his initial lectures. I experienced a feverish force with which my right arm shot up. Harry conferred a nod, inviting debate.

"But abusive parents already have low self-esteem," I stressed. "That's why they abuse their kids. And there's a generational pattern to abuse, and other factors like economics are at play. We need to *raise* their self-esteem, not lower it."

I couldn't hear his belabored response through my shock and bewilderment, though his tone maintained a calm thoughtfulness.

79

"…but don't let that affect your self-esteem," he concluded, simultaneously imparting a symbolic nudge and culminating his lecture.

"I won't," I retorted, confident, upset, puzzled.

More baffling than the Dean's proposed method for eradicating child abuse, none of my 100 peers —primed to combat authority with vigor at the slightest inkling of prejudice— weighed in, neither in class nor afterward. I couldn't believe it. Who are these people? What is this place?

Parkside Manor afforded a more pleasant, grounding contrast.

Noah and I began running into each other—when knocking on the other's door, for example. He invited me over for tea. I coaxed him to visit with an offer of "extra" brownies from a batch I baked (and ate half of) for me. And him.

We chatted at length on our respective couches, gazing with a fuzzy blur of attraction that sparred in both directions. I learned of Noah's semi-Jewish upbringing, ex-girlfriend in Pittsburgh who owned nine cats and sent him cat hair in her "goodbye" letter, and his grueling process to secure med-school residency.

As flirtations brewed in Parkside Manor, tensions broiled on campus.

One brave social welfare Teacher's Assistant facilitated a class discussion on the topic of date rape. A male peer, who sat directly behind me, curbed her from fully introducing the issue: "The problem with calling it 'rape'," he spouted, "is that there are multiple levels of consent involved. The woman keeps consenting to different levels of the suitor's behavior. There's consent to the date, then consent to the kiss, then consent to touching..." I spun around and witnessed his placement of one hand over the other, alternately, to illustrate his point. "...consent, consent, consent."

"That's a big leap," I snapped. "Kissing or touching doesn't equate with permission to penetrate."

The man pierced me with caustic eyes, blood surging from his red neck to his face. So I turned back around to converse with a more enlightened doctoral student.

"The problem with his argument," I didn't miss a beat, "is that it lends itself too easily to a blame-the-victim mentality."

She nodded and expanded, "True, society does tend to readily blame the victim, and that complicates the initial trauma." She continued with eloquence, as my breathing eased.

Fortunately, Redneck was the only classmate with whom I'd argue. I couldn't fathom why he'd partake in one of the most seemingly liberal programs at one of the most seemingly liberal schools on the planet. But he clearly coalesced with a small yet powerful segment of the department's administration. Little did I know, things would get worse.

At home, chemistry progressed to a dinner invite.

"How do you get your dishes so clean? They're so shiny." My inquiry followed a tasty meal of scallops and pasta, garlic bread, and red wine.

Noah carefully placed our spotless kitchenware, one by one, on a dishrack.

I stood nearby, gawking. "I mean they're just so perfectly clean. I can never get mine to look like that."

He wiped his hands on a washrag. "I use soap and water." He smiled. "Can I ask you a question?"

"Yeah."

"Are you seeing anyone?"

"No."

"Then…" he slowly stepped closer. "Can I kiss you?"

An excited nervousness pushed a "yes" out of my mouth.

Noah tenderly cupped my chin in his hands. He began poking my mouth with his tongue, and moved it ever so slightly to the right and then left. It was weird, so weird that the image of Noah attempting to budge a dead possum came to mind.

He merged us over to the futon couch, where we continued.

"You don't have to do anything. Don't even open your mouth," Noah instructed.

Keep my mouth closed and do nothing? Like a corpse? I wondered about Noah's leanings towards necrophilia.

Still, we liked each other. He was respectful enough to ask if he could kiss me, and he made dinner. Best yet, I kept thinking, he lives next door.

"Sorry," Noah said, sensing my caution. "Are you okay with this?"

"Yeah, I just need to take it slow that's all."

"Sure. Okay." He placed his hand on mine, as we made plans for another date. Noah walked me to the door and granted an affectionate "goodnight" hug.

My relationship with Noah settled into a holding pattern of sorts. We'd end the school days with a knock on the neighbor's door, a shared bite to eat, and the resumption of a horizontal position for holding time. This involved lounging on his couch or mine, our arms wrapped around each other for hours. There was limited kissing and no groping.

In retrospect, it's rather strange—both in our twenties, with easy access to each other's bodies throughout the night, yet perfectly content to engage in holding and nothing more. At the time, though, I was relieved we didn't even kiss much. Moreover, I was glad not to have had to negotiate, or even discuss, sex.

Looking back, perhaps two virgins were entwined in that holding pattern.

One evening, Noah and I laid along my couch, blissfully relaxed in an eye lock, our arms resting on each other's backs. Noah gently coiled ringlets of my hair through his fingers.

"I don't even know. What's your last name?" he asked softly.

"Engel. It means 'angel' in German."

"You are." Noah pulled me closer. I let my eyelids drift closed, as he gingerly planted kisses on my forehead, cheeks, and chin. I felt at once safe, nurtured and cared for. Devon had predicted 13 months, I thought, but maybe it took closer to 13 days.

October 23, 1992: Dear Di, I can't believe I met such a wonderful man right after I left L.A., and he's on the other side of the wall as I write this! It feels like we were meant to be. Noah's so incredibly sweet and smart and caring. We lay in each other's arms for hours. And it's heavenly being in his arms, Di. It's the nicest place I've ever been.

As the holidays rolled around, I drove to L.A. Home, though, was no longer home. Per an unspoken rule, the Engels had ceased all holiday celebrations after Mom's death. So I stayed with Kathryn and her family. Her mom, who I affectionately called "ma," always fed me well.

Christmas meals were the best. "Come on, eat more. Can I give you some more ham, or mashed potatoes or stuffing? What would you like dear?"

"Just more candied yams, ma. They're SO good! I can't stop," I reached for the spatula to serve myself some more. "Nobody else wants any, right?" I chided.

After my candied yam fix for the season, I was glad to re-enter Parkside Manor, where phone-calls with Noah floated me through the remainder of winter break. Noah was with his parents in New York but didn't hesitate to call long-distance. As his vacation was ending, he made a monumental request. Next to a marriage proposal, there's no greater defining aspect to a couple's commitment, or so I figured: the airport pick-up.

"Sure, no problem," I said, "I'll greet you at the gate."

With heightened excitement, I'd cover all bases. The night before Noah's return, I'd arise three hours prior to his arrival. That would allow plenty of time to get ready, check and re-check his flight information in case of changes, drive nine miles to Oakland airport, and walk to the gate.

When the alarm sounded the next morning, I jumped up and snapped into action. I showered, dressed, ate Maple and Brown Sugar oatmeal, brushed my teeth, and called the airport; his flight would arrive on time. But there might be heavy traffic, I told myself; you never know. So I grabbed my purse and left by 9:15 a.m. Noah's plane wouldn't arrive until 11:20 a.m.

I found myself ridiculously early, as I drove along Hegenberger Road towards the airport. Embarrassed by my over-zealousness regarding the airport pick-up, I pulled into the parking lot of a Chinese buffet. I could see the airport from there. So I paid for a leisurely meal of all-you-can-eat egg drop soup, fried won-tons, sweet and sour chicken, chow mein, and whatever else I could waste my time and appetite on. The food tasted like it had been festering in stale airplane fueled toxic air for days. Take this grub in slowly, I told myself. You have 75 minutes to kill. That I did.

At 10:45a.m., I aimed for the airport. Traffic suddenly appeared, and I realized I hadn't thought through a parking plan. I circled the airport twice before locating a Public Parking entrance. Then, I drove through the lot for minutes of cursing and escalating blood pressure in search of a vacant parking space. Once I managed to park, the clock screamed "11:00 a.m." Shit!

I jet to the crosswalk. A blaring "No Walk" command seemed to prohibit movement for hours.

Alas, I scrambled for the doors. People nuzzled me as they moved towards the curb. Wrong doors. I shuffled to the ones featuring "Enter." Made it in.

Pre-9/11, I wasn't stalled by lines or the need to remove my shoes. I thus maintained a rapid jog through Oakland Airport's United Airlines terminal. I found the Arrival listings. Oops, those are Departures. Damn, where—oh, on the other side. The letters were so small. There's his flight, arriving on time at Gate 22.

It took a bit of time to find the arrows for Gate 22. As I did, I brushed by a little boy who was ambling with a stuffed purple and green Barney in one hand, his Mommy's hand in the other.

"Sorry, honey," I slowed to say.

Shit, my watch now read 11:19, and it was a long stretch to the Gate.

I pushed myself onward, "Chariots of Fire" running through my head, and I arrived breathless. My body froze as I watched a woman in an official navy blue uniform shut the doors to the passenger walkway. They'd disembarked. Noah was nowhere in sight.

"Robyn Engel, please pick up the white courtesy phone. Robyn Engel..." Shit, where's the phone? It was like that nightmare in which you keep dialing and dialing but your fingers instantly freeze so you can't ever complete the call. Or the line gets disconnected the second the killer enters the scene. Or the call's picked up but you've suddenly contacted laryngitis and can't talk anymore. Where's the damn phone?

I finally spotted the courtesy phones beyond a slew of weary travelers several yards to my right. I rushed over, breathing heavily, and picked up.

"Hello Noah?" Damn dial tone. He must have left.

I sped home, fraught with guilt and anxiety. Is he okay? He can't walk all the way home. What if he takes a cab and gets killed? It'll be my fault. I fuckin killed my boyfriend for the sake of gross chow mein.

Home now, I knocked on his door but Noah didn't answer. Damnit! I really blew it. Poor Noah. Please, please be okay. It's all my fault. I really blew it.

I waited in the lobby, hoping he'd appear.

Eventually, a tattered, weary emotionless traveler trudged in, lugging a large suitcase and mid-sized travel bag.

"I'm SO sorry," I rushed over to him. "I was too early, so I took my time, but then I was too late, and then I missed your call and, wait, how did you get home? I'm so sorry."

Noah was neither angry nor happy to see me. "I took a cab. It's alright, I'm just going to take a long nap right now."

That was the beginning of the end for us. Holding time diminished in duration, coziness, and frequency. Yet Noah maintained optimism about his future. Any day now, he informed, he'd find out about residency.

I replied with the only words that popped into my head, "When you leave, I mean, if we're still together, what happens to us?"

"What do you mean? Why do you ask?"

"Because I want to know."

"You can't be asking for a commitment after only three months, Robyn. Nobody does that. I'm going to be thousands of miles away."

"So," my voice faded, "you mean this is it? We're going to be through?"

"Long distance relationships don't work."

"They can if you want them too," I pressed. Love is all you need, right?

"No, they can't," he insisted.

I sat up and moved a few inches from him. My heart rattled with shock and upset.

"So what do we do now?" I asked.

"That's up to you."

I sauntered to Lake Merritt the next day, to decide. The glistening water both soothed me and instilled clarity. As a few teardrops dampened my face, I turned back to Parkside Manor.

Inside my apartment, I pulled open the refrigerator door. I removed Noah's ketchup bottle that had somehow migrated to my fridge. I walked to his door and knocked. He opened immediately.

"I can't do this. Here's your ketchup." I extended my arm and he took the Heinz.

I responded by launching into a mad masochistic jealous craze.

With both hands, I scrunched up all the hairs in the vicinity of my left ear, then tucked them tightly behind my ear. I pulled a Q-tip from my bathroom cabinet, thrust it into my ear and twisted frenetically, until I was certain I'd cleared out all remnants of excess wax.

I entered the closet that bordered our apartments. In perhaps the most undignified moment of my life, upstaging my slipper-slippage-into-ladder ensemble, I pressed my ear against the closet wall and held my breath to hear exactly what was going on.

Truth is, I detected nothing but free-flowing high-pitched sound bites mixed with an occasional deeper toned blurb. But I convinced myself otherwise. They were going at it, I was sure. After a few minutes of eavesdropping, I couldn't stand it any longer. I came out of the closet, secured a box of Kleenex and plopped down next to my phone.

"Ka, Kathryn, it's Robyn. Am I bothering you?" I blew my nose into a tissue. "I just, I need a friend. Is this an okay time?"

"Of course Robyn. Are you alright?"

"No, I'm a mess. You know how I told you Noah's never going to move out?"

"Yeah. Why? What's going on?"

"God, Kat, I was finally getting over him, but then I heard some stupid whiny bitch at his door saying —I pinched my nostrils to best imitate her— 'God, I had such an awful day!' And he'd rather be with her than me? What the hell! Then he fuckin' invites her in for a fuckin' drink and they're on his couch now in *our* spot and I just know he's fucking her brains out." I blew snot into a gob of tissue. "Sorry. Ugh. I can't believe I did this but I went into my closet to listen to them. I don't know what came over me, I couldn't help it. What the hell was I thinking, Kat, dating my next-door neighbor that" —sniffle— "bastard?"

"Oh Robyn, you'll get through this. Hey I've seen you through much worse honey. And I've been through worse. Remember my roommate a couple years ago, Zack? I told you that story, right?"

"Oh my God, Kat, that guy was a freak. But a cute one. I don't remember. What's the story?" My tone lightened.

"Oh boy. He came home one night and told me his girlfriend dumped him. He was really depressed too, so we had a drink. And we had another drink. And we kept drinking. Pretty soon he was looking really, really hot and he was coming onto me big-time."

"Woohoo!" I exclaimed, excited for her and forgetting my woes.

"Anyway, we, well, we ended up in bed. I tell you, Robyn, it was good and all but the guy was deranged. The next day when I got home from work, he acted like nothing happened. I'm thinking 'okay, if you're gonna be that way, I will too.' Then he laughed and said he was back on, or maybe off and on, with his girlfriend."

"Oh shit," I interjected.

"Yeah a few nights later, I came home and they were on alright. She was on him on the kitchen table." Kathryn continued, describing a yelling match. It took her weeks to kick the guy out. He insisted on staying. Worse, his girlfriend practically moved in.

Kathryn had to eventually call the cops.

For the moment, I wasn't going berserk. My life wasn't even *exiciting* at all. That was a very good thing, and Kathryn was a very good friend.

Perhaps everything would be alright.

Chapter Six: Penthouse View

During my two year stint at Cal, the women's movement journeyed an erratic course. I managed to land at the intersection of two factors: (1) my research on an incredibly destructive psychosocial phenomenon and (2) an historic issue of Penthouse Magazine.

- October, 1992: Madonna's first book, Sex, was branded soft-core porn. Within days of publication, sales soared to 1.5 million, and Sex became the world's most popular coffee-table book of all time.

- June, 1993: The United Nations World Conference on Human Rights affirmed that human rights do in fact include women's rights.

- September, 1993: A topless pole-dancing Carrie Ann Inaba opened Madonna's Girlie World Tour, which rapidly grossed an estimated $70 million.

- September, 1994: Authored by Senator Joseph Biden and signed by President Bill Clinton, the Violence Against Women Act poured $1.6 billion into an array of efforts to deter violence against women and support female victims of violent crimes.

  -Wikipedia

- Also in September, 1994: Penthouse Magazine celebrated its 25th anniversary with a 350-page Collector's Edition. A young social worker, Robyn Alana Engel, is referenced and quoted on page 38 of this issue.

--

At home, avoidance mode kicked in. When readying to leave in the mornings, I wrapped my bag handle across my right shoulder, clenched the doorknob, and waited before turning it. If I heard

Noah's door open, I stood still long enough for him to exit the building. If I didn't hear him leave, I departed quickly. Luck was on my side in terms of the whiny bitch; I didn't hear her anymore, though I tried.

I couldn't always dodge Noah, though. We crossed paths occasionally, between Parkside Manor and the 19th Street BART station. When face-to-face, I'd give a curt "hi," turn my head, and walk on briskly.

Meanwhile I enjoyed friendly chatter with other neighbors like Vince, down the hall, an undergrad studying biology. Vince moved from San Diego, and he planned to return there after graduation.

Despite getting to know Vince and a few others at Parkside Manor, I remained oblivious to the couple next-door, until one night…

I'd sunk into my study spot on the chocolate brown couch, adjacent to the wall between our apartments. As I trudged through a chapter on social welfare policy, noises startled me.

"No! No don't hit me! Stop!" she shouted.

Shit.

"I told you not to! Why'd you fuck me over like that?" His voice fumed with rage.

Despite fear, I knew what I had to do. So I crept over to my phone at the foot of the bed, picked up the receiver and pressed 9-1-1.

"…I'm calling to report domestic violence in the apartment next-door. The woman shouted at the man to stop hitting her. He's been yelling back. I still hear him."

"…123 Bay Place, apartment 223…Okay, thank you."

I sat in angst, wondering how long it would take.

Quiet resumed. What could this mean?

Twelve excruciating minutes later, a blunt knock simultaneously jolted and relieved me. Two deep voices recited the words, "Oakland Police."

The neighbors' door swung open as she said, "We were just playing."

The officers left. That was it.

Damnit, lady! I risk my safety for yours, and you let the beast off the hook.

Fraught with fear that he'd figure out who made the call, I entertained the thought of carrying a weapon. What could I use? A steak-knife? Scissors? I have that old hammer in the closet. Good Lord, I was deranged by paranoia. This isn't right, I realized.

I purchased pepper-spray at Long's Drugstore on my way to campus the next morning.

A few evenings later, sounds of a different sort propelled me back into high alert.

"You're the only neighbor I've met." I recognized the voice; it was the woman next door. "I've seen that lady around but never talked to her," she said to Noah. "Do you know her?"

Wow. They're actually discussing me, just inches from my door. Do you people not know how thin these walls are? Girlfriend, you haven't a clue what I did for you! And you sir, don't, don't, just don't get me started!

"That's Robyn," Noah replied. "She's a sweet person unless you cross her, but I didn't do anything. We dated a little and I was honest about my situation, but she's acting like I'm the enemy."

"Mm mm, I know what you mean. My boyfriend's the same way too sometimes. He's kinda got a short fuse but we're cool. He's a great guy. You met him?"

"No. Sometime, though."

I pictured Noah digging into his pocket for his keys. "Well, I'll see you later."

"Bye, bye."

The doors to my right and left closed in unison.

Sweet unless you cross me? I shifted towards my closet, his place. In a cold controlled tone, I informed, "I'm always sweet, you fuckin' bastard necrophiliac!"

And then there was school. And more weird tensions.

Professor Neil Gilbert's lecture room buzzed with embitterment. Students either challenged him through relevant retort, or derailed him by random announcements.

I sat in the back rows with a cluster of friends; we'd keep a safe distance. It's not that my peers and I wished to ostracize the department stronghold. It's just that we knew Neil Gilbert had authored the controversial 1991 article, "The phantom epidemic of sexual assault."

Once, as he was about to begin a lecture, our class cheerleader made an announcement: "The Social Welfare Graduate Assembly is sponsoring an Ultimate Frisbee tournament at one o'clock this Saturday at Strawberry Canyon. We'll provide water and sodas. Please bring snacks to share. It's going to be a lot of fun! See y'all there!"

"Enough!" Redneck barked from the front row. He shot up and spun around to address the class. "I'm sick and tired of all these interruptions when the professor has something valuable to say!" Redneck turned back around, dropped into his seat, and looked up towards the podium.

As Neil Gilbert proceeded to reference a striking discrepancy in reports of rape when comparing FBI statistics to numbers that he claimed had been grossly inflated by a "radical feminist agenda," I envisioned Redneck sharing cold beers with Gilbert on an expansive grassy field. Chuckling, they elbow-nudged each other in appreciation of a rousing game of Ultimate Frisbee played by bouncy, bikini-clad bronze grad students.

Following an uneventful chunk of self-imposed reading time at the Haviland Library that weekend, I meandered by the Ultimate gathering. What a mundane scene, not what I imagined. A few folks tossed a fluorescent green Frisbee, and a lone bottle of water rested in an ice-chest that pinned down a stack of flyers. I took the cold bottle, along with a flyer. It pitched an upcoming mixer hosted by SFSU's Social Work Graduate Program.

Maybe I need to venture to San Francisco for a man or just some normalcy, I thought. Note to self: If normalcy is to be found anywhere, San Francisco would not be the place.

Johnny greeted me as soon as I entered his lavish 9th floor apartment on the San Francisco Waterfront. A clean-cut, Richie Cunningham type, I was instantly attracted.

Despite a growing crowd in his home, we focused on each other.

"My sister's in the Social Work program," he told me. "I'm at Hastings. I like to host parties so I offered my place." He turned towards a pair of wide windows that boasted a picture postcard scene of the Bay Bridge stretched across a subdued gray-blue blanket of water.

"Not too shabby," I affirmed. A law student who practically lives in a Penthouse. Have I met Prince Charming?

"Yeah, I can't complain," he responded.

We sat on his sectional, connecting over childhood memories of life in LA: boogie-boarding at Toes beach in El Segundo —what a strange name for a beach; and the La Brea Tar Pits, the number one default field-trip spot for all of L.A. Unified. I was fascinated at first. But it became no surprise to see the dinosaurs still stuck in tar year after year.

Then there's the humungous cement donut atop Randy's Donuts in Inglewood. You couldn't eye that thing without craving donuts for the next three hours or months, yet the cravings were never strong enough to actually stop in to buy one. We'd both heard the donuts weren't all that good anyway.

By the end of the evening, I'd secured a date for Friday night.

Johnny suggested the movie, "The Age of Innocence."

"Sure," I said, just excited to have a date.

I sat next to Johnny in the theatre thinking, he's liking it but I'm not sophisticated enough to appreciate this intensely boring movie. I did, however, appreciate a yet unexpressed sexual tension between us.

When "The Age of Innocence" ended, Johnny took my hand and led us into a small independent bookstore. He walked directly to a bookshelf in a back corner, reached up and retrieved Sex by Madonna, as if part of his daily routine.

When he opened to a photo of Madonna appearing to get intimate with a canine, I announced I'd be in the self-help section.

"Uh, mm," he murmured.

"Co-Dependent No More"? I could use this, and it was half off. I skimmed through the book and decided to buy it. Johnny approached, appearing sated.

"Ready?" he asked.

"Oh, yeah, if you are, sure." I can't make you wait while I buy this, because yeah, I'm co-dependent no more. I returned the book to the shelves, imprinting the author's name—Melody Beattie—in my memory.

Back at the entrance to the South Beach Marina Apartments, Johnny invited me up to his place for tea. Enticed by a rising tension, and being a tea fan, I agreed.

Inside, I stood at his living room windows admiring the view. Johnny stroked my hair, and rubbed his hand up and down my back. He then escorted me to the plush sectional a few yards away.

"It's our spot," Johnny flirted.

"So it is." I smirked.

He took the two large mauve pillows on either end of the sofa and placed them side by side in the nearest corner. Johnny eased himself onto the sectional, seductively, confidently, settling in with his body sideways and facing me.

"Come here." He patted the cushion by his chest.

I guess I'm not getting any Earl Grey, I thought, but this could be more fun. I slipped off my shoes and carefully nestled in. Our lips touched, and kissing began with Johnny's tongue flapping rapidly in my mouth like an arthritic sprinkler head. Weird, I thought.

Despite our close quarters, our bodies barely touched. I only felt the up and down, and occasional sideways, erratic movement of his tongue. Johnny slowed to a stop, shifted onto his back, with a glowing face – as if he'd conquered the world.

A vertical object caught the corner of my eye. I glanced downwards and there it was: a proud upright penis, freely unleashed and towering over Johnny's horizontal frame. He took my hand to its hard, rubbery surface, then let go.

As did I. I was stilled, shocked and perplexed.

Johnny pierced me with a look of patronizing scrutiny. "How weird!" he stated.

How weird that Johnny said "How weird," as if I was the one who'd committed a penile oddity.

"Well, I think I'll get going now." I moved to collect my shoes.

Johnny zipped up his pants and walked me to the door.

A cursory peck "goodbye" preceded no contact ever again.

Always quick to dive into schoolwork as a means of forgetting things like a penile mishap, I shifted focus to our second year research project—a dreaded project, especially because it involved computer statistics.

Students typically explored topics related to their internship placements, and I'd been matched with Jewish Family and Children's Services. Since I couldn't fathom a marginally fun researchable Jewish topic, I went for meaningful and relevant.

My Professor at the time—we'll call him Footinmouth—met with us individually to discuss our topics.

"I'm thinking of exploring anti-Semitism on the Berkeley campus," I told Footinmouth.

Without pause, Footinmouth replied, "I was hoping you'd pick a topic more people care about."

In that instant, a sharp and weighty pain took residence in the core of my veins. I had no response but to depart Footinmouth's office.

The next day, I met with the Assistant Dean, who —with compassion and diplomacy—expedited my transfer to a new class. Professor Yu-Wen Ying would provide the brilliant, caring guidance I needed for the rest of the chapter.

A few days later, Footinmouth called me back into his office to make amends. Fumbling for words, he appeared sincerely sorry and explained that his kids swim at the Jewish Community Center. He has nothing against Jewish people, he asserted. Yet Footinmouth offered no viable explanation.

"Okay," I said. "Thanks."

Amid months of laborious research, I interviewed a handful of professionals in the Jewish community. Shady granted ninety minutes of her time and input. Her enthusiasm about my project boosted my own. Grateful and naive, I handed Shady a copy of my paper.

"It's just a draft," I clarified. "I'm going to try to get it published when I'm done, but I'm not quite there."

Note to self: Don't trust people you will later name "Shady" when you write about them.

The remainder of the school year passed without incident. In a nutshell, so to speak, I successfully dodged Noah and penises.

Like all big days, it seemed it would never arrive, until it did. And then it seemed to have arrived suddenly. Family, friends and peers roared as I crossed the stage. I proudly strode by Neil Gilbert and other faculty members who'd marked their official ceremonial posts in official ceremonial attire. Dean Harry Specht handed me a rolled up slip of paper. We exchanged a handshake and warm grin. Water under the bridge, I thought. You go about your business teaching others to lower the self-worth of abusive parents. I'm outta here. "Thank you!"

The all-around energy was one of unabashed thrill for each other.

In the midst of the jubilant crowd post-ceremony, my eyes met Redneck's. I smiled at him. He countered with a glare that said a lot, excepting "Congratulations to you too!" Good luck to the field of child welfare, Redneck – the niche that now has you as their ally. And to all the women in your life, my sympathies.

As I pressed a photograph into my graduation album, a week or two later, the phone-call came.

"Hello...Yes, this is Robyn. You're a reporter from where? Penthouse Magazine?" My eyes popped open wide. "Sure, you can interview me...Now is fine. I'm just wondering, how did you find out about my research?"

Shady sent my draft to, of all places, Penthouse Magazine. They were writing about, of all issues for Penthouse Magazine to address, anti-Semitism on college campuses. My interview would appear in Penthouse Magazine's 25th Anniversary issue, to be released in late July of 1994.

When my friendly interview with the reporter concluded, I called Shady to ask about forwarding my paper to Penthouse Magazine.

"That's ridiculous Robyn," Shady defended. "It's 23-pages long. How could I send it so quickly?" Despite the fact that FAX machines, scanners and FedEx had long since been established, I saw no point in arguing. In fact, I might have thanked Shady had she not been so…shady.

Next, I called everyone I knew. All offered to shop for Penthouse upon its release, to spare me any embarrassment. I thanked them for their generosity but expressed a need to get ahold of it myself.

I was highly methodical about the task. For weeks leading up to its release, I investigated prospective retailers. The quaint and clean convenience store on 20th actually carried it. Better yet, they didn't know me; I'd never bought anything there. Plus they sold tame items like chewing gum.

When I entered to make the purchase, my heart racing, I casually located some Trident spearmint gum. Then I slowly moved to the magazine rack, found the silver covered issue, slid it under my left arm, and meandered for at least one more item. A small pink hairbrush would do.

I took five steps over to the cashier and placed the items down in front of her, with Penthouse on the bottom, face down. I can do this. I can do this. I'm almost there.

The young cashier scanned the chewing gum. Then the hairbrush. She looked at the Magazine nonchalantly.

"I'm only buying that because I'm in it," I explained, as if that justified my purchase.

She shot me a blank look that said, "Whatever, pay up." But you didn't even ask for my I.D.? You mean, I look my age? Blasphemy is this easy?

I left disheartened, clenching the bag with all the tightness of my proper being. I walked home briskly.

The second I shut the apartment door behind me, I thrust the magazine out of the bag and perused its pages for typeface.

There it was, in big bold letters that centered page 38: a quote by me, but a misleading one that was taken out of context. I quickly began reading the full-page article on the phenomenon of anti-Semitism on college campuses. Wait, I didn't say that, not exactly, I thought…And that wording is wrong too, and —crap! I was mortified by a slew of inaccuracies. Yet not too mortified to stifle myself from zipping to Long's Drug Store to make a dozen copies of page 38.

In a polite letter to Penthouse Editor Peter Bloch, I corrected him on a number of items, requesting that he "kindly note these clarifications." I'm not sure if he did. Regardless, I found myself swirling in media mayhem.

One Jewish publication after another contacted me for interviews. The Hillel Jewish Student Center's administration, clearly facing backlash, claimed my study had little significance in the context of greater campus life.

More upsetting was the fact that they were upset. I'd grown close to them and wanted my research to be helpful, not stress-inducing.

The worst it all was George, a stranger from across the country. "I'm in Tennessee," George told me when he called. He asked about my research methodology in less scientific terms. "How did you get your information?"

In turn, I asked George how he knew about my study. As if I needed to ask. George ignored the question. After bidding George and abrupt farewell, I had my number unlisted.

By the time my paper was published in a reputable Journal, the Journal of Jewish Communal Service, in the summer of 1995, excitement had waned. Nobody expressed interest, not reporters, not family, nor friends. Talk of Penthouse had ceased. I was fine with that. It wasn't a pleasant Penthouse view.

In fact, I didn't think for a moment that perhaps I might continue to follow a writer's path. I just wanted to crawl into a hole and forget it ever happened.

But I had one more thing to do first...I picked it up. Who could I give it to? It would be too weird to offer it to a blood relation. I looked towards my front door. Yes, Vince down the hall. He's between girlfriends. I stuffed the Collector's Edition into a brown bag and walked to the other end of the building.

"I have something for you, Vince," I said, handing him the bag. "I'm in there on page 38, but there's no picture, so you don't care about that. I don't feel right keeping it, so it's all yours."

As Vince peered into the bag, a smile dominated his face, as though he'd just uncovered Willy Wonka's fifth and final Golden Ticket. He fought to restrain his elation.

"Um, thank you, Robyn." He laughed.

"Sure, Vince." I giggled.

<u>January 12, 1995</u>: Dear Di, I still think about Johnny. I shouldn't have gone to his place, but I just wanted to explore our chemistry. I want to feel normal, like a normal adult who dates and gets sexual. But hell, I didn't know he'd unleash and make me touch it. It's not my fault. Or is it? God damnit! I'm so embarrassed to even write "penis" when I'm writing to you, Di. Shit, I hate this. I wish I wasn't so naïve, embarrassed about sexuality, and embarrassed that I'm embarrassed about sexuality. I mean, I'm an adult, not a teen. And now, what the hell? I'm in Penthouse Magazine. What could the universe be telling me? Crap, nobody cares that I'm being published in the Journal of Jewish Communal Service. They just wanted to see my name in Penthouse. Yeah, like hell they did. They wanted an excuse to buy it. It's so gross, though, Di. So demeaning of women. Why was I so excited? I guess because it's Penthouse—same reason I'm so ashamed. It's a really weird time, Di. Really weird. Thanks for being here.

<u>Chapter endnote:</u>
At the time of this writing, one can obtain Penthouse Magazine's 25th Anniversary Collector's Edition for as low as $2.98 at www.Amazon.com. Copies are used; handle with care. Kindly skip page 38.

Chapter Seven: Mindless Meanderings

How would the world's most perfect couple have described themselves through personal ads, had they not met at the ball? I imagine something like this:

Name:	Cindy Rella
Sex:	Oh no, not until marriage *giggling and blushing*.
Appearance:	They say I'm beautiful - perfect height, weight, figure and feet.
Hobbies:	Talking to birds, playing with mice, sewing, cooking, and cleaning.
Seeking:	Male; any age, religion, ethnicity, and employment status. Criminal and substance abuse history don't matter. Relationship history doesn't matter. Kids or no kids doesn't matter. Looks and money a plus.
First date preferences:	Marriage.

Name:	Prince Charming
Sex:	Please, frequently and often.
Appearance:	Gorgeous, manly, and extremely handsome.
Hobbies:	Waltzing.
Seeking:	Beautiful female – perfect height, weight, figure and feet. Nothing else matters.
First date preferences:	Family is pressuring me to marry. I just wanna get laid.

And so a woman (i.e., me) meandered mindlessly in search of a man, because she's supposed to have a man in her life and get married. We've been taught that it's better to be in a relationship than not, regardless of the nature of that relationship. A gal is deemed worthy when she has a man by her side, especially when that man is her husband and regardless of what type of person he is.

Remember a few chapters ago when I nonchalantly mentioned, "I dated and started antidepressants" (in the early nineties)? Yeah, I was trying to manipulate time like other authors do so flawlessly. That move was neither discrete nor fair on my part. I didn't even mention names. Here they are: Prozac, Paxil, Zoloft, Wellbutrin, Imipramine and, alas, the antidepressant I stuck with, Effexor.

As far as men, the list started with Alejandro, when I still lived in L.A., and would span various locales and names well into the 21st century.

Anticipating delectable dessert, I slithered into my little black dress and drove to The Cheesecake Factory in Redondo Beach, where Gary hosted a New Year's bash.

Gary is the type of friend a woman keeps around, at least temporarily. He doesn't exude a sexual vibe, never talks about dating or relationships, and supports his gal pals through their dramatics. He's a sensitive guy with some feminine mannerisms—the type I suspected might be gay but unwilling to acknowledge this even to himself.

Back to my story, I wasn't sitting alone at the Cheesecake Factory for long before Alejandro conspicuously slid onto the chair to my left. We proceeded to chat and share a generous portion of white chocolate cheesecake decorated in elaborately swirled dark cocoa and sparkled with almond slivers. Alejandro noticed that I really enjoyed it, so he let me finish his portion too.

On cue (i.e., as soon as I licked the last remnants off my fork), he asked if I wanted to dance.

Alejandro took my hand and led me to the dance floor. We spent the next several hours grooving to 1991's best: Paula Abdul, Madonna, Boys II Men, Michael Jackson, and—still popular then—Celine Dion.

At the midnight hour, we separated to endure obligatory rounds, forcing insincerely loving hugs onto everyone in the vicinity.

Alas, Alejandro and I were thrilled to reunite minutes later.

After some more and slower dancing, he started to make his move.

He stroked and brushed my hair away from my ear and neck, I wrote on January 1, 1992. Then he kissed up and down my neck. It felt a little weird and wet, but great too. Then Alejandro stole a kiss on the lips, SO quick and SO sweet, Di! The next thing I knew, his whole mouth was on mine, shaking, with his tongue inside my mouth. It was just happening. I didn't know what I was supposed to do. I figured I should close my eyes and put my tongue in his mouth too, so I did. We kept kissing and kissing. It felt naughty and exciting. We finally stopped. Alejandro looked and me and asked, "Where'd you learn to kiss like that?" I told him, "From you."

I'd define our kissing as flawless fun. It lasted hours but felt like minutes. Alejandro and I kissed where-ever we went: on a lifeguard stand at Santa Monica Beach under the stars, in the back row of Manhattan Village Cinema during "Beauty and the Beast," on my pink bean bag chair in my bedroom, and in his car or mine.

He didn't push boundaries; he simply hinted devilishly at sex on a few occasions. It was a relationship comprised of kissing for the sake

111

of kissing, with no real pressure to get to second base, much less hit one out of the park. Mm, those were the days.

<u>January 7, 1992</u>: It's really happening this time, Di. I'm really falling for someone who's falling for me. It's been a romantic week. It's a dream, but it's real. I can't believe it's so real. He's a sweetheart. He holds me. He tells me I'm safe with him, that he won't leave me, that I'm special to him, that I'm beautiful and desirable. We kiss like there's no tomorrow. He held me on his lap in his car the other night, at the beach, in the rain. He told me not to be afraid of anything. He's honest and open, very sweet and giving. I can't believe any of this.

Truth be told, I didn't kiss Alejandro for the pure thrill of it. I had another agenda. I needed to shut him up. Talking was not his strong suit. The words emanating from Alejandro's facial orifice irritated, confused, and contradicted themselves, me, and the greater stratosphere.

There was the message, "I'll pick you up at seven," when, in fact, he did not arrive until nine-thirty.

There were the words, "I'm going to take you to Disneyland next Saturday. We'll get a locker there, for our stuff." A locker? I was baffled by this nuance; however, intrigued. In all of my ventures to the Magic Kingdom, I'd never been privy to a Disneyland locker. That must be something special!

Two days later, Alejandro said casually, "By the way, the Disney trip isn't happening." What? No, no locker?

"An apology would be nice," I asserted.

With a grumble and heavy sigh, Alejandro sputtered, "I'm sorry, but it's not my fault."

Between the kissing and irksome vociferations, our romance ebbed and flowed into its thirteenth day.

On January 13, 1992, Alejandro invited me to the Santa Monica Boardwalk for, perhaps, his most dramatic performance to date.

"It's just not working," he announced, displaying the agony of a soap opera character whose evil twin —the one that died in a plane crash fifteen years earlier— just reappeared; having survived on a small tropical island unknown to scientists, Oprah and the CIA; to avenge all who wronged him, starting with blood relations.

"I feel like I have to work too hard. You don't talk to me," he sighed. "We're stopping each other from seeing other people. And okay, I'm a jerk, I made a lunch date with someone else."

You don't shut up, jerk. "You haven't even given me a chance."

"That's not the point," he proclaimed. "And I don't believe in second chances, but I still want to be friends."

"Well, I don't," I responded.

I turned my back on him and headed for my car.

I'd heard that the first break-up is the hardest, so I knew I needed to take it easy on myself. I thus drove to the Santa Monica Mall and walked, in a slightly disoriented but okay state. When I saw and smelled some breathtaking chocolate fudge, I stopped walking.

As I bit into a fat chunk of soft, creamy, rich and potently sweet dark-chocolate fudge with those little marshmallows that make hot chocolate such a treat, I thought about how easily I could endure a lifetime of break-ups, you know, if I had to.

It's over, I wrote in my Diary. But it was a very nice 13 days until he dumped me. I want to be kissed like that again, but I want it to be more real. And I want it to last, maybe even forever.

Five months later, as I drove my Festiva to my job, I saw him through my rearview mirror.

Alejandro gave an I'm-no-longer-attached-to-you-even-though-I-decided-to-go-out-of-my-way-to-drive-by-your-place wave, while he trailed me in his car to my worksite eight miles away.

Am I being stalked? What the hell? I drove as fast as possible, while staying below the speed limit.

When I arrived at the lot, Alejandro continued south on Westwood Boulevard, perhaps disappointed that I didn't pull over and jump into his arms.

Several years later, when I was living in the San Francisco Bay Area, Gary called. Alejandro had a wedding to attend in the Bay Area. He'd asked Gary for my number, and Gary refused to oblige. It was sweet and protective on Gary's part.

At the time, though, I was flattered by Alejandro's attempts at contact and recalled how nice the kissing was. "You can give him my number if he asks for it again," I told Gary.

"You know, Robyn, the guy's a jerk. And who does he think he is for breaking up with you in the first place! He probably just didn't want to be seen without a date at the wedding."

"You're right. You did me a favor, Gary." I scoffed. "Thanks."

114

Gary giggled.

"God, it's weird," I continued. "The guy had no problems ending our 13-day romance with a dramatic performance years ago, but he's been unable to let go of me ever since. It's kinda freaky. Did I tell you about the time he followed me to work one day?"

Perched on a sun-warmed spot of stone overlooking the cliffs at Pirates Cove, Negril Jamaica, I was privy to an influx of magnificent sights. While this "no worries" isle boasts resplendent scenes, one specimen instantaneously claimed top of my list.

A seasoned diver leapt from steep cliffs and floated downward in elegantly angled positions, splashing with equal grace and poise, into a welcoming ocean forty feet below.

I sat a few yards from his launching point to my right, and even closer to the ladder that brought him to land.

Upon returning from his fifth magnificent display, the diver halted nearby. He glanced my way, and I reciprocated. I couldn't help it. The man appeared a delicious chunk of dark chocolate sculptured by Michelangelo, radiating sunrays from the most intimate of crevices and dressed in black spandex for public viewing.

"Hi, I'm Omar." He extended a hand.

"I, hi, I'm Robyn."

"Come with me." Like a puppy in heat, I pranced behind.

Focused on the subtle shifting of his tight buttocks, I followed Omar down a metal ladder into an underwater cave.

We landed in an active, chilly ocean, sheltered atop and along the sides by dark stone walls and opening up to a glorious view of the fading blue sky streaked with yellows, oranges and reds.

The waves nudged me, as I fought to secure my footing.

Omar planted himself in deeper water and I inched closer to him amid brief flirtations.

"No husband or boyfriend?"

"No, I came here alone, just to get away. They're crazy."

"Do you make them crazy?" He teased.

"No." Maybe. "I think they started off that way." But maybe not.

By this time we stood facing each other, little room in-between.

With waves crashing against the rock, sun resting in the backdrop, and the titillating grazing of our warming bodies, Omar's luscious lips met mine.

Incredible.

Suddenly, rough waters forced me off-kilter, tossing me back towards the cave's walls. My forehead crashed against sharp-edged rock. I decided, when a momentary little shrill of pain skimmed my forehead, that I was perfectly fine.

Omar stood giggling, still planted firmly in the sand.

He meandered towards me. Rather than offering aid, Omar motioned me to follow him back up the ladder.

I was perfectly fine, after all, so I climbed the ladder back up to safety.

Blasting reggae tunes from a small radio greeted us.

Omar and his equally scrumptious diver friend engaged me in some reggae dancing. I boogied on top of the world, in complete denial of my little accident, and fully appreciative for how Stella got her groove.

Omar's friend departed to start diving again.

Shortly thereafter, my time with Omar ended on a promise to meet at Margaritaville Saturday night.

Come Saturday night, he never showed. Instead, I was stuck dancing to endless repetitions of "One Love" with a dweeb so doped up he could barely keep his eyes open.

We were panting and sweating during the initial encounter. Still, he was really good and made it seem effortless. I, on the other hand, struggled to keep up. In synchronicity with a hottie, though, fire charged through me. My every movement took on a ravenous life of its own.

"I'm Robyn, by the way," I said between breaths.

"I'm Basil."

Basil? I pondered. Who's named Basil? His parents must've loved natural herbs. But he's darn cute, in an intellectual Clark Kent kind of way. It could be worse. I could be lusting after a Paprika.

We pressed on for another 20 minutes or so, at which point he stopped and got off. I slowed down.

"Well, I'll see you next time, Robyn."

"Okay, yeah. Have a good one," I responded, as if content to go at it solo for the rest of the night.

When I saw Basil again on the elliptical machines at the Alameda Athletic Club, he asked if I'd like to go for dinner Friday night. I immediately agreed, stuffing my excitement underneath hard breaths and a constant flow of perspiration.

"Meet me at Park Ave Pub n Grill. I've started a tab," he texted. I'm no drinker. But Basil was cute, and a good 10 years younger than me, I figured. Thoughts of cougardom thrust my right foot down on the gas pedal.

Twelve minutes later, I arrived in peppy spirits. Two shiny empty beer bottles centered the reddish wood tabletop.

We ordered, then struck up carefree banter over sandwiches and fries. By the time I finished my meal, I'd witnessed Basil polish off three beers.

Directing my gaze to his meaty biceps, I took a couple of slow sips of my rum and coke. "Go light on the alcohol, please," I'd told the bartender.

"Wanna walk around?" he suggested after paying the bill.

"Sure."

Basil and I strolled along Piedmont Avenue. A quiet cautiousness brewed within, as the guy expelled stories involving intoxication. There were countless frat parties and raves, severe migraines induced by a 72-hour hangover, and a time when he got lost for hours in Emeryville because he was "really wasted."

"But I'm always a safe driver," he claimed. "To hell with seatbelt laws." Whoa. Where did that come from? "The government can't tell me what to do! I don't need to wear a seatbelt if I don't want to. It's my choice; I have certain freedoms."

Drinking and driving unseatbelted? Not a life-enhancing formula. "You really need to wear a seatbelt." I lectured, my right arm moving up and down radically with my index finger extended. "The laws exist for a reason." I scolded like a school teacher or worse, his mother.

Basil quieted, and I realized I'd said too much. We found ourselves staring into the window of a frozen yogurt shop and agreed to go inside. "Do you want frozen yogurt?" He broke the tension.

"Sure, great."

At the counter, Basil joked that he'd like to taste a beer flavored yogurt. Unrestrained, I blurted out, "Are you an alcoholic?"

"No," he immediately defended. "I drink the average, three to five drinks per week. Or is that per day?...Just with dinner, and, wait, there's lunchtime drinks too."

Basil studied his open palms, slowly counting while folding in one finger at a time. When he got to the left middle finger, he abruptly excused himself to add rainbow sprinkles to his chocolate mint fudge.

Basil practically sprinted north on Piedmont upon seeing me off. When my Festiva was within sight, he stopped. The man maintained a football field's distance between us to declare, "Well, I'll see ya when I see ya."

119

A few days later, Basil was working up a sweat when I entered the cardio room. This time, I wouldn't sweat next to him. Instead I chose the treadmill across the way, affording him a view of my, well, semi-toned and slightly drooping butt in blue spandex.

He left shortly thereafter. No doubt, it was five o'clock somewhere.

"Robyn, Manny's a really sweet guy. Are you open to a set-up?" Leah always kept me in mind for her boyfriend du-jour's single best bud.

Really? A guy? Sign me up! "Yeah, I guess you can give him my email."

A cold, clammy hand touched mine, as I sat to join Manny at a quaint corner booth in Mexicali Rose.

At first sight, what impressed me about Manny was a prominent receding hairline drawing attention to a very long forehead. Don't be so shallow, I told myself. That's why you're still single. If a woman's still single into her thirties, they say, she's too picky. Come on, you know it's the insides that count. He's really sweet. Remember?

I couldn't help but wonder if he knows that he has a huge forehead. And do men with big foreheads have big other-body-parts? Ew, don't go there. Why'd you go there?

"Robyn?"

Oops. He asked me a question. "Oh, sorry. I spaced out for a moment, guess I'm a little tired."

120

He chuckled awkwardly. "I asked what you do for a living."

"Oh, I'm a social worker."

"Cool." He guffawed, followed by a high-pitched snort. "You get paid to, like, be social. I wouldn't mind that job."

"Well, yeah, I mean it's not all fun and games but it pays the bills. Actually, it barely pays the bills, with no cushion for a nice pair of socks or a really cool stash of paperclips." Manny showed no response. "But I like what I do. Usually…" I paused and grinned. "No, it's nice" —my tone integrated authenticity— "I can end my days knowing I made a difference in people's lives. It feels good and meaningful. You know?"

He shrugged.

"What do you do, Manny?"

"Oh, I'm a professional student." He laughed, confidently, as if to embark on a well-rehearsed speech. "I got my first degree in English. Did some small office jobs after that. That's all I could find. Talk about a useless degree. Now I'm at Cal State Hay—"

I counted three definitive wrinkle lines crossing his wide, pale forehead.

I looked down at my plate, now empty. I don't remember eating those tacos. Damn. I had to find something else to do with my time.

I looked back up and decided those wrinkles must be a good 4.5, no 4.75 inches in length, 1/4 or maybe 1/8 inch wide. Crap. What if I get major wrinkles like that before I die? And a receding hairline? I'd die.

"You know?" he asked.

121

"Oh yeah, I know." I nodded in agreement. "I know."

Manny opened his mouth wide, displaying a grotesque mixture of pinto beans, guacamole, onion, salsa, cheese, and saliva. He took another bite of his fat burrito, as bits of salsa dropped to his knuckles. Resting the burrito on his plate, Manny ran his tongue across his right, then left set of knuckles.

"Mm, my mom taught me not to waste food." He grunted, or laughed, with a snort or a hiccup or a sneeze or burp or something. I'm not sure how to categorize it.

An exceedingly high level of aversion dominated my being. The guy looked at me in a friendly manner. I returned a pleasant smile.

He abruptly grasped his stomach with one hand and dropped his big forehead into the other, partly hiding a reddened, scrunched up face. "Ouch! God, that hurts!"

"Are you okay?" What the hell am I supposed to do? Is he having a heart attack? I hope not. I don't wanna do mouth-to-mouth on him. And I'm certified in CPR so I'd feel extra guilty if he died because I didn't even try to save him.

"Oww!" He breathed out deeply. "Oh this hurts. I think I have indigestion."

Lovely.

Manny turned towards the register and signaled the waiter to bring the check. "Hurry, please."

The waiter shined a courteous glance, walked over briskly and handed Manny the bill. "Take your time. Thank you."

Manny examined it and placed the bill face-up on the table directly under my nose: a non-subtle hint.

"Can I pay my part?" Please say "no". Please say "no".

"Yeah, sure." Of course I can! Manny picked up the check again. "Half plus tip is seven, uh, seven dollars and sixty-five cents."

I dug through a bundle of ones in my purse. "I don't have change."

"That's okay, you can just give me eight."

Cheap-ass, weird-ass, gas-ass. Half grinning, and attempting not to inhale, I gave the man eight bucks. He tossed his and my cash onto the table, then stood up.

"I'm going to get some, oh, ouch!" Manny clasped his hands together over his belly— "Rolaids. Will you come with me? It'll only, oh man, take a minute."

"Okay." Oh-kay, I am actually going now to get some Rolaids with my date because he needs Rolaids because he has indigestion. What the hell is wrong with me, him, him, me?!

He babbled and groaned all the way to a little convenience store in Oakland's downtown Civic Center.

Manny picked up a roll of Rolaids from the shelves, and pulled out his wallet. "Darn" —he looked at me— "Oh never mind, you said you don't have change. I hate using my ATM card for such a small purchase." Dude, just buy the damn thing.

As I watched the cashier run Manny's card, and saw Manny clench his stomach with one hand, reaching out with the other to take his card back, I thought: this has got to be the most undignified moment of my life, knocking down a notch the Q-tip-cleansed-ear-to-wall-to-spy-on-ex-boyfriend, which far outshined the slipper-slippage-into-ladder debut. Yep, I'd hit a new low.

We departed the store. "Where's your car, Robyn?"

"Back on 14th Street."

"Oh, well, I'm this way." He pointed in the opposite direction. Manny extended his hand and said, "It was nice meeting you."

I didn't want to shake his hand, but I did. "Okay, nice meeting you too." That's it? Got company on your Rolaids venture and that's it?

Thank goodness. Hope your gas goes away. Far, far away.

In lieu of a sex life, I often defaulted to the less threatening but nearly as addicting Latin dance venue —replete with seduction, physical intimacy, and male attention in correlation with cleavage exposure.

In time, I became a decent dancer, at least within Jewish circles. "You wouldn't think so by looking at her, but she's a really good salsa dancer," they'd say of me when I hosted dance events for a Bay Area group that I founded, the Bay Area DJs/Dancing Jews.

Events were well attended and fun. It went great for a few years. I even ignited a marriage, after two friends met at one of the events. Predictably, I wasn't so lucky.

I met Len at Emeryville's Allegro Ballroom, where I danced off-and-on for over a decade. Len was a bad dancer, and he reeked of nicotine. Len couldn't endure more than two songs before taking a cigarette break.

We were both 32 then, in 1998, but Len's graying black hair and serious demeanor made him look a lot older. Worse yet, he forgot to bend his elbows when dancing, yanking my arms with up-and-down abruptness as if to activate my control over air-traffic throughout the Western hemisphere. I was pained and annoyed but, until that time, had never refused a dance; I couldn't be rude.

Eventually Len began asking me out for coffee, a drink, whatever came to mind, including a bite at Denny's. For over a year, I said "No thanks" each time. Once I'd carelessly mentioned a recent birthday, so he tried a new angle and insisted on treating me to a post-birthday meal. This time I obliged, providing we'd dine platonically and not at Denny's.

The night of our date, I stopped at his place and he drove from there. I'd known Len long enough to feel safe in the passenger's seat.

Dinner itself, at Kincaid's in Oakland's Jack London Square, included red wine and a tasty seafood pasta dish. The company involved irritating blather. Len talked in tedious detail about his job doing some high-tech stuff that I didn't care to try to understand, and he continued to ramble about other less interesting matters. Eventually he picked up the bill. I thanked him and suggested we leave.

Back in the parking lot at his place, I bid Len "good night" and turned to the car door. He leaned over and warmly kissed my cheek and then my neck. I fingered the door handle, reiterating "Just friends."

Len said, "I know. You keep saying that."

He puckered again and kissed my lips. I dropped my defenses momentarily and reveled in the kissing. Then Len's hand slid up my leg and found its way to less explored terrain.

I found myself in that moment of sexual versus intellectual forces—one we all face. It's a conflict for which women are berated whichever side we take.

Humans are sexual beings, yet if a woman embraces or merely accepts this fact, she's labeled promiscuous, and in some places, unworthy of life.

When we choose to not have sex, we're considered heartless teases. How dare we leave men high and dry? They deserve sex whenever they want it, it's believed, and boys will be boys. A woman who doesn't have sex with her husband or boyfriend—regardless of how he treats her—gives him complete and total freedom to have sex with others. Yet there's no excuse for female infidelity.

So long as misogyny exists throughout the world, there's no resolution to this conflict. The shame that's fed by societal messages feeds the shame women carry whatever choices we make regarding sexuality. Even when we're robbed of a choice.

In that moment in the car with Len, a hot tension between us, I stopped kissing him and reached for the door handle.

"Just friends," I said once again, realizing how ridiculous that sounded at the time. "I'm going home now," I asserted, and pushed the door ajar.

I stepped out and closed the car door.

Len did the same and approached. He grazed my arm and urged, "Come inside with me. I know you want to."

I stepped away from him and towards the back of his car, where my purse had been safely stored.

"No, I'm going now. Thanks for birthday dinner. Please open the trunk."

Len trailed me to the back of his car and stood still.

"Open the trunk," I instructed. "I need my purse."

Len ignored my request. "I should just take you inside. Come on."

He stretched his arms around me from behind and with force, in a manner that was more determined than playful. Len proceeded to lift me a few inches off the ground.

I squirmed and pushed away, grounding my feet on the pavement.

"Stop it! Open the trunk! I'm going home."

"Come on, come upstairs with me."

"No!" With an open palm, I pushed his chest. The impact created safe distance between us.

Len's eyes widened.

He sighed and manipulated his keys.

"I guess it's my loss," Len mumbled, opening the trunk.

I grabbed my purse and walked briskly to my car.

After locking the doors and driving down his street, I kept peeking into the rear-view mirror, worried that Len might not have given up. But he had, at least that night.

The next Sunday, Len approached me for a dance –utterly clueless. I refused.

He called the following day to find out why I wouldn't dance with him.

"You're too pushy. When a woman says 'no,' she means it."

"Too pushy? No other lady ever told me that."

"I don't care, I'm saying it now."

We talked in circles for a bit.

Twisted sensations consumed me as I hung up. Len's kiss and touch had excited me, and I did, after all, permit it. I just wouldn't have sex with him and he just (almost) wouldn't accept that.

I re-enacted this dating scenario with many others, too many to mention. I'd get sexual, because it feels so damn good, but would not have sex, because it scared me so damn much.

I prefer not to expel details of those incidents. I don't want you to think that I'm a cruel man-hater, or a sleaze or tease or anything like that.

I'm simply a human who, like most of us, has made efforts to explore my sexuality, despite my conflicts regarding sexuality, within my own comfort zones.

When Valentine's Day rolled around, months after my date with Len, I arrived home from work to a nice surprise.

February 14, 1999 I can't believe it. A vase with a beautiful bouquet of a dozen long stem roses mixed with six lively daisies was at my door when I arrived, Diary! I pulled the card out, anxiously. It was unsigned and with no message. A call to the flower shop and I was told, "Sorry we don't know who it's from. He didn't leave a message. You'll have to guess."

The phone rang. Len called to ask if I liked the roses. Damnit.

"Yes, there wasn't a name. Did you do that on purpose?"

Len said he'd given his name and didn't know why they omitted it. I thanked him for the roses and said clearly, "I won't dance with you or date you again."

Finally, he seemed resigned. "I guess I'll wish you the best."

"You too, Len. Take care."

After hanging up, I wiped a few tears that meandered slowly down my face. Then I entered the kitchen and eyed the rosy ensemble that I'd placed in a vase on the counter.

They weren't so pretty any more.

Chapter Eight: Keeping the Faith

In the early 2000s, San Francisco Bay Area's East Bay was a great place to be. I adored my one-bedroom apartment on San Jose Avenue in charming, small town Alameda. The glorious bay was a short walk away. When I drove locally, except to San Francisco, traffic and parking were non-issues. I couldn't ask for more, though I did (naturally).

I steadily placed a pair of faded silver candlestick holders on the off-white kitchen counter of my home in Alameda, transfixed on a memory...

As rain hammered the windowsills that Friday night, Mom suggested we stay home instead of trekking to Temple Jeremiah for Shabbat services. Nobody argued. Instead, the six of us gathered eagerly around the slick white oblong kitchen table. Just a bit left of its center, Mom placed a pair of tarnished silver candle holders sprouting half burnt white sticks.

I peered mesmerized as Mom pulled a matchbox out of the silverware drawer. She plucked a match, struck it, and lit both wicks in a swift, graceful manner.

That was Mom, ever calm and capable. She could do anything. She knew I could too. We likely had more confidence in each other than we did in ourselves.

Without thinking, I got lost in the magical orange and blue flames that drew me into a peaceful unity with the Jewish world.

Dawn broke the mood. "Teacher Sylvia told us about inner-fate marriage."

"Honey, you mean inter-faith marriage," Mom clarified.

I had no idea what they were talking about.

"Yeah, that," Dawn continued. "She said we should only marry someone Jewish. Too many Jews are marrying the Goys.[5] Is that true?"

Her question reminded me of the popular, pseudo-underground version of "Lo Yisa Goy"[6]: *Don't kiss a boy if he's a Goy. He won't kiss you if you're a Jew.* The words troubled me. Desperately wanting to fit in, though, I sang along with my Jewish peers. Temple School Teachers often joined the chorus.

A mere blip in time since the Holocaust, I understand sensitivity to factors that might threaten Jewish survival, though I've never been convinced that interfaith marriage is one of them. To the contrary, I think it's likely strengthened the Jewish population. Regardless, I attempted to heed these teachings like a good Jewish girl.

That night at the kitchen table, Dad answered Dawn's inquiry. "It's true. If you kids don't marry Jews, your Mother and I will disown you."

Mom nodded in agreement.

Disown? Dis-own? What? You own me?

I couldn't imagine how disownment would play out, and I'm pretty sure they meant that as a threat. Yet I kind of elated in the concept.

I can get kicked out? I never fit in anyway. Maybe I could be a Partridge or a Brady or I can live with Uncle Bill, Mrs. Beasley, and Mr. French. In the mornings, Mr. French would hand me a silver tray. On it, a plateful of pancakes covered in fresh, hot maple syrup,

131

with ripe strawberries on the side; and a can of whipped cream, so that I could spray it myself.

Sigh...If only I could find a Goy to marry me.

Many years later, however, I found myself comfortably entwined with a strong sense of Jewish pride. This fueled countless excursions through the Bay Area Jewish single's scene on a quest to find that mensch[7] who'd bestow a happiness I'd never known.

So, like hundreds of thousands of single marriage-minded Jews worldwide, I registered with Jdate dot com. This highly popular Jewish dating site assures "no more blind date blahs".

To think, I could avoid the intimidating pick-up scene and deal with rejection in the privacy of my own home. What could go wrong?

For one, there was Harold.

Harold described himself as an accomplished photographer, well-traveled, and financially stable. The basics were covered. Plus, he was cute, when I squinted and imagined a non-jagged hair line, two eyebrows instead of one, and a less elongated forehead. Looks don't matter; I'm not superficial. He might be the one I'm looking for, I told myself.

I arrived a bit early to Starbuck's on Park Street. Within minutes, I knew it. I saw Harold enter the café, and I just knew...that I'm superficial. Looks matter.

"Hi. What would you like to drink?" Harold asked without hesitation, flaunting his generous offer to purchase my beverage.

Note: Harold had suggested a coffee date because he doesn't eat dinner after 5pm. It's "too late in the day for a meal," he'd said. As the owner of a home in the North Oakland Hills, a cup of tea would not likely have plummeted him into bankruptcy.

"These are together," he boasted to the cashier as she placed both our drinks on the counter. Harold then dug into his wallet and whipped out what I can only assume was a buy-10-get-1-free card. I looked away, embarrassed, so I'm not sure. Generosity had reached a shameful low.

To be fair, Harold proceeded to impress me greatly. In our brief, painstaking discourse, he displayed a substantial number of traits on my checklist. My Red Flag checklist, that is. This list ran through my mind as he talked.

1) Harold discussed the ex in excess. It was "Marcia this, Marcia that, Marcia, Marcia, Marcia!"
2) Infidelity. "I only cheated once, with my first girlfriend. It was horrible for the relationship. I'll never do it again." I wasn't as surprised by the fact that he shared this—though it seemed a peculiar first date strategy—as I was by the concept of two women simultaneously vying for Harold's affections.
3) Talker's Syndrome. He kept talking and talking in one longwinded never-ending run-on sentence like this one but it was a lot longer and a more boring and spewed in a completely monotone and stoic manner with no break between words or sentences but one that afforded me time to study my watch, finish my tea, and contemplate my holiday gift list for next December and the upcoming decade.
4) Self-indulgence. Harold reached into his briefcase, pulling out each and every photography book he'd contributed to, showing me each and every Table of Contents, his favorite pictures in each and every book, accompanied with explanation as to why a few photos didn't turn out better: Marcia, though well-intentioned, isn't a skilled photographer.
5) Bigotry. "I'm not racist. I only tell racial jokes with my friends, and we know we're just kidding." I thought, yeah, you're not homophobic either. After all, I'm sure you occasionally

watch "How I Met Your Mother" starring Neil Patrick Harris.

6) <u>Anger issues.</u> "I have a sharp tongue. I've had many friends turned enemies because of it." I imagined myself standing up to demonstrate real rage: "You ain't seen nothing yet dude! Oh, I'm sorry. Did I just spill the rest of my hot tea on your lap?" In reality, I held a grin.

Harold finally paused and said, "I've had a nice time. Would you like to get together again?"

Of course he had a nice time. Who doesn't appreciate a docile female audience for ninety minutes at the cost of one tea purchased via a frequent-buyer-coffee-discount-whatever card?

"It feels like just a friendly connection," I replied.

Dejected, he hung his head low and began stuffing all his books back into his briefcase.

This is a bit awkward, I realized. Do I say something else? Plant a big wet one on his cheek as a no-hard-feelings gesture? Go back to the counter for some chocolate?

I decided to leave casually, after watching Harold depart.

Most of us would much rather meet someone in-person versus on-line. Of course, I tried this too.

San Francisco's Jewish single's scene comprises massive amounts of hopefuls in their 20's and 30's, and three men well over 45, who convene in a display of concern for some aspect of Judaism. Espressos and Blackberries in hand even during worship, they'd scan the crowds for the one – the one they're somewhat sure they haven't already met through Jdate. And that one must (a) look hot, (b) live within 5 miles, and (c) hate country music.

Being a non-native didn't serve me, as the Bay Area's full of Southern California transplants. Nor did I gain points in other categories: I was a country music fan; a non-hot and non-sexy one; and I lived in the East Bay.

One Sabbath evening, I was greeted by a friendly brunette upon entering a posh home in San Francisco's Nob Hill district.

"Hi, I'm Shira. We're playing tell us what you do for a living; feel free to make something up."

"Okay." I didn't miss a beat. "I'm Robyn and I'm a professional basketball player."

Shira laughed, as did a short handsome man with whom it appeared she'd been chatting. Two lanky guys focused on a halogen lamp in the corner, and conferred unaffected glances in my direction.

"Robyn, this is Ilan," Shira said.

The three of us chatted for a while. My hopes flew as I studied Ilan's almond brown eyes. But my heart sank when, minutes later, Shira and Ilan casually discussed plans that didn't include me. It seemed, though, that maybe they were already friends. I wasn't sure.

Before I left, Shira and I exchanged contact information.

She called a week later. I initially feigned excitement for her when she mentioned having recently had coffee with Ilan.

"You went out with him? That's great! How'd it go?"

"No Robyn. All he talked about was you. He thinks you're really cute." That's unfamiliar, I thought, blushing.

"He's concerned about dating someone across the bridge, though, but I told him that's silly. A good woman's worth it, and you seem like a good one, Robyn."

"Ah, that's sweet. Thanks, Shira."

I'd never heard about the bridge factor. The Bay Bridge spans 4.5 miles. At that time, in the mid-1990s, traffic was a breeze and the toll, a mere $3.

"Well, I can see how the Bay Bridge might be an obstacle, I guess, if we got married, or divorced with split custody arrangements or something," I joked.

We both giggled.

Ilan had clearly considered Shira's input. He emailed a day later asking for a date and specifying San Francisco as the date's locale. I eagerly accepted.

In retrospect, I'd already started a dating pattern of happily—but not really—doing the driving, paying, and other things I preferred not to do, up to but not including sexual favors.

Ilan held my hand during our first-date movie, "American Beauty."

Dinner discourse was more than decent, and the after-dinner activity on his couch was less than decent. As passions mounted, he reached for the remote. "I need to watch Melrose Place," Ilan reported.

Now I have no qualms admitting that Heather Locklear is/was hot. But as Ilan and I snuggled on his couch, his arms wrapped around me, my bra strap and a few buttons undone, his odds with me were significantly higher than his chances with Heather—until he fondled the remote, which nearly evened the score.

At the next commercial break, I stuffed the last scrap of my ego into my purse and departed.

Still, I'd give Ilan another chance. Let's face it, once a good make-out session has occurred, the attachment has begun, at least for the woman.

Since I planned to be in San Francisco mid-week for a group discussion about grief and loss at Congregation Beth Sholom, Ilan and I would grab a bite afterwards.

Ilan surprised me by showing up at the synagogue to join me.

Afterwards, we strolled to a nearby Thai restaurant. Ilan took my hand from across the table. Things seemed promising, as Heather Locklear was nowhere in sight.

The bill came. "Oh, hmm, I don't have cash or my credit card on me. I forgot." Ilan hadn't even taken out his wallet to check it. He was so rehearsed, so ready to deliver that line.

"No worries," I said with a grin, placing my credit card on the bill.

Back at his place, a steamy make-out session brought my spirits back up, especially when Ilan agreed to cross the bridge for our next date. We hadn't specified a time but he'd spend the day with me on the upcoming Sunday.

Our big day arrived. I got up extra early and called Ilan at 9 a.m. No answer.

I emailed and called and called and emailed every four minutes or so for the next two hours, to no avail.

It was 11:30 a.m. by the time we finally connected.

"What's going on, Ilan? I've been trying to reach you all morning."

"Oh, I, I was out taking a walk."

"Well, what's the plan? Are you still coming over?"

"I don't, I dunno."

I was fuming at this point and suspected his bridge-phobia had taken its toll.

"What? I've been looking forward to this and was trying to reach you all morning. You said you'd come over. I crossed the bridge the last two times. I'm only five miles away!"

"I just don't think I have enough time. Dave's coming by tonight. We're going for dinner."

"At what time?"

"I don't know, like 7:30."

"Eight hours isn't enough time to see me? What the hell is wrong with you?"

"I, uh, I…this isn't working."

"Good luck to you," I said, resolved.

Ilan's voice softened with relief: "Good luck to you too."

Three years later I sat by Ilan at another Shabbat dinner in San Francisco. As I conspicuously chomped chopped-liver while talking to him, Ilan said he'd soon make Aliyah.[8] Our discourse was light-hearted, so I didn't have the heart to inform Ilan that Israel is more than five miles away. I'm guessing he learned that during the sixteen-hour flight. I'm also guessing he flew out of the San Francisco airport to avoid crossing the Bay Bridge.

My clock ticking like an irate Big Ben when the big 3-0 entered view, my friend Barbara encouraged me to join her on a visit to a local Jewish matchmaker.

At age 45, Barbara still harbored the fairytale of meeting her dream man, getting pregnant, having it all. I'm not saying it's impossible, but I thought she'd have done well to be realistic and consider other options.

Barbara was far from happy and constantly complaining about loneliness. I'd do and pay anything to avoid ending up like her.

So we drove to the yenta's[9] office in San Francisco.

Barbara met with the matchmaker first, as I sat in a narrow hallway to await my turn.

Fifteen or so minutes later, Barbara stepped out. "Not good," she reported. "There really aren't options for me at this age. Men always want to go younger, so the pool I'm looking at are pretty much dead." She sighed. "Well at least she was honest with me and saved me the money," Barbara added.

My turn came.

139

I viewed page after page of handsome, well-educated men in my age group. And for just eleven-hundred dollars, I could date any or all of them, the matchmaker promised. "Your beshert[10] might just be one of them," she glowed.

Without hesitation, I handed the yenta a whopping check. (This was when I had money saved. Those were the days.)

A week later, the matchmaker called with my "perfect match." Stewart's 32, she said; attractive and a very nice man. I agreed to have her forward my number.

Stewart's speech was belabored, with lengthy pauses between words, so our first phone conversation was a bit challenging. I surmised this was due to his being attentive and thoughtful. Perhaps he *was* my perfect match.

A few days later, Stewart and I met at Java Rama in Alameda. He appeared handsome, with a nice broad smile. It was downhill from there.

We sat with glasses of hot tea in front of us. Stewart grabbed a napkin from the napkin-holder on our table and meticulously opened it then lay it on the table between us. He was a swimmer, Stewart reported, and he needed to always be careful to prevent swimmer's ear.

Stewart took a pen from his jacket pocket and drew a set of parallel lines on the napkin. That was the ear canal, he taught. He scribbled in circles to illustrate the process by which water builds up and bacteria grows, when you don't shake your ears out after a swim. The problem, he continued, was that this could lead to a bad infection.

My date curbed tedious monologue about the eardrum and other bodily intricacies. (I wasn't paying attention, so I don't know what these other things were. I could guess, but I don't want to bore you.) He needed to use the restroom. Said restroom, as I'd learned during a previous visit to Java Rama, existed through the back door and at the end of a walkway.

Minutes later, Stewart returned to report that he was unable to figure out how to open the back door. He apparently did not realize he needed to push on it. I offered directives, but Stewart sat back down.

"Are you sure? You just have to push hard."

"No. It's okay," he said.

My best strategy, it seemed, would involve taking over the conversation. If Stewart got more nervous, he might not be able to control his bladder. That would embarrass him even more.

I told Stewart I'd taught preschool for several years.

He looked inquisitive. "Does preschool come before or after kindergarten?"

Are you for real? "It comes first," I informed. "That's why it's called pre-school."

Alas, I took a final sip of my Lemon Zinger.

"Can I ask you a question?" Stewart said.

"Sure."

"You don't seem interested in me."

True, but what's the question? "Well, you're nice. I'm just not really sure if we have a romantic connection." I work with people who have special needs, I continued in my mind, and I don't want my personal life to mirror my professional life. Oh and it's not ethical for counselors to date clients. There's that. It'd be a breach of professional ethics. Phew.

Stewart didn't seem to register my response. "Do you wanna walk to the beach from here?" he asked.

Alameda's Crowne Beach was just a few short blocks away, and it was a beautiful day. I thus politely told him that I needed to go to the market but pointed towards the water. "Just walk straight down Park Street, that way."

We shook hands, and I watched Stewart stroll towards the water. I hope he made it there by now.

With apologies, dear reader, here's the moral to this story: You can lead a date to water, but you can't make him think.

By my estimation, Stewart's most redeeming quality was his failure to be a stereotypical high-powered, intelligent Jewish business executive or Hollywood film director. I appreciate him for that. It's good to squelch stereotypes. They only serve to hurt, fester and destroy.

Barbara, to the contrary, was not only a whiny, nagging Jewish woman, she was your classic Jewish American Princess—a Beverly Hills prima donna through and through. When I told her about Harold and then Stewart, though, she had a charitable thought.

"I'm thinking of setting you up with Simon," she said. "He's my ex-boyfriend, Robyn. We dated for three years."

Barb described Simon as "a nice Jewish man, attractive, kind, and very smart."

"So why didn't things work out for you?" I had to ask the obvious question.

"Really, the only thing about him, Robyn, is that he didn't take me out to nice dinners. I mean, I don't need lobster every night, but on weekends, I want to be treated to a fancy meal, or to see the opera or a musical. You know? He complained about finances, and that he'd rather stay in and snuggle in front of the TV. I'm just accustomed to being treated better."

He'd rather snuggle than go to the opera? "Sure, I'd go out with him, Barb. Thanks for thinking of me."

☐ It was painful to witness, like watching Quagmire get hit with a seizure attack. The guy's fingers were trembling so erratically, he could barely lift his coffee mug.

How I wished to ease his pain. I envisioned myself graciously raising the cup for Simon, then tossing the hot coffee at his face. But I held back, classy as I am. I'm not sure why I was so irritated. Perhaps it's because Simon was blind date number 12,462. Or maybe it's because Barbara had billed him as the idyllic keeper. Did she not notice he's exceptionally awkward? I guess not.

So there we sat at Java Rama, engaging in the typical first (and last)-date-with-the-friend's-ex conversation: "How do you know

143

(Barbara)? She's great, isn't she? Yeah, and hot too. Really hot. God, I miss being with her…"

After thirty-two minutes of this, we walked down Park Street to the Alameda Beach. I felt obligated to be polite.

The beach stroll was actually peaceful, though. We meandered through the sand, making small talk and glancing at the glistening water.

Suddenly, Simon—towering at 6 feet of lanky cowardice—crisscrossed his arms overhead and made a mad dash back towards Park Street.

"The pigeons! The pigeons!" he screeched in holy terror.

"Um, those birds flying overhead would be called 'seagulls,' you dumb ass," I asserted, trudging through the sand many yards behind him. "They aren't likely to crap on you, dude, but if they do, it won't kill you." I felt embarrassed for both of us.

On a happy note, the date was over, as I watched Simon dash for his car. "Go get him, pigeons! Go get him!"

"How was it, Robyn? Isn't he nice?" Barbara was excited to learn my impressions.

"Well, he's nice and all, but he seemed kind of nervous. Did you notice he's jittery?"

"Oh, I guess I got so used to it, I didn't mind. I think it's some neuromuscular condition."

"I mean," I continued, "that was fine, just a little awkward. But we went to the beach, Barb, to walk around, and he got freaked out by a swarm of seagulls."

"What? Really? That's odd."

"Does he have a bird phobia or something, Barbara?"

"Not that I know of. Why? What did he do?"

"Well, he ran and screamed like a flailing idiot, 'the pigeons!' 'the pigeons!' I've never seen a grown man do something like that."

Barb sat silently on the phone. "I don't know what that was about, but he's a nice, sensitive man. Don't you think?"

"Yeah, he is nice," I responded, rolling my eyes, "just not for me. Thank you for thinking of me, Barb."

"Sure, Robyn. I'm sorry it didn't work out."

My track record with Jewish men wasn't a winning one. Nor was my track record with men in general. But I kept faith, staying in the single's scene and continuing to look at on-line ads.

Here's one memorable example.

Headline: NOT OJSIMPSON.

I clicked on the ad. With an opener like that, I had to read more. This followed:

Disclaimer: It is a fact that every woman on every dating site failed miserably at maintaining their last relationship: because if you had been successful-you wouldn't be here.

Interesting pick-up strategy, I thought.

NotOJ messaged me. "I see you viewed my profile. You're an attractive lady and I'd very much like to be friends. But I didn't say

145

hello, because I also noticed you are Jewish. And I didn't think Jewish women spoke to anyone except other Jews."

Every ounce of my Jewish blood boiling, I responded with the restraint and eloquence of my oppressed people—a people so oppressed that we don't dare acknowledge we've a history as victims of genocide. This acknowledgement means we're whiny snobs.

"Yep," I wrote, "we Jews have even been known to intermarry. We just don't enjoy corresponding with people who stereotype us. Good luck to you. –Robyn"

NotOJ responded: "Though in my heart I know that I was not stereotyping you...I'm as normal as they come...A truth which is actually borne out by my textual faux pas in the regards that a 'normal' person becomes habituated to expect a certain action after having witnessed said action manifest...Be nice. Say hello. And you will be surprised at how 'normal' and not inclined to stereotype people that I am. I hope I hear from you. And if not, good luck, and do forgive me for being an idiot."

"I accept and appreciate your apology. Thank you. Still, I don't wish to pursue a connection. All the best, -Robyn"

"Very good. – NotOJ."

I felt victorious at having successfully educated a man. He did admit to idiocy. He's a good judge of character and not at all a bad guy. Just not one for me. As usual.

Discourse about my Jewish faith didn't usually go so well. Other prospective suitors declared that Israelis should just relocate to Iowa or some other state; Jews control Hollywood; we're all frugal and materialistic, etcetera. It's hurtful, exhausting, and a bit shocking to me that these beliefs continue to thrive.

Truth be told, though, I've done a lot of flip-flopping on the issue of interfaith dating. In more recent years, I've landed on the other side of the spectrum. I like it here.

That is, it hasn't mattered to me what religious group, if any, my date affiliates with. After-all, a person's religious label tells me little or nothing about their character. It also fails to provide assurances regarding values or anything else, for that matter.

While it's nice to share religious beliefs, practices and cultural nuances with someone, it's not a be-all, end-all. We find wonderful people, in addition to vicious lunatics, in every segment of the population.

In both the micro and macro scheme of things, it's all about harmonious relations. This is, in fact, a central tenet to the world's main religions: our ill-forgotten common ground.

Lo yisa goy el goy cherev.

Nation shall not lift up sword against nation.

Lo yil m'du od milchama.

Neither shall they learn war anymore.

Chapter Nine: Losing It

Hysteria over Y2K piqued; Prince's song, "1999," aired on all the hip stations; and I learned I'd passed an oral exam that granted me a license to practice therapy in the state of California. The new millennium brought promise.

Prior to midnight, I'd only been using my computer to send occasional emails and thus didn't get caught up in the Y2K fervor. I knew only that internet and all technical systems would shut down in 2000. Ramifications would likely be disastrous; banking systems, traffic lights, computer desktops, and anything technical would freeze. Computer technicians had been working laboriously against the clock, to prevent utter chaos.

So it was rather anticlimactic when nothing of the sort happened at the midnight hour or later. Y2K was a farce, it seemed. As 2000 arrived, the big ball dropped, I hugged a few friends I'd gone dancing with at a club in San Francisco, and the internet snoozed. No individuals or organizations reported having been struck by the Y2K virus. Pasadena's New Year's Day Rose Parade proceeded as scheduled. All the hype and frenzy was for naught.

"So I guess Y2K didn't break the internet?" I said to Dave, joking.

"No. We were ready for it," he giggled sweetly, awkwardly.

Dave's shyness endeared me.

We stood by the pool at a friend's New Year's Day gathering. Dave offered to get me a soda and stuck around thereafter, despite seeing some of his friends.

Before I left, we exchanged business cards.

Dave and I proceeded to send email messages, which escalated to friendly phone conversations that continued for weeks.

Finally, per my suggestion, he visited me in Alameda. We walked along the ocean, played Scrabble at my place, laughed a lot, and got along great. I felt a chemistry building.

Valentine's Day neared, and I decided to take the plunge and ask him for a dinner date. I swore I'd never do that again, after Brad (sort of) rejected me for the high school prom, but Dave was special. I really liked him, and it seemed he simply needed a nudge.

"Dear Dave," I wrote in an email message, "Would you do me the honor of having dinner with me on...um...I don't know, say, - GULP- February 14th? PS Will you be my Valentine? Please say 'yes.' Please say 'yes.' GULP. ~Robyn"

One long and anxious day later, I read his response.

"Dear Robyn, I just checked my calendar and it appears that I have a date with a nice lady on Valentine's Day. I'll be calling her soon to make plans. Be it known that gulping isn't necessary, except to drink, because I'm the one who's honored. PS Yes! Yes! PPS Thank-you for asking. ~Dave"

Dave greeted me at his door with a Valentine's gift.

"Aw, how sweet," I gushed, taking the green pencil. It was sharpened on one end. A tiny plastic pink fabric rose, maybe three inches long and two wide, sprouted from the other end.

The fact that he gave me something meant the world to me, and I'd treasure this pencil for a day or two.

After sharing a pizza, we drove to his place to watch a movie of Dave's choosing: Austin Powers. Not so romantic, I thought. But I like him. It's Valentine's Day, so I'm easy, I thought. I mean, his movie choice was fine with me.

We sat close together on one end of his couch.

Well into the show, there was still no romance. At one point, Dave got up to adjust the volume. I secretly moved a smidge, so we'd be sitting a little bit closer.

Dave sat back down. "Did you move over?"

"Uh, I guess a little."

At some point before the final credits, Dave started kissing me. He didn't really have a choice. With no room to breathe, his only means of survival was to share oxygen. For the next half hour or so, Dave's lips were tasty and his hands, excitedly busy. My clothing got disheveled as we got bundled in a horizontal kiss-and-grope fest. A real Valentine's date, finally, I thought. Heavenly.

But Dave stopped abruptly, patted his head, as if I'd messed up his thick brunette hair, and said, "I have to go out and feed the dog."

Feed the dog? Are you kidding me? You're rejecting me for a canine? "Well, alright."

I sat up and slipped my shoes back on.

Dave walked me to the front door, kissed me quickly, and turned towards the back door.

Feed the fuckin dog, I thought, walking to my car.

"Feed that fuckin dog!" I said aloud, after shutting my car door, and numerous times on the drive home.

"Feed that fuckin dog!"

Still, I really liked him, and dating weirdness was a normal experience for me. The kissing was great, so when Dave called the next day, I was happy.

Our conversations got easier, actually, and make-out sessions, more fun and steamy. He didn't mention dog feedings again, thankfully.

One night, Dave and I pulled over into a parking lot in Mountain View. We'd bought tickets for a movie, but it wouldn't start for forty minutes.

"What do you want to do?" Dave asked.

I looked at him, suggestively.

We crawled into the back seat of his car, and the games began. Kissing quickly deepened, and Dave unhooked my bra-strap. I started unbuttoning his shirt.

Suddenly, a bright light glared in our faces.

Shit.

We looked out the window and there he was: a police officer shining his flashlight on us. At age 34, I worried that I'd be thrown in jail for necking in the backseat of a car.

Slightly embarrassed, I instantly wrapped my arms around my chest and shifted my shirt down.

Dave jumped into the front seat and rolled down the window. "Hi," he said to the officer.

The cop simply nodded and said sternly, "We don't do that here."

"Oh, okay. Sorry," Dave responded.

The officer switched off his flashlight, turned around and left.

"Slow night in Mountain View?" I laughed, crawling back into the passenger seat. "They don't do that here—what the hell?" I beamed at Dave, my hand on his thigh. "Nobody makes-out in this town? It's against the law to make-out in the privacy of your own vehicle in a public parking lot?"

Dave emitted a brief chuckle, appearing ashamed. "I guess we'll get going."

I didn't know what his deal was. We really liked each other, loved the groping and foreplay, but something wasn't right. Sex wasn't on the table (or in the bed, on the floor or elsewhere). In that way, Dave was safe for me. Perhaps too safe.

One night, I was supposed to meet Dave's parents. He suggested we'd all have dinner together. Dave would pick me up.

But that night, I waited and waited, growing increasingly angry and anxious.

I started calling and left one message after another. "Where are you? You were supposed to be here at 7 tonight. It's 7:30…8:00, 8:10, 8:30."

Tears streamed forth. Damn him.

His call came after 10 p.m.

"What's going on?" I asked, angrily. "Are you okay, because if you are, I'm going to kill you!"

"I'm okay. I was just thinking about us,"

"Alright. Well that doesn't explain why you bailed on me! You could've at least called to tell me you weren't coming!"

"I didn't know what to say," he sputtered. "I was just thinking about how to tell you."

I huffed. "Tell me what?"

"I don't want to date you anymore because you're not a dog person, so I wouldn't marry you."

What the hell? "What are you talking about? We never talked about marriage or pet-care even. What does that have to do with anything?"

"It's just where I'm at, Robyn. I don't want to keep seeing you because I only want to date somebody I'd marry. I take dating seriously."

"You're being stupid." I didn't want Dave to hear my tears. "Okay, you made up your mind...Bye."

"Bye Robyn."

Alan told me that he worked in "occupuncture." I wanted to scream whenever he mentioned his job: "It's akk, akk, as in Axl Rose! How can you do it if you can't even say it?!

But something about him was alluring. Plus, Alan gave me chocolate on our first (and last) two dates—good stuff too, Lindt and Toblerone.

I invited him up to my apartment when he dropped me off after our second date.

One thing led to another and...

"We need to stop," he pulled away when our tongues threatened to touch. "I'm not ready to make-out. That involves commitment. It's been three years since I made out with a woman."

"We're just kissing," I said shyly.

"We need time to build the relationship first."

"Okay, that's alright. How much time do you need?" I glanced at my watch.

"I don't know. I can't tell you that."

Then why would I want to date you? And why are you dating at all? And don't you think, at age 44, that it's time to start to become a man—one with testosterone, for example?

"I don't like it Alan, but I accept it. I'm not going to argue with you."

Alan left, leaving me bewildered and frustrated.

He called the next day and suggested we get together for a movie. I told him that I was sorry but it just wasn't working for me.

Upon hanging up, I shouted at the phone, "P.S., It's 'ack-you-punk-sure!'"

Kenny's creative silliness and depth of character depicted the man I wanted but couldn't have. For years, he dated a steady stream of women with no apparent breaks in-between. When I started seeing him at East Bay social venues more often, Laura was the lucky one. Though they seemed an odd match—she was aloof and awkward, while he was warm and gregarious—they appeared inseparable.

But things changed quickly when I learned they'd broken up. I didn't plan on replacing Laura. It just started happening that night. Those fantasy feelings became realized with every passing moment that we spent talking at Le Cheval, after our mutual friends had departed from a birthday dinner.

I'll never forget our 2 a.m. drive to Mt. Diablo, to best view a lunar eclipse. Kenny sang to me all the way there and back, as I faded in and out of a dreamlike state.

At the top of the mountain, we reclined on the hood of his Chevy under a blanket of stars. Kenny countered the biting air by heating me; first, with his jacket, and next, with his arms and lips.

We never saw an eclipse that night, but it was all so incredibly romantic that I can't begin to reconcile it with his agonizing neuroses.

Specifically, I lacked the skills to adequately fold his triple-A maps. "It's all in the corners," he lectured with a map in hand to demonstrate. "You have to line them up like this."

Why do you need a map anyway, I wondered, Mr. I-have-an-amazing-sense-of-direction-and-can-find-my-way-out-of-IKEA-in-record-time?

I guess it's a mere fluke when you drive down the wrong streets trying to find my place, every time you visit Alameda. And it was purely misfortune when you got lost trying to take me Le Cheval in downtown Oakland, where our initial spark was ignited, though you were certain you knew how to get there. Plus, you only live five minutes from it.

Dare I mention the harsh weather conditions that caused you to become terribly flustered upon driving through the Mojave Desert that night? I wanted a warm bed to sleep in, Kenny. Alone, preferably. Instead, we were stuck in three feet of mud in the middle of the desert, no cell-phone reception or indication of life anywhere in sight. You offered no comfort, except one stale Oreo cookie that you scrounged from the glove compartment. [Thank you for that, by the way.]

There's more, dear reader. Like one astonishing moment when Kenny silently and robotically reached into the dark recesses of my kitchen trashcan and pulled out a milk carton. How dare I trash a recyclable item? I loved him, but I forgot why.

As tenacious as I was frustrated, I began conjuring means for rekindling our romance.

"I like red roses," I declared in the midst of a home-cooked meal that I'd prepared. "They're my favorite." It was a natural deviation from the food: pasta with blood-red spaghetti sauce.

These pronouncements mattered not. I'd mentioned my affinity for red roses many times. And what woman doesn't like red roses? Instead, though, Kenny had gifted me with a four-inch tall bamboo shoot from an excursion to Truckee. "Thank you," I said, underwhelmed.

My collection of plant life grew in our months together to include a baby cactus from Salt Lake City, four birds of paradise that looked oddly similar to the ones that used to be in his neighbor's front yard, and your basic indoor plant with three wilting leaves.

Alas, one day, I returned home from work to one dozen long stem red roses. He did remember! Timing wasn't Kenny's strong suit, though. I'd ended our relationship the night before. The break-up had left me depleted…

"I just can't do this anymore. I'm sorry," I told him. "It's taking too much work, Kenny. I love you and I wish you the best but—"

Kenny dropped to his knees in dramatic, tearful desperation. "I don't want to lose you. I can't believe you're doing this to me."

"Get a grip, Kenny!" I snapped. "Nothing lasts forever."

"That's not true," he argued. Kenny's hysteria intensified. "You're so cold and unforgiving! Please, please just give me one more chance!" He covered his face with his hands, lowered his head onto the carpet, and continued spewing anguish.

"I'm sorry. It's over." I reiterated. "And I have to get up early for work tomorrow, so you need to leave."

"You're breaking up with me, and now you're making me drive home!"

"It takes you fifteen minutes to get home, Kenny. But if you're not safe driving, you can sleep on my couch. Pull yourself together! You're a grown man."

I got up and removed a spare comforter from my hallway closet. Kenny was flat on the floor, belly down, still wailing, as I rested the comforter on the couch.

"I'm going to sleep now," I said loudly. He quieted. "If you want to sleep on the couch, here's a comforter. If you leave tonight, lock the door behind you."

I went into my room and prepared for bed. Though shocked by Kenny's histrionics, I was exhausted. My eyelids drooped closed fairly immediately.

Soft knocking awoke me. "Yes?" I asked.

"It's me. Can I come in?"

I opened the door to a defenseless Kenny. "Can I lay down with you?" he inquired, like an innocent child.

"I don't know. I need to get a good night's sleep, Kenny."

"I know. I'm going to leave soon."

"Alright."

He followed me to my bed and lay alongside me. I turned my head to face the wall, as our bodies relaxed into our final moments together.

I'd started drifting to sleep, when I felt his lips on the back of my head, imparting one last kiss.

Kenny whispered, "I think I loved you even more than I loved Laura," and then left.

So when I picked up the bouquet that greeted me at my door the next day, I didn't know what to feel. An accompanying card included a plea to start anew.

I unlocked the door and studied the flowers. They are beautiful, I reasoned. And they're red. They are, after all, long-stem roses. I counted twelve, a perfect dozen, deeply red, sweet smelling, and in half-bloom.

While reaching for a vase in the upper kitchen cabinet, I noticed a bright red spot on my left index finger. I dropped my head toward the stems.

"Thorns!" Damn blood inducing thorns! I let go of the bunch over my trashcan. "I'm not recycling those damn things!"

By this time, I'd nearly given up on men. What kept me charging back into the dating arena, though, wasn't so much my tenacity, nor my hormones, but a painful desperation that I'd rightfully call loneliness.

While I loved, and even found solace in, being alone much of the time, solitude also served to exacerbate my long-standing feelings of worthlessness and shame. I hated being unmarried, without kids, and a thirty-something year old virgin. I felt like there was something horribly, embarrassingly wrong with me.

These feelings unleashed the huge weight of my lifelong depression, especially when I wasn't dating and had the time to be bulldozed by it.

Being in the right relationship, and having the whole shebang, I was sure, would fill my deep void and make everything alright.

April 2, 2000: Dear Diary, shit! Am I the only adult virgin left in this world besides Gary Coleman?[11] I'm scared of sex, but I'm more scared of not having sex. Not ever. That I'll die first. What's wrong with these fuckin' bozos? What's wrong with me?

"Chivalry isn't dead!" the dating ad claimed. Richard described himself as gentlemanly, hard-working, and in search of a long-term relationship. As with Dave, his soft side drew me in.

At first meeting, Richard's face flushed giddily. In a quiet, confident voice he said, "You're even prettier in person."

We spent hours relaxing on the sands of Crowne Beach, getting to know each other that warm afternoon. Richard hated his troubled ex, I learned.

I liked the idea of being the right one for him, the one to prove that not all women are crazed drama queens. Even better, I liked the possibility of having found my Prince Charming.

Over the next several months, Richard and I enthusiastically partook in picnics and barbeques with friends, Shakespeare in the Park, jazz concerts and lengthy doses of kissing in public and private. He cooked meals for me and sporadically handed me bouquets of flowers "just because."

At day's end, Richard would melt into his most endearing state, take my hands and ask, "Who made you so beautiful?" What a vomit-inducing and bizarre question! At the time, though, I was moved to smother him with affection.

We slept together regularly, but that only meant falling asleep in bed together. Regarding sex, I figured it would eventually happen between us. We were just taking things slowly.

Signs of trouble tiptoed through my naïve bliss. While discussing past relationships, Richard described a breaking-point for him: "She didn't even thank me after I mowed her lawn! She didn't even offer me a glass of water! That selfish bitch took a nap while I did the hard work," he fumed. "Thank God she's someone else's problem now!"

I was likely more relieved than I realized at the time, when Richard drew clear lines one night. "We won't have sex, not for a while at least. That only complicates things. I don't want to get too attached, if we're going to break up." I didn't respond.

Sleeping next to him became difficult. Richard's daily angry outbursts had grown furious and frequent. I tossed and turned one night, then grabbed my squishy white teddy bear and took it with me to the living room sofa. There, I snuggled with it and cried silently. A few minutes later, Richard entered the room.

"Oh I'm sorry, sweetie," I said softly. "I was trying not to wake you."

"What's wrong?"

"Nothing. I just can't sleep."

"Because of me?" he asked.

"No." Of course it was. "I guess I just miss my Mom."

"Close your eyes, honey. You can be with her anytime if you just close your eyes." I dropped my teddy bear, and Richard held me tight.

"I never really felt loved before," I shared, my head resting on Richard's chest. "I mean, by my Mom, but then she died. I used the word with someone else before, but I don't think we really meant it."

"But you're so loveable." This was exactly what I needed to hear in order to sleep until daybreak.

161

Richard's tenderness posed a striking contrast to his heated rage. On June 28, 2002, we sat for dinner at a busy Italian eatery in San Francisco's Sunset District. Richard had ordered a bottle of wine. Lifting his glass, he swished the liquid around and stared at it.

"You know, if I wanted to buy milk at 2 am, I could. But if I wanted to buy alcohol I couldn't," he ranted. "It's ridiculous. What if I want a beer at 2:30 in the morning? I'd have to drive to Nevada!" His face reddened. "What the hell's the difference between 1:30 in the morning and 2:30 in the morning?"

"Honey," I calmly interjected, "alcohol is related to car accidents and crimes and after two in the morning there's a peak—"

"That's just stupid!" He pounded the table with a closed fist. "Besides—"

"Sweetie, please. You hardly ever drink anyway. What's this about?"

"That's not the point!"

"Richard, it's my birthday. Please. Let's just have a nice dinner. Okay?"

His fury simmered to a halt, only to kick-in again on the drive home.

Crossing the Bay Bridge, Richard swerved to avoid a semi-truck that merged in front of us, nearly crashing into a blue sedan that zipped by to the left.

"Learn how to drive, assholes!"

"Be careful honey."

"Robyn, you aren't in the driver's seat! You don't see what I see, so don't tell me what to do!"

I stared out the window. It was pitch-black outside. Home seemed so far away.

Richard stopped, finally, in front of my place. He glared at me and said nothing. I picked up my purse and left.

"Unhappy birthday to me!" I should've stayed home alone. In fact, I should've stayed alone. Single, that is. It's better than this shit.

I planned the break-up that night, and followed through the next day.

I still believed in true love. And that marriage can work. My parents loved each other, I was sure. I'm still certain of that, though I don't know that I would've tolerated half of what Mom put up with.

There are good men in the world, nonetheless. For one, Mike's attractive, loyal, stable and smart. He married Susan, my college roommate and long-time close friend. By this time, they had two kids. Then there's Tyler, I realized. Kathryn nabbed a quirky but responsible one in him. They seem to be doing well. And Shira's fiancée, Ian, is a keeper—a gourmet cook who's outgoing, sensitive, and generous.

Thus, I never thought that there aren't any good men out there. I know they exist; my friends found every last one of them.

Occasionally, too, I'd see couples at Safeway Supermarket—for example—wherein the woman nags, nags, and nags the tame fellow.

He listens patiently, continuing to hold her hand or keep his hand on the curve of her back. It takes all I have in me to not force myself in-between them and elbow her in the rib cage, so that I can take over from there. Were I not so nice, I'd have snagged a good one in produce years earlier.

But I am nice, so I started thinking about adoption. I still loved kids and wanted to become a Mommy. Through my work in the foster care and adoptions field, I knew the ins and outs. I interviewed several friends who adopted as single moms. I even got so far as to decide on the agency I'd use.

Meanwhile, my hormones squealed loudly. Frustration met its breaking point. I needed to take action and just do it.

So I went to where all the free-loving former or current California hippies go: Harbin Hot Springs. This popular retreat center tucked away in a beautifully isolated area, decorated by luxurious pools of water from the depths of the earth, is clothing-optional in the pool area.

I opted to keep my bathing suit on when I arrived at the hot tubs, but instantly felt ostracized by stares. I noticed too that some or most of the people staring at me didn't have gorgeous bodies. They didn't care about letting it all hang out. Why should I? I was the only one wearing anything too.

So I took off my bathing suit. It felt freeing, actually. Nobody looked my way, except Mark, after I crawled into the warm pool.

Mark was cute, with dirty blonde hair and a nicely toned chest. I didn't see the rest of him, as we stood in the water. He asked me the basics: name, age, where I live, what I do. Mark told me he was divorced, 35, and that he lived and worked in San Francisco. After talking for a while, Mark offered me a massage, and I readily accepted.

Shared shoulder massages were nice.

Then kissing was too. Eventually, he asked where I was staying for the night.

"I have my own room at Manzanita," I told him. "What about you?"

Mark was camping outdoors but, pulling me closer by the waist, he'd rather share my bed.

I was conflicted. He was nice, and this was what I wanted. Right? I dreamed of and then met him, just like in a Harlequin. I needed to finally just do it, and here was my opportunity. I wasn't meeting anyone to marry much less date or fall in love with, otherwise. Time to take the chance and get it behind me.

In my room, he somewhat awkwardly, and readily, undressed.

"I should tell you," I interrupted, "I haven't…this is embarrassing…I haven't done this before."

He stopped for a moment, looked at me, unaffected. "It's alright."

Mark kissed me, maneuvered us onto the bed, and focused on the task of the evening.

He took a while to put a condom on.

That's a strange event, I must say: to sit (or lay) and watch. Isn't it? But a responsible one, and I wasn't going to have it any other way.

With condom on, and him atop me, Mark tried and tried.

"You're supposed to help me with this," he grunted.

I am? I'm supposed to help operate your penis? Are you supposed to need help? Okay, I guess. I tried to assist with gentle guidance and leadership, but it wouldn't cooperate.

So what did I do? Apologize. "I'm sorry. I guess I'm…I guess I'm too tight."

Mark finally gave up and laid by my side.

"I'm sorry," I repeated.

"With my first girlfriend," he disclosed, "she was a virgin and we took weeks. It hurt her and a little for me too, actually."

"Really? I didn't know it'd be so hard." Poor choice of words.

"It can be."

Mark kissed my lips, lightly and much less passionately than he had earlier. He sighed, resigned, and rolled over onto his back facing the ceiling.

"To tell you the truth, Robyn," his words slow and serious, "I'm still married."

What the hell? "You're still married? I thought you were divorced?"

"We're getting a divorce. It's just taking a long time. But I'm not getting back with her, if that's what you think. At least, I don't think we will. She's the one who filed."

"No, it's not that. But married is married and divorced is divorced, Mark."

"Not really, Robyn. You don't understand how long it takes, since you haven't been through it."

"I wish you'd been honest with me, and it doesn't even sound like you let go of her."

"What do you want from me? I'm being honest now." After you couldn't activate it, thank God. "She made it clear that it's over. It's not a big deal, really."

I was at a loss for words. To think I was going to have sex for the first time with a married man.

"Maybe it's best," he suggested, "that I sleep outside like I planned tonight."

"Yeah, I'd be most comfortable with that."

When I got home, I really needed to talk to a girlfriend.

"Kathryn, you wouldn't believe where I went this weekend. It's so not me."

"You went to Harbin Hot Springs."

"How'd you know?" We both laughed.

"Lucky guess. So, did you get lucky?"

"Oh God, Kat. I tried. I'm so tired of being a virgin. It's like excess baggage. Shit, this is so embarrassing…" I told her the details.

She laughed. "He's the one with the problem, Robyn. He has penis issues, and the fucker felt guilty for having lied to you."

"Yeah, thank goodness he couldn't even get it straightened out."

"Oh Robyn, don't feel bad. My first time, I was drunk and it hurt a little and I bled and it was all weird and hell if I remember his name.

But you're brave and you went to Harbin and you tried, safely and all." She giggled in a non-shaming way. "Good for you, girl."

"Actually, it was pretty cool, Kat. I mean, I looked around at all these naked people with bulging bellies, boobs sagging down to their knees, and long shlongs, thinking, 'you probably shouldn't even get naked for a private shower,' and it gave me confidence to strip down too. I was mostly self-conscious 'cuz I'm so damn white. I sprayed myself with sunblock 250 or something." I belted out a guffaw. "It is really pretty there."

"Yeah, did I tell you that Tyler and I got kicked out of Harbin?"

"Are you serious? Only you two!"

"Yeah, really. I mean, everyone has sex there. This was when we first got together, when we used to do it all the time." I started feeling comforted. "But we were, well, kinda loud, in broad daylight by one of the lodges and I guess there was some group meditation going on and we had it going on, and he was groaning and I was all screeching and sighing. Well, I guess we interrupted the mediation, and the people inside started coming out and we didn't notice for a while but ooh, they were pissed. Someone went and complained."

"Probably just jealous."

We laughed.

After striking out with Mark, you'd think I'd give up. No. I was more determined than ever.

Losing it became my mission.

Chris and I had a strong chemistry. He seemed a nice, respectful guy.

After a few weeks, things progressed towards home-plate. "I'm not going in all the way," he stated. Chris proceeded to lightly, and with a lot of control, barely lower his penis into my vulva, slowly raise it, and repeat this sequence several times.

Maybe I wasn't clear that I wanted to have sex? This isn't sex, is it? "Are you…are you afraid to have sex?" I asked.

"I'm not answering that."

That answered that.

In a society so refrained from discussing sex in a healthy way, how can we expect men to be Casanovas? Then again, I didn't. I merely expected sex to take the form of sex.

Randy was 38 and athletic, so I didn't think he'd have these problems.

When he stripped down on my couch one hot summer afternoon, he tried and tried to straighten things out. Randy's face looked as though he was painfully constipated. I tried to help budge it, but it rested like a limp spaghetti noodle.

Thing is, Randy had a lot of psychological issues that he refused to deal with. He'd been the victim of a violent gang-related assault, and his childhood sounded like an utter mess.

Like many, he proudly said "I don't believe in counseling." How can you not believe in counseling? That's like saying global warming doesn't exist, or oxygen is a myth, or Donald Trump's hair doesn't need its own zoning laws.

Anyway, I realized with thanks to Randy, if you can't work it out in your bigger head, you can't work it out in the smaller one.

We bring our emotional lives fully into sexual relationships, and most of the pressure is on the men. As it should be, I suppose, at least to some extent. They're the ones with penises. Second, society expects the man to take charge, especially in the bedroom. But this is a tall order for a sensitive, caring man with unresolved issues.

Phil and I met at a writer's Meet-up in San Francisco. A fellow writer who's working on publication—very cool, I thought.

As we rolled lustfully across my living room carpet one evening, I invited Phil to spend the night.

"Sure, yeah, but we won't have sex," he responded.

"Okay, not tonight...Or do you mean not ever?"

"I don't know." He sat up, breathed heavily, and looked down at his lap. "My last girlfriend, she tied me up. I just, it was scary."

"Okay, it's okay. We won't use rope. Don't worry." I stroked his face lovingly. "Do you want to talk about it?"

Stupefied, Phil didn't respond.

When I encountered Larry at Café Cocomo in San Francisco, I was as happy to have met a potential dance partner as I was a prospective lover. He was dark and debonair, and a fairly good dancer. Surely, he knew how to make it work. Right?

On our third date, I looked towards him from my bed, as I lay on my back. He'd knelt down so I could only see his upper half. Larry worked somewhat effortlessly, so this would work. Yes?

He sighed, frustrated. "That confirms things."

On our next date, Larry told me that his doctor had prescribed Viagra.

We'd try again. And again. Larry got hard and horny frequently and often.

But he had yet to break in. "You're really big," I told him.

"Am I?"

"Yeah, I've never seen one so big. Not that I've seen that many. I've seen…a few. Yours is by far the biggest. It's really huge." I knew this was supposed to be a good thing, but it didn't seem so good at the time.

We gave up again.

Larry called his former girlfriend the next day. He reported that she said, "Yes, you're really big." Larry then understood why, when he was a child, his pediatrician told his parents, "Your boy is going to please the ladies."

Larry and I kept trying, made some progress, and as he slowly made entry one night, I thought, is this the moment? Or is it happening now? Wait, I'm no longer a virgin, right now, right? Or was it earlier? Or has it happened yet? When did that life-altering moment actually occur? I had no clue.

That was it? That's what I held out for all these years? That's what all the fuss is about!?

At home, a few months later, the phone rang when I'd just stepped in after jogging along the Alameda Beach.

Shira invited me to join her and Ian, and a group of his buddies, on a camping trip to Ukiah.

"Me?" I laughed. "I don't have a sleeping bag or tent or anything. You know I'm not much into roughing-it. But I'll supply the s'more makings."

She guffawed. "You do that, Robyn. Don't skimp on the chocolate."

"You know I won't, Shira. When is it?"

As I transferred the information from a post-it to my datebook, I engaged myself in discourse:

"Maybe I'll meet someone there."

Then I said, "Quit it! You always think that way, and it's just disappointing."

"I know. I can't help it."

"Well, stop. You're pathetic."

"Well, so are you."

"Whatever! Goodnight."

"Yeah, yeah, goodnight. Don't go dreaming about him now. He doesn't exist."

"Oh, hush!"

Chapter Ten: At Last

I shifted subtly in the car seat and looked towards my lap to study the seat-belt clasp. I'd never analyzed a seat-belt part before. I now knew why; it was a highly mundane activity, but I needed a new focus. The content and duration of the driver's ramblings induced a date-like pain, yet I wasn't even on a date.

"...and I realized I needed to switch backpacks and bring the framed one instead. Those don't stress the body unduly because they distribute one's weight evenly and allow ample space for items supplying necessary nutrition and hydration —"

Oh, God. This is the longest, most excruciatingly boring carpool situation I've ever been stuck in. It seemed like a good idea last week, when I responded to his e-mail. He said he was going alone and had space for a passenger. Since he's a he, and I didn't want to do the driving, I took him up on it. Wish I hadn't.

"Shira said someone, Howard or maybe Valerie or Justin or someone needed to borrow a tent but that was last Tuesday and so maybe they have one by now but I brought my four-man Coleman just in case. I was at work until 6:15pm. After that, I had to wash up and take a quick nap and go to Whole Foods to get food for this trip before I packed up my car. But then my mom called. She's been suffering with chronic lower back problems and tendonitis from sitting at the keyboard for long stretches of time –"

Hell, I'm confined to a car for a 127 mile trip to Ukiah with Mr. Camptastic.

My eyelids fell heavy, and I drifted into a nap. Irritating sound-bites plagued my dreamscape, but I managed to sleep long enough.

I was abruptly shaken by boisterous cheer.

A dust cloud enveloped the windshield, and a small group applauded our entry. We were the last to arrive; they'd been waiting for hours, Shira shouted.

Exasperated, I stepped out of the car, and she wrapped her arm around me. "That was the most fucking annoying long-ass ride, Shira," I said under my breath. "Thank God I fell asleep. Who the hell is this dude?"

She laughed. "Oh, Phillip? I really don't know him. He's a friend of one of Ian's co-workers. I'm sorry Robyn, but you can ride home with us. And Justin and I set up a tent for you."

"Thanks, I'm beat. Who's Justin?"

"Come with me, I'll introduce you."

Shira led me to a picnic table in the middle of the campsite.

There, a man focused peacefully on an open book that was propped against a lantern. He appeared short and with fair features.

Justin wore a tan cowboy hat and dark leather jacket zipped up just enough to reveal a silver Mogen David.[12] I've never been drawn to the Boot Barn type before, but he looked like a nice guy. And he gets bonus points for being Jewish, I thought.

Shira broke his silence. "Justin, this is Robyn. Robyn, Justin."

He placed the opened book face down. Justin's eyes twinkled of an amber or hazel, I couldn't quite tell at night. His smile was warm, as was his handshake.

I looked down at his book and immediately knew that a connection with Justin not only invited, but required, my banter. "'Fabulous Small Jews by Joseph Epstein?' Talk about a short book. Are you in there?"

Shira chuckled at my quip and looked towards the tents, likely contemplating leaving us alone.

"I don't know yet," he smirked. "I'm still reading."

"What's that?" Shira asked, pointing at a mound of something resting near the fire-pit several yards away.

Justin and I watched her walk over to it. Shira giggled, while she lifted two little things that looked like stunted logs.

"Well, there's a bootless little cowboy running around these here parts," she joked, walking back to us with a pair of children's cowboy boots.

"Oh, those are so cute and tiny!" I remarked.

"Might they be yours, Miss Robyn?" Justin asked.

"Very funny, Mr. Fabulous Small Jew."

And so it had begun.

At last.

Sleeping in a tent by myself is always so damn lonely, I thought, while squirreling into my sleeping bag. And it's so damn cold, I want someone to heat me up.

Somehow, I managed to steal a couple meager pockets of shut-eye.

Hours into the night, a harsh chill skimmed the side of my face, prompting me to sit up. But a second waft of air compelled me to sink back into the sleeping bag, when my eyes caught the presence of something near the tent's entry. A skinny object stood guarding me, about one foot tall.

I wiped my groggy eyes and two of them, side-by-side, came into view: little tiny cowboy boots that had somehow, at some point, moseyed into my tent.

How odd. Did someone drop off a donation for my kids? (At that time, I was the director of a therapeutic preschool.) Wait, that's ridiculous. I'm in Ukiah on a camping trip. Who's gonna find me here?

Oh, duh. Those are the ones Shira found. Justin's the culprit. "Very funny, Justin."

I buried myself in my sleeping bag with a smile and plan for retribution.

After a breakfast of soggy scrambled eggs and semi-blackened bacon, Justin, Phillip, Valerie and Howard headed downhill for a swim in the lake. Shira and Ian took off for a hike, and I opted to soak up some sun in Phillip's precious camp chair.

"Anyone's welcome to use my reclining folding ergonomic outdoor chair," he'd declared, pointing at the chair he'd positioned near the fire-pit. "It's padded and sturdy with a stainless steel frame. The armrests can be adjusted into three different positions, and there's an insulated drink-holder on the right arm. It's a little tricky for lefties, but it's very comfortable, so it's worth making accommodations given the utility factor. I only request that you don't get it dirty. My mom got it for me for my thirtieth birthday."

With every molecule of my being, I refrained from giving Shira an eye-roll.

Finally, everyone had left.

Now was the opportune time to hide the cowboy boots. I walked to my tent, picked up the boots, and meandered into Justin's tent. There, I found a large purple duffle bag. I unzipped the bag and stuffed the boots inside. Mission accomplished.

Time for sunbathing.

As I melted into Phillip's precious chair, I stated, "Mr. Camptastic is right. This reclining, folding ergo-whatever-the-fuck chair is damn fuckin comfortable!"

A deep blue canopy of sky, and the sun's generously warm rays, afforded an added layer of snugness. Since I hadn't slept soundly the night before, I intended to enjoy a solid snooze. And I achieved this effortlessly.

I don't know how much time had passed, likely an hour or two, when I awoke to a beaming sun and the crunching of twigs. As I opened my eyes, I saw Justin gazing at me with that look a man imparts when he sees a woman he enjoys the sight of, from a few yards away. Justin abruptly walked away.

I thereafter pretended I hadn't noticed Justin having noticed me.

As we began packing our things the next morning, I glanced towards my car to find Justin with one hand on the hatchback, two tiny little cowboy boots in his other hand.

"Justin what are you doing?" I blurted, as if I didn't know.

"Oh, um..." Caught in the act, he changed his story. "I'm just going to hand these boots over to the ranger. We don't want the little cowboy to run around barefooted."

Justin headed for the camp office.

He returned a few minutes later with empty hands and a victorious demeanor.

"You did the right thing, Justin," I affirmed.

"I always do, Miss Robyn." He grinned.

"Somehow I doubt that." I responded, and we went our separate ways, but only for the moment.

Email correspondence began the next afternoon.

Dear Miss Robyn,
I hope you don't mind that I did some sleuthing to ascertain your email. Do not worry, as I don't yet have your phone number or address. If I did, I would personally deliver this note to you. At any rate, it was nice meeting you over the weekend, and I admit that I have been thinking about you. What I have been thinking about you is this: I think that you are the perfect combination of Cruella De Vil and Charlie Brown's red-headed girl. With that, I shall close.
PS I would be honored if you would kindly forward your phone number.
Justin

Dear Justin Case,
Cruella De Vil and Charlie Brown's red-headed girl? Do you mean to say that I'm a mix of a villainous puppy-murdering she-devil and a stunted pre-pubescent scarlet hussy? Why, thank you!
PS My number might be the number that I've typed in the subject line. Or maybe not. The risk is yours.
Miss Robyn aka Bea Ware

Justin called that evening, expressing relief that the phone number worked.

"I had to make you squirm a little," I told him. "It's the Cruella De Red Head in me." He chuckled and had no come-back line. I could tell he was nervous, and I liked that.

We made plans for dinner that weekend.

As I walked towards the entrance of Barnes and Noble, one minute before 6 p.m., I thought, "He better be here. I better not be getting stood-up, or have to wait."

And there he was, in his tan leather jacket, reclining against the walls of the bookstore with his arms crossed in a faux relaxed manner. He smiled broadly and approached me with a hug.

We looked around and decided on Hahn's Hibachi for dinner.

Inside, a freckle-faced brunette boy sat with his parents at a nearby table. I watched Justin's face light up when he noticed the child. I'd never seen a man react to kids the same way I do.

"So do you have your own, or an ex-wife? What's your story, Mr. Case?"

I learned that he has an ex-wife, an evil, crazy one, and no kids of his own. I shared that I'd been planning on adopting. He liked the idea, and it turned out we'd both babysat for a mutual friend who adopted from Kazakhstan.

"There are too many kids in need of homes. Plus, I don't want to pass my genes on," I added.

"Oh you mean because you're—" Justin extended his arm towards the floor, palm faced-down, as if to guard the head of a small child.

"No, not because I'm short, because of diseases and other family stuff." My tone was matter-of-fact; I was annoyed but tried to let it go.

After dinner, we wandered the book store aisles.

Realizing we had different tastes, we agreed to meet near the entrance in 15 minutes. Justin got lost in the History section, fascinated by war books, while I was drawn to Humor.

When taking in Sedaris' "Me Talk Pretty One Day," I heard, "There you are." Justin had been looking for me. "You're not so easy to find, because you're kind of, you know—"

"Okay, Justin. Enough of the short jokes. I don't like that."

He changed the subject.

We chatted about our respective book interests, as Justin walked me to my car.

Justin gave me a caring peck on the lips and asked for a second date.

"I don't know. I really don't like all the jabs about my height."

"I'm sorry. I hope you'll reconsider. I was kind of nervous."

We said, "good night," and I didn't know what to make of the evening.

At home, I found myself sitting on my couch stupefied, tears crawling down my face. What's going on? I've never felt this way after a date.

One thought crystallized: either Justin is a jerk or I'm already falling in love. I didn't consider that it might not be an either-or matter.

I called Shira.

"He said that, Robyn? Is he just stupid?!"

"I know. I mean, I don't know. Even after I clearly wasn't humored, he made the second comment. But why do I feel this way? It's like, I don't know, really deep. I can't describe it. I'm just feeling so much."

"What are you going to do if he calls you, Robyn?"

"I don't know."

Dear Robyn,

I'm very sorry for my insensitive comments and for hurting your feelings last night. It's no excuse but I sometimes say thoughtless things when I'm nervous. I hope it goes without saying that you're very pretty. Actually, I think you are impossibly cute. I should've just said that instead of making senseless remarks.

I would like to make it up to you by taking you on a maiden voyage in my new car. We can drive up to Occidental, along the ocean, and I'll treat you to dinner at one of my favorite restaurants.

Everyone deserves a second chance, and I really hope you'll give me one. Either way, you're a wonderful woman and I wish you the best.

Justin

I didn't know what to do. They say that women are supposed to forgive, so I knew that much. Mom said it too. She, Dawn, and I were in the car on the way to school when a radio host discussed extramarital affairs with wives who'd been cheated on. Dawn asked Mom what the women should do in that situation. "You just forgive," Mom said, as if she had. (Perhaps she had.) I didn't agree then, and I still don't.

But forgiveness over a much lesser offense differs greatly from excusing infidelity. Plus we're supposed to follow our hearts. Justin had already invaded mine.

Nobody teaches us to follow our brains when dating. We're not taught to love intelligently. Then again, I thought, Justin's a smart choice: a lawyer, sincere, playful, smart, quick-witted, and handsome. He was nervous because he likes me. And I feel such strong emotions already. There's something intense there. They say that happens when you meet "the one."

What if I'm on the verge of my happily-ever-after? At last. Regardless, I shouldn't rule a man out because he says some stupid things. Shit, I'd never date again! This book would end here. You'd get a raw deal, and I'd run out of space for battery-operated gadgets.

Dear Mr. Justin Case,
You're lucky I'm so forgiving. But if you blow it again, I'll unleash my Cruella in full force. It won't be pretty.
Be warned.
Be scared,
Bea Ware
PS Call me.

Staring at the face of my watch, I didn't realize how nervous I was until Justin's knock shook me. He was precisely on time.

I swooped up my purse handle to greet him. Justin's careful smile conveyed his inner discourse: "I'm not going to blow it this time. I hope not. I'll try not to. I better not. Don't blow it, me!"

"Hi, Justin."

"Hi. Are you ready?"

"Yeah, sure, let me just lock up."

I turned the dead-bolt and dropped my keys back into my purse. As I followed Justin along the narrow walkway towards the street, I enjoyed the view. Justin strode in the same tan cowboy boots and leather jacket he wore at the campsite. And his dark blue jeans fit snuggly. Nice butt, I thought.

He stopped at the curb, turned and smiled proudly. Justin stood in front of a shiny new golden Jaguar.

"Wow. That's your new car? Very nice."

He opened the passenger door for me.

I sunk into the plush seat. This was so much nicer than Kenny's beat up old Chevy. That tightwad insisted I give him my registration sticker. (The DMV had mistakenly sent me a second one). I wouldn't oblige, and he moaned about it for days. Then I recalled a blind date during which I dinged the guy's new car door by opening it too wide and hitting it against the parking meter. "Oops, sorry." He politely brushed it off, but I'd just blemished his new baby—not even one week old! Oh, well. It was only a Kia. He was a nice guy, and I never heard from him again. None of it mattered because I was dating in style now: the passenger in a Jaguar. Justin would open the door for me too, so I wouldn't do that again.

He scooted into the driver's seat. "It's my dream buggy. My boss gave me a good deal. You can say it's a company car." Justin explained that he was paying out of his paycheck monthly, at a reasonable rate.

This seemed an odd arrangement, but who cares? I'd enjoy the dreamy transport.

"Etta James okay with you, Robyn?"

Etta who? "Yeah, sure."

He slid the cd into the player and began the drive.

"I like this song," I remarked. "She has an amazing voice."

"Yeah, she's one of my favorites."

The words "At last" resonated with me, and perhaps with Justin.

We wound our way along Highway 116 inspired by majestic pines, the sun's rays that streamed through a blanket of blue, and easy conversation.

I turned towards the window. "It's so gorgeous around here. I wanna bottle the pine air, take it home and inhale it whenever I need a fix."

He grinned. "I'm glad to hear it, because I can't get enough of this area. I have so many good memories. My folks and all our Bay Area relatives rented cabins up here every summer." Justin stole a quick glance out the driver's seat window. "We did a lot of hiking, went tubing on the Russian River, and Dad taught me to fish there. My Mom and all my aunts— talk about your stereotypical division of labor—stayed in baking pies."

"Sounds great. Makes me think about Engel family vacations to Camp Blue in Yosemite. We loved pool-time and ping pong, the campfires, making s'mores and then s'more s'mores. But the best part" —my voice enlivened—"was those little mini individual cereal boxes on the dining hall tables for breakfast. I had to act fast to grab the Cocoa Puffs. It was my goal every morning. I usually won. People learned not to get between me and Cocoa Puffs."

"Note to self," he teased, "don't touch any chocolate that's Robyn's. P.S. to self, ALL chocolate is Robyn's."

"You're a fast learner, Mr. Case!"

Justin stopped the car at a deep red house with black trim along the door and windows. "That's the one we rented." He stared silently for a few moments, and I sensed a sadness.

"It's hard not to miss those days," I said. "I'm glad you have the memories."

"Thank you, Robyn. I'm glad you have yours too."

"Yeah…but it's like the Engel family died with my Mom."

"I'm so sorry." Justin touched his hand to my thigh, supportively, and I gently placed my hand on his.

"I know how that is, Robyn. My sister Gayle and I fought bitterly over Mom's inheritance. I haven't talked to her since. I don't even know where she is, and I don't care to."

"Wow, I'm sorry. It's a shame tragedy tears families apart. It's like…like a second tragedy, almost as bad or maybe worse, what it does to families that weren't solid to begin with…Oy," I added. "I'm sorry for being a Debbie Downer on such a nice day."

"Not at all," he assured. "I'm having a wonderful time." Justin looked at me as if about to kiss me but held back.

He turned his hand over slowly, interlocking his fingers with mine. We sat for several moments in a cozy lull.

"So, Miss Robyn, aka Bea Ware—"

"Yes, Mr. Justin, Just in case?"

"How about a bite for you and the rest for me, at the best Italian eatery outside of Rome? It's family style. Enough to feed the mafia. Or me. Sound good?"

"I'd say that sounds good, but I'd like to vie for two bites."

"Deal."

As soon as we entered Negri's, a plump little old woman, as wide as she was tall, brightened up and waddled towards Justin. "Little J!" she said excitedly, "it's been ages!"

The woman gave Justin a suffocating hug and a kiss on both cheeks. "How you been? How's the family? So good, good, good to see you!" She pinched his cheek and he flushed.

"I'm great. Everyone's fine, Evelyn. It's good to see you too, sweetie!" Justin turned towards me. "This is Robyn."

Evelyn glanced at me, then back at Justin. She seemed to know I was special to him. And before I knew it, I was the recipient of a very loving, garlic smelling, Italian version of the Jewish Bubbeh-I-can-barely-breathe-so-kindly-set-my-ribcage-free-now! hug.

Finally, she dropped her arms and led us to a table by the front windows. A minute later, our waiter brought over a bottle of Rosé. He announced that it was on the house.

Justin had known Evie for over thirty years, he said. His family frequented Negri's every summer. They became very close with Evie's family; he was very glad the place was still going strong.

I soon understood why. The ravioli and garlic bread were scrumptious, and the portions, humungous. Sweet red wine added the perfect touch. Shortly after we began eating, Justin told the waiter, "We might as well get our to-go boxes now."

I finally ate all I could, took another bite of garlic bread, and excused myself to use the restroom.

When I began walking back to the table, our eyes met. Justin's face rested on the palm of his hand, his elbow nearly touching his plate. He sat staring at me with a broad, glowing smile.

I sat back down, across from him. "What? What's that look for?"

"You're just so amazingly cute."

I glanced down at my plate, flattered and embarrassed, not used to this kind of attention from a man who's not a creep. I liked it, though, and I definitely liked him. Then it struck me how comfortable I was with Justin, as I slipped off my shoes, straightened my legs—under the table—and rested my feet on his lap. Justin pushed his nearly empty plate towards the table's edge and massaged my feet.

As if scripted, the waiter took a long time to bring our check.

The sun appeared to melt into the ocean, while we meandered towards our final stop: the beach at Bodega Bay. A peaceful stretch of Highway 1 paved the way. When we arrived, we giddily asked a young woman walking by if she'd take our picture. She smiled in agreement, and Justin handed her his camera.

We posed in front of his car, our arms around each other and a magnificent expanse of shimmering ocean in the background.

"Thank you," we said in unison.

He retrieved his camera, pocketed it, and asked, "Shall we?"

"Let's go!"

We walked hand in hand through the sand, and then I followed Justin up and down a series of enormous rocks—jagged and worn by time and the ocean. Justin slowed to a pause, looked back at me, but then proceeded to move forward. I sensed he was inclined to kiss me but wanted to find the idyllic spot.

Alas, we came upon a spacious patch of level land. From there, we looked out at sailboats gliding along the water. Seagulls drifted overhead. Justin stepped closer to me, gently anchored me in his arms, and eased me up against his chest.

He stroked the side of my face, leaned in and kissed me.

We kissed passionately, lovingly, somehow knowing this was it, the one—the kiss that ignited our happily-ever-after. Our bodies swayed as one with the breeze.

"We're dancing," he whispered. Justin's face overflowed with joy.

We kissed again and again, charged by a blazing inertia.

A smile eclipsed my face during moments of breath. I was happier than I ever imagined I could be, with Justin, because of Justin.

As Justin drove us into the Bay Area, day transformed to night. I didn't want our time to end.

"How about we pick up a video and watch a movie at your place?" He suggested. A perfect plan.

"Sure, yeah, there's a little video store on Park Street. I have a membership card. We can stop there."

He pulled into a parking spot by the video store, just as an employee inside was flipping the window sign over to display the word: "Closed."

"Drats!" I exclaimed. "Alameda slumbers early, even on weekends. Sorry."

"That's alright. Some other time, Robyn." His hint of a future date reassured me.

When we reached my place, I still hadn't thought of another excuse for subtly extending the evening. Justin opened the passenger's side door and walked me to my apartment. An alluring tension strolled with us.

"Well, um,"—I fumbled for my keys—"You're welcome to come in, I mean, for tea or water or"—my voice dropped—"something."

"I'd like that."

We found ourselves inches from each other and my plush burgundy sofa. Justin's hands captured either side of my waist.

"You know, Robyn,"—he looked at me with deep sincerity—"I really didn't care to watch a movie. I just wanted to spend more time with you."

I guffawed. "Me too, Justin. I mean, I wanted to spend more time with you. In fact, I"—he lightly kissed the hollow of my neck—"I actually hate," I continued, determined to finish my statement.

Justin planted sensual kisses along the side of my neck, his tongue ascending towards my ear, where it lingered—"vid"—he hoisted me up, laid me across the sofa and joined me, as if through one flawless motion—"eos!" By now, our tongues were entangled and bodies aligned. Our fingers rushed each other's fevered skin, as buttons came undone.

"Mmm, Justin,"—he kissed me along my collarbone, then a tad lower—"this feels"—and again—"so good!"—his hands met at the small of my back, then slid carefully up along my spine to unhook my bra—"I've, I've never felt"—then flowed along my ribcage towards my breasts—"like this before. Let's go to my bedroom now!"

Justin swooped me up and snuggled me in his arms.

He carried me down the hallway and into my room. He lowered me onto my bed, and I rested my head on a crimson pillow.

As Justin stood by the bed and tossed his shirt towards the door, I jumped up—always thinking practically—dug out a pack of Trojans from my dresser drawer, and placed it on the nightstand by my headboard.

"Good thing these last for years," I joked, bouncing back into my position on the bed. "It's so rare they come in handy."

Justin chuckled. "God, you're so beautiful...everything about you." He reached down to un-button my jeans and slowly disrobe me.

I watched the curves of my thighs reflect a glimmer of light that broke through the curtains above, as my legs moved apart. He kissed and licked.

"Mm, I really like that."

"I don't even, really know what I'm doing," he admitted.

Surprised, I savored the fact that Justin was that innocent, that inflamed by our connection, that intent on taking care of me. I'd never affected a man like that.

"Yes you do, baby," I whispered. "It feels wonderful."

The night, like the day, nested pure enchantment. Nothing but *us* mattered, none of the men from my past, the countless tiresome irritating dates between lengthy bouts of celibacy; not Dad's failure to love me like a child should be loved by their parent; none of the guys who overlooked me to go after someone else who was taller or cuter or more confident. Sadness and loneliness no longer defined me. None of that mattered.

Or maybe it mattered a lot. Maybe that package contributed to a remarkably magical evening, one I'd been longing for all my life because it contrasted so strikingly with everything I'd formerly known. It changed everything.

Justin changed everything.

As he lay atop me in the early morning hours, I felt our heartbeats race in rapid succession. I also felt an ardent, precious love.

I was in love with Justin. I already knew it. Yet I'd refrain from telling him. It was way too soon, and I couldn't risk saying it first.

In that moment, though, he stilled his body and gazed deep into my eyes. "I love you, Robyn," he said softly.

"I love you too, Justin," I breathed back.

At last.

Chapter Eleven: Triskaidekaphobia = fear of the number 13.

Justin was a lot older than me, thirteen years to be exact. We didn't meet until I approached 40. Thirty-nine was a difficult number to wrap my brain around—until I found out he was 52.

I forgave our age difference because of our chemistry. Plus, Justin looked a lot younger. I suppose there was something parental about the discrepancy too. He'd fill a loving fatherly role.

Of course, I wasn't conscious of that and hate even admitting it now. It's pretty twisted, but our unconscious has more control over us than we'd care to acknowledge.

At any rate, Justin's presence in my life made for a happy entrance into the forties. Thinking back, twenty-nine had been much more difficult to accept.

One decade pre-Justin, I'd hosted my 29th birthday party. Friends had clustered in the living room, claiming various chairs, patches of sofa, and flimsy amber floor pillows that accented a cream carpet. Lively conversation and the intoxicating aroma of fresh baked brownies permeated my apartment in Alameda.

A boisterous knock startled us, and I excused myself to answer the door. At my doorstep stood a strange female donning a brightly tie-dyed sundress, stringy brown hair that flowed down to her kneecaps, flip-flops, and a burlap handbag. Nicole, who I'd befriended at UC Berkeley, stood slightly behind her.

"Robyn, this is Glory," Nicole took a step sideways to introduce her friend. "We work together." Glory gave me a quick handshake and walked inside. Strange. I was unaffected, knowing Nicole is the type who befriends all.

"Good to see you, Nicole! It's been a while."

"You too." She imparted a friendly hug.

I turned around and noticed that Glory had already made her way to the kitchen counter and began munching a brownie. "Mm, these are really hot but delish, Robyn!"

"Oh thanks, Glory. Yeah, help yourself, everyone."

The woman's commanding presence quieted the room. Still chewing, Glory looked at me and announced, "My gift for your birthday is a Tarot card reading."

She plopped herself down on the carpet, dropped the rest of her brownie into her handbag and pulled out a deck of cards. Glory patted a space of carpet in front of her. "Sit here, Robyn."

"Great. I've never done this before." I smiled, thinking I might be better off had she sprung for a Hallmark.

Glory spread the cards out along the carpet face-down, told me to pick one, then to show her, then to put it back in the deck. I did as told.

She scrunched up her face and closed her eyes for a moment, then reordered the cards (face down) painstakingly, as if guided by a divine spirit.

"Now think of a 'yes' or 'no' question, but don't say it out loud. Tell me when you have it."

All eyes studied me. Not a sound could be heard but the grating ticking of my biological clock. It was, after all, my 29th birthday.

And I was, after all, still single. Naturally, I wondered if I'd end up with the Old Maid card or if I'd ever meet my Prince Charming. "Okay, Glory I have my question."

She did some more hocus pocus with the cards and turned a few over one-by-one. Glory then blurted out: "The answer to your question is 'No! Absolutely not!'"

With that, she crushed my insides. "That's just mean," was all I could muster.

How dare she kill my dream, on my birthday. It's not that I wanted to bear children. I just wanted to meet my Prince and we'd adopt, when I was still fairly young. Then we'd live hap…we all know the rest.

I pushed myself up to a stand and told my guests to eat and enjoy – while fantasizing about wrapping Glory's long locks very, very tightly around her pale neck; tying the ends together very, very securely into a large, permanent, decorative bow.

Now, ten years later, I could safely say I'd disproved Glory's edict.

I remembered, too, Devon's prediction: "You're going to meet someone in 13 months, Robyn." Though I had met Justin on August 13, but it wasn't thirteen months after my move to Oakland. It was…I calculated on my fingers, slowly raising them one by one, to count the numbers between 2005 and 1992…13 years.

Devon got the number, just not the unit of time. I'd never been superstitious, but 13 seemed to be playing a big role in my life these days. A good one at that.

By now, I seemed to have everything I'd always pined for.

Justin and I couldn't refrain from giggling, kissing, touching, dancing, making love, and talking by phone when apart for more than two minutes. I wanted to shout to the world that my time had come. Instead, I sent an email to a handful of my closest girlfriends.

October 3, 2005: Dear Friends, I hope you're well. I'm great for a change. Believe it or not, all my whining about being single and lonely, my jealousy of all the lovey-dovey couples out there (including some of your relationships), is finally over! I'm very happy to report that I've been in one of those vomit-inducing happy-go-lucky couples. It feels really right, and we believe we have a future. His name is Justin. He's a lawyer, an honest one, and very sweet. We're falling more in love every day. Can't wait for you to meet him! Excuse my self-centeredness. I just needed to share!
Be well.
I love ya,
Robyn

Being with Justin made me feel "normal," like the rest of the world. Ironic, given nobody's "normal." Moreover, romance feasts off of the last crumbs of one's sanity, taking a person light-years away from their more stable footing. But I'd believed that my former footing wasn't stable mostly because I wasn't in a romantic relationship. Yet I wasn't in a romantic relationship mostly because I was abnormal, so I believed. As my Bubbeh would say, "It's meshugenah!"[13]

"Normalcy" also meant having a close-knit family. So I created this, in my mind, and readily introduced Justin to the Engels on a trip to LA. Justin had no family to speak of, so I felt proud and generous in offering mine.

Following a cordial dinner at El Torito with Dad and his long-term girlfriend, Irene, she and Justin meandered towards the exit. Dad conferred a nod with the words, "He's a good pick, Robyn." That meant a lot, especially since Mom wasn't alive to meet him.

I knew Mom would have approved too. They were both lawyers focused on justice, not money, and they shared a sensitive spirit that appreciated life's details: young kids in thick-framed glasses, a smile from the postman, and an extra juicy plum.

Incidentally, Mom would've approved of Jonathan's pick too; baby brother had also met his match. "She's just so easy to be with," Jonathan said of Angela.

The four of us ventured to Jonathan and Angela's favorite place: Disneyland. It wasn't much of a double-date, though. We immediately split up so they could hit the real rides.

Justin and I took off for Fantasyland.

While in line for Peter Pan, I rested my head against Justin's chest, our arms folded around each other's waists, and Justin kissed the top of my head.

"Look at you two, so in love!" an elderly man with his granddaughter in tow remarked from ahead of us in line. "That's something truly special."

"Thank you," we chimed, glowing.

"Let me take your picture for you."

Justin plucked the camera strap off his shoulder and handed it to this stranger— a stranger who voluntarily preserved the moment, our connection, forever.

There've been too many times when I was that stranger in observation of a loving couple. Rather than stepping out of myself and being happy for them, I broiled with putrid nausea and homicidal venom. Damn them for the getting the happily-ever-after that I never seemed to find. So, now that it was my turn, I'd joyously lose myself in it. Hell, I'd get even by flaunting it.

Bubbling with giggles, Justin and I gazed into each other's eyes.

"We're so darn cute!" I blurted.

"I just love us!" Justin added.

I tossed my arms around his neck and pressed my lips to his. We kissed and kissed until we noticed that the people in front of us were yards away, and our stranger-friend was helping his granddaughter onto the ride.

"Come on, Never Never Land awaits!" I gleefully took his hand and we skipped to close the gap between us and the family in front of us.

But Fantasyland exists in a confined space.

Weeks after the trip, Justin called to break plans for dinner.

"I can't make it. I have a migraine."

"A migraine? You've never mentioned migraines. You sound bad. What's going on?"

"No. Nothing. I'll be alright. I just need to stay in tonight."

"Justin, do you need anything? I'll come over. I want to see you."

"No, don't. I just need some time alone."

"Damnit, Justin! You're scaring me. I'm going over there if you don't tell me what's going on."

He sighed deeply. "Baby, I lost my job today."

"Oh God. I'm so sorry, honey. You'll be okay. We'll be okay. What happened, babe?"

He said that his boss complained about Justin leaving too many unattended loose ends, taking too long to wrap up cases, and that he'd given him enough chances. Justin said he had to return the Jaguar and take the bus home. The thought of such a humiliating experience moved me to tears.

"Honey, I love you. You didn't deserve any of that. He's psycho. We knew that. You lasted longer than any of the others. Sweetie, you're a great lawyer."

"No I'm not!"

"Yes you are, Justin. His excuses were bullshit. He was trying to save a buck at your—at OUR—expense. We'll get through this."

Justin paused momentarily. "Why do you have to be so nice?"

Month's end approached, and Justin took the bus to visit me, as he'd gotten into the habit of doing. It meant a lot that he wasn't depending on me to drive to him all the time.

He walked in, chewing on his lip.

I gave Justin an abrupt kiss. "Honey, what's wrong?"

"Nothing. Well, I'm a little stressed." He placed his jacket on the arm of the sofa. "Rent's due. I don't want to lose the place." Justin pulled me close. "Baby, I want it to be our home. I'll repaint the second bathroom pink for you." He grinned. "And you've seen the

office. I was thinking that could be a third bedroom for, you know"
—Justin slowly whispered, "pit-ter, pat-ter."

I smiled half-heartedly. "I want that too. It WILL be our home, sweet-love. But why are you worried? You can't make rent?"

Justin took a heavy breath. "No, I can't," his words emitting anger and shame. "Robyn, Suzanne took control over finances. I handed over all my paychecks to her."

"So you had nothing after the divorce?"

"Not a damn thing."

What a bitch, I thought. "Well I'm not like that."

"I know you're not, sweetie. But I'm trying to climb out of a huge debt. I'm still paying off law school loans. Golden Gate's a private school. It cost a fortune."

I sighed and took Justin's hand. We sat down on the couch, when an idea struck. "Why don't you move in here, love?"

"Your place is way too small for all my stuff, Robyn."

"Yeah, but," my voice faded, "It's a solution. I mean, we need to do something. Your rent is due tomorrow." It seemed I was more nervous about this fact than he was. "What are you going to do, Justin?"

"I don't know."

"Well, how much is your rent?"

"Thirteen hundred." Good God, that's almost twice mine, I realized. But I had savings. I'd been working hard for many years and rarely spent money on myself.

"I'll be right back." I entered my bedroom, pulled my checkbook out from the dresser drawer, and scrawled on it. I walked over to Justin. "Here, sweet-love. Just address it."

"No, Robyn. I can't let you do that."

"It's just a temporary situation. What choice do you have?" Frustration and angst rattled me. "Do you know anyone else you could borrow from, or can you take out a loan?"

"No. No. I don't. I can't." Justin begrudgingly took the check from my hand and stashed it in his wallet. "I'm going to pay you back. You know that, right?"

"I know, babe."

Justin and I would do the rent-check tango for several more months: The 30th arrived, I wrote the check, he refused the check, I insisted, he accepted begrudgingly and promised to pay me back. We ate dinner in an air of reticent tension.

But he was worth the investment, I had no doubts. We loved each other too much to let petty money issues destroy us. Besides, as a Bay Area attorney, Justin would surely be making a nearly six-digit salary when he secured a new job. And I was always financially responsible.

We'd be okay. More than okay. We'd have the dream we both deserved and had been searching for all our lives.

"Honey, all couples go through hard times. We'll come out of it and be fine," I assured him.

"I know, baby." He turned to me and gently eased his fingertips down my face. "I love you very much, Robyn."

200

"I love you bundles too, Justin."

A tender embrace escalated into seductive kissing, then passionate sex.

Three months trudged by. Justin took some cases from former colleagues and had patches of part-time work, but still lacked a full-time position.

He started breaking plans, scaled down on phone-calls, and, eventually, stopped corresponding with me altogether.

Four days of this, and I couldn't take it anymore. I drove straight to Justin's apartment after work, unannounced.

The door crept open and Justin looked bad. For the first time, I noticed a few gray hairs. His vacant expression lightened a smidge when our eyes met.

"I don't want to lose you," I immediately cried.

"Ssh, ssh" Justin pushed the door wide open and pulled me against his chest.

We moved to his living room and sat on the love-seat.

"This is driving me crazy," I told him. "I can't lose you."

"Baby, it's taking too long. I can't find a job. I can't take care of you. I can't even take care of myself."

"But we'll get through this together. It's just a dark time."

Justin sighed loudly, decisively. "I think you're better off without me. I don't deserve you."

"But I don't want to live without you!" Tears drenched my face. "We're so happy together," I argued. "At least we were before you

201

lost your job. You'll get a new one. You're a wonderful man and a wonderful lawyer."

"Don't say that!"

"Why not? It's true, Justin."

"No it's not. I'm just going to disappoint you."

"Only if you're giving up. Justin, don't do this to us! I thought we had a future. Why are you doing this?"

He looked away from me, contemplative. Then his eyes verged on tearfulness.

"Do you want me to leave, Justin? Do you want to *never* see me again?" I pulled a tissue from my pants pocket and wiped my face with it. "This is fuckin ridiculous!"

He shifted towards me. "I AM being a fool. I don't want to lose you. Not ever. I just want to do right by you."

"You will. You do."

I fell into Justin's arms and we held on tightly. He wouldn't let me go, he said, lest someone else would snatch me up.

I excused myself to wash my tear-stained face in the bathroom. When examining its drab white walls, I thought, this bathroom needs a splash of pink.

That night, we agreed I'd move in with Justin.

Piles of carefully packaged cardboard boxes spanned the width of my living room. "It's never as much as you think it is until you think it's too much because you're packing to move," I said out loud and to myself.

Justin had classy, elaborate furniture, most of which he'd inherited from his parents' estate. This meant I didn't need to bring furniture. There was no room for it anyway.

I'd made a dozen or so trips to Goodwill with donations. My neighbor, who was struggling financially, gratefully took the sofa.

I opened the door to greet Justin, who'd just parked the U-Haul.

"Hi, sweet-love. Come over here!" I said giddily, leading Justin inside and towards a lengthy, wide stretch of bubble-wrap. "There's extra! Ready?"

Justin hovered down with knees bent and fists clenched, as if he was about to ski down a black diamond slope. "Okay, I'm ready," he said in a playfully serious manner.

"One, two, three, go!" We jumped up and down in an aerobic frenzy, like Richard Simmons and his midget stunt-double with Tourette's.

I was laughing so hard that I made little progress, so I stopped to watch Justin crush the bubbles with his boot heels.

Pop! Pop! A demonic, expression covered his face.

"Get the last corner, honey! There's still more!"

Pop! "There's one more bastard." Pop!

"Woohoo! Mazel Tov!" I cheered.

Justin kissed my forehead. "Now that I've burst your bubbles, baby, I'm taking you home with me."

"Sounds just right."

Justin spared me from handling the heavier items— boxes filled with books and albums, my full length mirror, and vacuum cleaner. Otherwise, there was no rhyme or reason to our labor. We just kept shoving box after box, item after item, into the truck.

Three hours later, I wiped droplets of sweat off my brow and dropped my keys into the manager's mail slot.

Justin and I jumped into the truck. "I can't believe we're doing this. I'm really moving in with you!" Happy days are here again. "Take me home, Mr. Case."

"Yes, ma'am, Ms. Bea Ware. We'll be there before dawn."

I looked at my watch. "Silly. It's only 2:05. We're making good time today."

He smiled and revved the gas pedal.

Along Grand Avenue, I glanced nostalgically at Lake Merritt. "I love this lake. It was my first stop when I moved to the Bay Area in 1992. I really am coming home."

"Of course you are, baby. Home with me."

Justin pulled the truck into the driveway at 200 Montecito, and switched off the ignition.

"We'll unload here, unless someone kicks us out. Parking's a bear in this neighborhood."

"I know," I laughed. "I read that it's comparable to trying to find parking in Tokyo. I'm glad you have that spot in the garage. My car's small. I'll be okay if I have to walk a bit."

"No, honey, that parking spot is yours. I'll park on the street."

"You're so sweet, Justin." I leaned in for a kiss, sat back and looked at my watch. "We made it at 2:18. It took thirteen minutes to get here."

Thirteen.

Chapter Twelve: Jeopardy

Perhaps it was risky to move in with Justin before he proposed marriage. But I hadn't done the research and thus hadn't heard of the "cohabitation effect."

"Couples who cohabit before marriage (and especially before an engagement or an otherwise clear commitment) tend to be less satisfied with their marriages — and more likely to divorce — than couples who do not. These negative outcomes are called the cohabitation effect." NY Times, 2012, Meg Jay

---

"Shh-it," I whispered, crouched over to adjust the narrow black shoe strap that suffocated my right foot. "God I hate heels!"

Pain hustled through my right pinkie toe to the surface of my foot, and then back down to my ankle. My left foot was fine, though. Weird. It must be stronger, skinnier, or less sensitive than its dominant counterpart.

Justin strode through the courtyard yards ahead.

"Honey, wait for me," I urged.

He paused, leaned against a palm tree, and huffed. I chalked that up to nervousness. We'd never gone to a wedding together, and this was my family.

"Come on, Robyn! You were rushing me and now you're making us late. The photographer's waiting."

"I'm doing my best, Mr. Grumpy Grump Grumpster!"

Fortunately, the nickname amused him. It was the only way I could comfortably point out that Justin was being a pain in the ass when he was being a pain in the ass. I'd tagged him "Mr. Triple G." a few weeks earlier when we trekked around Lake Merritt. It took a lot to motivate him to make the three-mile walk. He'd started putting on weight and incessantly moaned about exercising. Meanwhile, I'd been inviting him to walk the lake with me once or twice a week. When he finally agreed, I was ecstatic.

Halfway around, though, Justin lost his sole. That is, I watched Justin lift his left foot. All but the base of his sneaker moved with that foot. His shoe's sole remained on the path behind him.

I was in stitches. "Justin, you just lost your sole!"

He looked peeved.

"I'm sorry, hon," I chuckled. "It's extra funny because we're halfway around. It's not like we can turn back and spare you from any of the walking."

Justin picked up his failed sole.

"Babe, you have to admit this is pretty funny! Those shoes were like older than God anyway. We'll get you new ones."

Justin tossed his flimsy sole into the water.

"Come on, sweetie." I gave him a hug.

He sighed, a tad more relaxed now, and resumed walking —with one sole-less shoe.

"I love you," I said playfully, "Mr. Grumpy Grump Grumpster. I'll call you triple G. for short." Alas, he smirked and took my hand.

Now, at the LA Airport Embassy Suites, I teased, "I see that smile, and I'm moving as fast as I can. It's not easy to walk in four inch heels, sweet-love." Damn, how do models and drag queens do it?

Justin looked at his watch, as I struggled to increase my pace.

I finally caught up and reached out a hand. He smiled and secured my hand in his. With his free hand, Justin moved in to adjust my collar. He stepped back to look at me.

"It was a little uneven, Robby, but you look stunning. Everyone's going to be paying attention to you and not the bride."

Weeks earlier, Justin had helped me pick out a deep emerald green silk shirt in San Francisco's China town. We found the perfect black and emerald green choker to match. I completed the ensemble with a black wool skirt; sheer panty-hose (another torturous female garment no doubt invented by men), and black four inch heels.

I kissed Justin's cheek. "Thank you, babe. But Angela's gorgeous. It's her day. Well, and Jonathan's, but it's really about Angela. It's always the bride's day."

"I'll remember that."

"As you should, Justin. As you should."

We meandered through the courtyard, admiring the scene. The five-star hotel provided a picture-perfect wedding venue: sunshine striking through the ceiling windows, palm trees and greenery sprinkled throughout, miniature water-falls and pools of water lodging Japanese Koi.

Yards further, we landed at rows of white folding chairs, perfectly aligned to face the microphone that centered the floor. In the backdrop, gloriously tall windows permitted streams of light to showcase the happy couple.

"Hey kids!" Dad closed the guest book that he'd just signed. It rested on a podium to the right of the first line of chairs. Irene stood stiffly next to Dad, cracking a subtle grin.

"Hi, Dad," I said, as we hugged.

"Can't believe I'm marrying off my youngest child."

Hopefully, your second oldest too soon, I thought. "Yeah, it's hard to believe my baby brother's getting married."

"Congratulations, Jerry!" Justin stepped closer to Dad, offering a handshake and hug.

"Thank you, Justin."

I turned back to see Dawn walking in, a man to her side. She looked well put together, as always, graceful in heels too. The guy appeared an unassuming, nice nerdy type with brown-framed glasses, patches of freckles, and greased back hair, formally dressed in a suit and tie.

"Dad, Irene, Robyn and Justin, this is Doug."

Two by two, we said "hello" and selectively exchanged obligatory brief robotic hugs.

While the guys chatted, I nudged Dawn. "New boyfriend?"

"Nah, just a friend with benefits." She smirked. "Damn good benefits too."

"Cool!" I stifled a habitual surge of Jan Brady jealousy. What the hell am I thinking? I have the love of my life! Justin scooped up my hand.

"You look so hot, my Robby!"

"Ah, thank you, baby."

Thing is, I continued in silent discourse with myself, I'd never shared assets with a male friend. It sounded so sexy, but no guy friend ever wanted me that way. Then again, I probably wouldn't have been impressed with any of their benefits packages. Get your mind out of the gutter, girlfriend! You're here for a wedding in a cathedral-like place. So it's a romantic hotel, but it is your brother's wedding. Stop it! Clean thoughts. Clean thoughts.

Truth be told, our sex life was fading fast. At the time, I blatantly denied this. After-all, I was deeply in love, and marriage would make things even better. We'd have our best sex on our honeymoon. The fairytale was nearly ours.

"Let's sit here, Robby." Justin gestured towards two chairs in the first row, Dawn and Doug to our left.

I started to remove my jacket, and Justin took it off for me, placing it on the back of my chair.

"Thank you, sweet-love."

Chairs filled quickly with well dressed, joyous people.

Eventually, several hundreds of us awaited the grand event.

"You look so beautiful," Jonathan told Angela, during his vows, "I could kiss you right now."

The audience held onto Jonathan's heartfelt impromptu words, inspired by Angela's beauty during that precious moment. An enthusiastic male guest interrupted with a shout-out: "Go for it, Jonathan!"

I looked around to a room full of laugher and instantly liked this big, spunky family Jonathan was marrying into.

When the music slowed, I recognized some long-time friends on the other side of the reception hall. Justin was busily making use of the disposable cameras on the table, snapping pictures of people dancing. "Honey, I'll be back," I told him and proceeded to cross the room.

"So, Robyn, is there a wedding in your future? You two look pretty cozy. I could see the love from all the way over here," Rhonda teased.

Rhonda still lived on 84th Place. She exuded the same spunk as she had when coaching me to toss toilet paper into the neighbors' trees decades earlier. Now, despite some gray hair, she appeared unchanged.

"We're pretty happy, Rhonda. Yeah, I can't believe it. Maybe a wedding. We'll see. Right now, we're just doing the living-in-sin thing." I nudged her with my elbow playfully. We giggled. "So how are you and yours these days?"

Rhonda caught me up.

I returned to Justin to listen to Dad's toast.

Dad complimented Angela's large, spirited family in comparison to the six people representing Jonathan's side of the duo.

Irene and Dad danced to their favorite song: "I Just Called to Say I Love You."

Persuaded by the bride, I reluctantly participated in the bouquet toss. I always hated wedding rituals, and this one's among the worst. But I stepped in with the group of desperate competitive females vying for marriage.

Angela appeared to have taken note of my position. She looked at me, turned her back to us, tossed, and the bouquet landed at my feet. Admittedly, with a surge of competitive thrill now, I snatched it up and held it up just long enough for the brides' maids to grab it and insist on a do-over.

Gimme a break! You have to actually catch the bouquet?

Next, the Maid of Honor caught the do-over toss that was meant for me. Bitch.

Back in Oakland, I lounged on our sofa, while Justin was busily making noises with pots and pans in the kitchen.

Day shifted to eve, and I found myself fading into a nap.

"Dinner is served, Madam."

My eyes popped open to a proudly smiling Justin. He handed me a healthy plate of food—fish, rice and broccoli.

I pushed up to seating position and took hold of my dinner. "Oh honey, this looks great. You're so good to me, my babushka. Thank you."

"My pleasure, but what did you just call me?"

Chuckling and stabbing the fish with my fork, I said, "I called you babushka. It just came out of my mouth."

"Do you know what that means, my pet?"

"Sure babe. It means you're my babushka, and I love you, babushka."

"Um, Robby," Justin informed, "Babushka means 'Russian grandmother'."

"Well, then," I chewed on a piece of tilapia, "You're the manliest babushka I've ever loved."

Thereafter when I'd call Justin my "babushka," he'd shout playfully, "I am NOT your Russian grandmother!" There was, for example: "Do you want to go window-shopping today, babushka?" and in response, "I am NOT your Russian grandmother!" or "I like that shirt you're wearing, babushka," and in response, "I am NOT your Russian grandmother!" (Even now, as I write about this years later, I'm laughing.)

Our bedtime routine comforted me too. After a goodnight kiss, Justin held my hand, as we lay side by side on our bellies. We wouldn't let go until I needed to reposition myself, like when his snoring began.

Although I continued to pay the bills and pick up the tab for most everything, and Justin had by this time owed me several thousand dollars, I'd convinced myself that all was well.

We stood at Best Buy staring at a computer mouse. "It's only nine bucks. I can't clear out my desk and get the desktop going without it. Then, I'll clean up the office."

"I'm not going to buy you a computer mouse, Justin. It's a mouse. You can buy it yourself."

"I don't have any money."

"Well then, buy it when you do. We have more important expenses than a computer mouse."

"I'm telling you I can't get organized like you want me to, without it. You know I don't have a job! I need this to work on getting a job so I can get out of debt. You know I'm going to pay you back."

I walked away, then turned around. "No!" Tears flowed. "I won't be your personal ATM machine!"

"Don't say that!" Justin exhaled hot air and stormed out to the car. A few people walked by, and I looked down at the parking lot pavement.

It was a long, tense drive home.

That night, Justin slept on the couch. I sleep in tears.

He called me at work the next day. "I don't see getting past this. I had the same problems with Suzanne. I want to share everything with you, Robyn. What's mine is yours. What's yours is mine. If you don't want it that way, I don't see how we can make it." Easy for you to say, you have nothing.

Fear seeped through me. "Justin, I don't want to lose you. I love you. But we're fighting over a damn computer mouse. If keeping you means buying a computer mouse, it's worth it. But I shouldn't have to. Something's wrong with that. I'm running out of money, and it's scaring me, honey."

"What are you worried about?" Justin retorted. "We're going to be making a six-figure salary between us."

My boss came to my office with a report in her hands. "I gotta go, Justin. Love you."

Justin and I didn't talk things through to resolution, not then nor generally. We just stopped fighting, exhausted. Yet we seemed to always find a way back to our loving connection. And when the phone-call came, all frustrations subsided.

"A job, a job, my babushka has a job!" I cheered. Justin had finally landed a full-time gig with a small, reputable law firm in Walnut Creek. We were thrilled.

"Yes, I got a job baby, but I am NOT your Russian grandmother!"

When he got his first paycheck, he wrote me a check for one-thousand dollars. "That's just a start, Robby. I know I owe you a lot more. I'm going to pay you back every cent," he promised.

"I know you will, babe. I trust you. I trust us, team J 'n R for the win!" I stretched out my arms. We held an embrace loosely, jumping up and down like silly kids.

Justin was a little off one morning. He seemed nervous, not in an agitated way, though. In a hopeful way. Plans were cryptic.

"We'll just go for a nice, long drive and spend the afternoon together," he said.

"Okay." I sifted through my t-shirts to find one that was clean and not stained by chocolate. "Where are we going?"

"I dunno." He paced back and forth through the hall. "I'll surprise you."

"Okay, hon." Maybe he's going to propose. Nah, I shut out the idea. That would be too good. If he does surprise me with a proposal, though, I'll pretend I'm surprised.

The trip bore a sentimental sweetness. Etta James' sultry voice provided background music. Justin easily navigated twists and turns—the Pacific Coast to the left and modest pine-dressed hills to the right. He didn't talk a lot, seemingly simultaneously nervous and assured.

An hour into the drive, Justin looked towards me. "It's been almost a year and a half since our first date."

"I know, babe. Can you believe it?"

He dropped his right hand from the wheel, inched it over to mine, and held on until the car met with a sharp bend on Highway 1.

I wasn't surprised to end at Bodega Bay, where we had our first kiss.

He opened the car door for me. "Let's go to our spot."

Our arms wrapped around each other, the wind against us, we climbed a series of solid rocks that would bring us to our patch of earth. This time, the journey was shorter and easier, more comfortable.

A mix of fading blues and pinks painted the sky. A group of seagulls landed on nearby sands.

We got to level land, and Justin climbed down a rock to sit a bit below me. He paused and simply stared at me, emotion-filled.

216

I stilled myself on a rock facing Justin and eased my hand along his face. "Honey, we're going to be just fine."

He sat contemplatively. "I believe it. I must believe it, because —" Justin's hand fidgeted and dipped into his jacket pocket. He pulled out a little black box and handed it to me.

I held the small ivory white jewelry box and slowly pulled it open.

Streams of rainbow colors sparkled from the opal —my favorite stone. "Oh my God." Tears trickled down my hands. I nervously slipped it onto my ring finger.

I sighed deeply, as I held my hand up to relish the beauty of the ring, of the moment.

I looked at Justin.

Tearful himself, he looked about to burst with pride but said nothing.

I waited for a question. That is, I waited for a marriage proposal. The moment every girl waits for and dreams about. It was here.

Justin still said nothing.

I could almost hear the Jeopardy theme song music crescendo from the waters below.

Our eyes remained moved by tears.

Justin remained silent...still nothing.

I couldn't contain myself any longer and burst out with a: "Yes, honey, I'll marry you!"

He lunged towards me, wrapped me in his arms, and kissed me. "Thank you. I love you so much, my Robby."

"I love you so much too, baby. I can't believe it! Thank you. It's so beautiful."

I loosened one of my arms and planted it on his chest. "Just one thing, my sweet love. I gave you an answer, but you never asked a question. I want a do-over, Alex, something like 'Will you marry me, Robyn, for the win?'"

Having realized he managed the proposal, but forgot to propose, Justin finally asked, "Robyn, will you marry me for the win?"

"Yes, Justin, I will marry you for the win. Team Justin and Robyn for the win! Woohoo!"

We marked our spot with profound excitement—smiling, laughing and kissing until the seagulls began to settle in for the night.

The moment Justin closed the passenger's side door, I scrounged for something to write on. This would do. I tore off a page near the back of my Hello Kitty appointment book.

"What are you doing with Miss Kitty?" Justin asked, playfully.

A smile remained pasted on my face. "I'm writing down the names of all my close girlfriends we're inviting to our wedding. Our wedding, baby! We're getting married. I can't wait to tell everyone."

He chuckled and grinned broadly all the way home.

As each name flew out of my head, I scribbled it down, until I couldn't think of any more.

Shira
Susan
Kathryn
Nicole
Leah
Barbara

Elizabeth
Felicia
Joanne
Judy
Genice
Becca
Lara

"One, two, three…" I counted. "…eleven, twelve, thirteen."

Thirteen.

Chapter Thirteen: My Day

Average cost of a bridal gown plus accessories:	$1,334.
Average cost of a groom's tuxedo:	$232.
Average cost of a wedding:	$28,730.

Numbers above refer to the average cost in the United States in 2007 (the year we married), according to www.TMSSpecialtyproducts.com and wwwtheweddingreport.com.

My brain-cells bustled with visuals of the perfect wedding dress: a vintage beauty, beaded, subtle but glamorous, off-white, devoid of a train or big poufy skirt, and no plunging neckline. I wouldn't spend too much on it, certainly not in the four-digits like the average wedding dress. A used one would do. I'd already done some research. In fact, Justin had caught me months prior to our engagement, perusing bridal gowns on EBay.

"Oh, crap!" I said, covering the computer screen with my arms when he walked into the room.

He teased, "I saw that, Robby. I saw what you were looking at."

"No, Justin. Crap!" I flushed with embarrassment. "No. It just popped up on my screen. I swear. I don't know how that happened!" I closed the page. Justin's grin suggested that he wasn't shaken by my Internet dreamscape.

Like many or most females, I'd been dreaming about the day as far back as I could recall. Now that I had my prince and the ring, it was time to find a dress. After all, the wedding day isn't so much focused on the couple's loving union as it is on the bride's beauty. And her beauty is defined by her gown. For that one magical day, I would be Cinderella.

The Saturday after our engagement, we drove to Alameda's Park Street, where Justin and I had trekked a well-worn path between the various antique shops; Books, Inc.; Java Rama; and Tucker's Ice Cream Parlor.

We landed at an open parking space in front of Pauline's Antiques. Justin and I rarely visited and never made a purchase there, but a mannequin drew me to the window. The lifeless model bore a sequined jacket that reminded me of Mom. Dawn and I used to play dress up with Mom's sequined jacket. We both wanted to wear it and be the village princess. Now it seemed as if Mom directed me into the store. "I kind of want to go in here, Justin. Is that okay?"

"Sure." Justin followed behind, as I passed dusty old clothes; stretches of glass-encased gaudy jewelry; racks of button-down collar shirts, blue jeans, and every-day, informal garments.

"I think wedding dresses might be in the back," I told Justin. "I'll just take a quick look, okay?"

"You're the boss." With his hand on my shoulder, Justin trailed behind.

Standing by a dress rack, I scoffed at a loud pink gown with bright gold sequins. Hideous Barbie bride's maid attire! I pulled and then pushed it along the rack to reveal the next one, and there she was: the most magnificent Victorian style wedding dress I'd ever seen, every square inch of her, an exquisite masterpiece.

I stood wide-eyed, as if relishing the vision of a double rainbow topping a lush green pasture in the wake of the season's worst thunderstorm. The dress shimmered modestly with a subtle golden aura. Her textured cream-colored lines flowed as if to form pearl rose gardens atop streams of softly blended jewels that danced on a bed of busily intricate lace and satin. I checked the tag: Size Small, $200. "I think I like this, Justin."

He peered at the dress, as I pulled it down from the rack and held it against me.

Justin nodded, impressed. "It might just be yours. Try it on, Robby."

I looked down and laughed. "Look how long it is. Well, I guess I could get it tailored if I have to. I'll go try it on quickly. Ok, hon?"

Justin led me to a small room, like a broom closet, that served as a dressing room. The door was cracked open. I poked my head in. The claustrophobic quarters screamed for a mirror.

"Stay close, okay hon? I'll have to come out to see that mirror," I told Justin, noting a mirror several yards behind him.

"I'll be right here, Robby."

I closed the door behind me and continued, "Well, it probably won't fit. But if it does, I'll need your honest opinion."

I pulled down the back zipper and stepped into the gown. I inched it up my frame. Squeeze in gut! Hold breath! Don't exhale! "You're not supposed to see me in my gown before the wedding, babe. It's bad luck, but I don't care. I need your opinion."

Once the dress was on, I was fairly comfortable. The sleeves weren't too long. I guess I have a Victorian body. "I don't know, honey, besides the length, it might work. You still there?"

"Yep, right here, Robby."

As I opened the door, a young woman walked by. She paused and glanced at me. "It's beautiful."

"Oh, thank you."

Justin froze. "Wow."

"Really?"

"It's your dress, baby."

I chuckled. "We don't even have a wedding date yet, but I found the perfect wedding dress without even trying!"

June 12, 2007: Dear Diary, I've ignored you for so long. I'm sorry, Di. I guess you've been my crutch in bad times and, well, things have been great. Justin and I are getting married next month, Di! I can't believe it's really happening to me. It's my turn! But damnit. I can't be fully happy. A sadness keeps creeping in and whispering, sometimes shouting, at me. God I miss Mom so much. It really hurts. I wish she was here now—to see my wedding dress and me in it, to walk me down the aisle, to cry happy tears for me. She and Justin never got to know each other. That's what breaks my heart the most right now.

Through it all, though, I couldn't help but feel Mom's presence in a way I'd never felt it before. While I don't believe in Heaven or an Afterlife per se, energy never dies. And I could feel Mom's calm, graceful energy through every step of the process. It's as if I embodied her. Mom was with me when I picked out the dress, and when I planned all the details of my big day. She accompanied me every step of the way. She kept smiling approvingly, as if to say, "See, I told you everything was going to be all right."

Mom wouldn't have been at all needy, the way some others got when it was my turn to shine.

I'd dropped by a little salon in the Alameda Town Center. There, Melissa scheduled me for a manicure and make-over on July 1, 2007, our wedding day.

"You're so calm. I've never seen a bride so calm on her wedding day," she exclaimed.

"I've never been so calm on my wedding day," I joked.

Truth is, I'm generally composed, except when I'm frantic. When it comes to big projects, I snap into hyper-organization mode, and I'm able to relax at the eleventh hour. I'd already made sure to address every detail. I wasn't going to make the day all about me, either. It would be memorable for everyone. I hadn't forgotten the DJ's birthday. I bought him a "Kiss me! It's my Birthday!" pin, which I'd give him when he arrived to set up. When we hired him three months earlier, he said he wouldn't forget the date; it's his birthday.

I'd neatly boxed all the vases with satin flowers, the program handouts that I wrote and printed up, mini-cymbal clanking wind-up monkeys, bubbles, and disposable cameras. Wedding gift-bags were labeled such that ladies got chocolates and sample size perfume; men got chocolates and sample size cologne; and the kids got chocolates, play-dough and crayons.

The night before, Justin had finally finished with his wedding project. We'd purchased two cases of Trader Joe's "Cheap Chuck's" (Charles Shaw) wine. He'd soaked the labels off and replaced them with homemade "J 'n R's finest". Listed ingredients included Arsenic, Pepto-Bismol, and Grey Poupon.

Melissa was applying eye make-up when my phone rang. "Dawn, can you get that? It's in my purse, at my feet."

It meant a great deal to me that my sister Dawn was by my side throughout the morning.

"Ok, I'll find it." Dawn scrounged for my phone and flipped it open. "Hello...no, this is Dawn. She's getting a make-over...Oh, um, hold on. I'll ask Robyn."

"Robyn, sorry. It's Nicole. She needs a ride to the Temple."

Oy vey. I'd mailed the invitations weeks earlier with very clear directions. There are taxi cabs and busses, and it's my wedding day. "Maybe Becca and Samuel can take her. Becca's number is in my phone contacts. I can't help right now. Sorry Melissa. I'm trying to stay still."

"It's okay." Melissa was very cheery. "You're doing fine." She dabbed blush along my cheekbones. "Almost done."

Dawn drove me from the nail salon to Temple Israel, where we'd meet up with Justin and the rest of the wedding party.

As we carried boxes of wedding supplies to the synagogue entrance, Dawn asked, "Is my dress cut too low? Will the Rabbi be offended?"

"Don't worry," I retorted, placing the boxes down by the front doors. "The Rabbi's gay. He won't notice your cleavage."

I opened the door and scooted a box over with my foot, to use as a door stop. "We'll leave them here for now. The reception hall is there"—I pointed to the right, "and," pointing straight ahead I said, "the ceremony's gonna be in the sanctuary. For now, we'll store things and prep in the Rabbi's office over here." I walked her to the door a few yards to our left.

"Easy enough," Dawn commented. "It's nice that you're having everything in one place."

"Yeah, easier this way. Can you run with me to the car now for my dress and stuff?"

"Sure."

I centered the ketubah[14] on the Rabbi's large desk; next to it, Justin's favorite pen, a shiny black Waterman fountain pen.

"Hi, Robyn." Nanette popped in, bubbly. Betty sauntered behind her, stern faced.

"Hi, ladies. Nanette and Betty, this is my sister, Dawn."

Dawn shook hands with each of them. Justin had met this duo in law school. They were no-nonsense, fierce yet sweet friends, like a tame version of Thelma and Louise. Nanette had loud red hair and about one and a half feet on Betty; who, at my height, was chubbier and more intense than me. "Where's the groom?" Nanette inquired.

"He'll be here soon. He told me this morning he'd drop off the wine bottles and then take his car through a car-wash. For some odd reason. I can't talk him out of anything he has his mind set on. Speaking of the devil."

Justin arrived, composed, dressed in his dark brown tuxedo, white shirt and gold bowtie. He took my hands. "Hi, my bride. Your dress is stunning." I leaned in for a kiss. I look beautiful too, right? I already know the dress is a winner. What about me? Your bride? He didn't say it. "Thank you, my groom."

"Hi ladies," Justin greeted the crew.

Dawn and Justin shared a cordial hug.

"Now that you're here," Nanette told him, "we need to have a chat." She nodded at Betty. "Right?"

"Yeah, let's take a little walk," Betty added.

Justin would later tell me about this Dragnet-style intervention. With him sandwiched between the two, they escorted him on a walk along Mecartney Avenue to Island Drive and back.

Betty echoed Nanette's words and mimicked her commanding tone. Lacking time to respond between sound-bites, Justin simply nodded repeatedly.

"Don't screw this one up!" Nanette said, snapping her head to glare at Justin for a split-second, then snapping back to attend to the sidewalk in front of her.

"Don't screw this one up!" repeated Betty in the same manner.

Nanette continued. "She's the best thing that ever happened to you."

"She's the best thing that ever happened to you," echoed Betty.

Nanette then expelled the golden rule. "The wife is always right, Justin."

"Yes, the wife is always right, Justin," Betty stressed.

"Buy her chocolate when you screw up."

"Chocolate. Buy her chocolate, Justin!" Betty raised her voice to a shout. "Chocolate makes everything better!"

Nanette started over, for emphasis. "Don't screw this up."

"Do not," Betty yelled, her face reddening, "screw this up!"

Justin came back frazzled, as Dawn helped attach my veil to my hair.

"I told them not to mess with the car. I'm going to run it over to the car-wash."

"What? Now? Justin, we're about to get married. Don't go to wash the car. That's crazy."

I still don't know why this was a necessity for Justin—something about his ego was tied with marriage and his car. Independence? Quick getaway? One last chance to cruise chicks as a bachelor?

Nanette flung open her make-up case. She pulled out a small cosmetic brush, tapped it on pink blush, and came at me.

"I just got a makeover. Please don't, Nanette. I don't want to ruin it."

Despite my pleas, Nanette painted my cheeks. "It's just a little touch-up for the pictures." I didn't want you to do that. I asked nicely. I'm the bride, and it's my face. You did it anyway.

Next, she switched the brush for a humongous one, twisted open a container of cake powder, and honed in on Justin.

228

"What are you doing? Men don't wear make-up!" Justin blurted.

"I'm just hiding the blemishes with a little face powder. Close your eyes and hold still."

Nanette briskly swiped Justin's face with powder, creating a dust-bowl of particles shooting out from his eyes and nasal region. "Jesus, Nanette. I think you sufficiently powdered my pupils!"

David, our photographer, arrived. "Robyn, your dress is beautiful!"

"Thanks, David." I look beautiful too, right? I mean, it's not just my dress. I look beautiful *in* my dress, right? He adjusted the camera lens.

"Oh, so I don't forget—" I pulled an envelope out of my purse and handed it to him. "This is for you." It contained the rest of the money we owed David, plus a hearty tip and "thank you" note. David stuffed it in his pocket. "Thank you, Robyn."

"You're welcome."

"Don't mind me" —he lifted his camera to eye-level— "I'll just be doing my job."

Justin stepped around David and quietly told me, "Honey, I'll be right back. It won't take long."

"No, don't, Justin. Please stay here. It's not the time for a car wash."

"Help! Somebody please help!" The caterer's cries stemmed from the social hall. I gasped.

Colleen, one of our wedding singers, appeared at the door-frame. "Hi, everyone."

"Hi, Colleen," I said. "What's going on? Is Phoebe alright?"

"Yes but she needs help. If any of you are free, she needs help unloading her truck."

I remained composed. "Why does she—"

Phoebe rushed into the office, one palm glued to her back and a distressed look on her face. "My assistant bailed on me and my back is killing me. It's a chronic pain that's been flaring up all week. I need help!

Dad and Irene arrived and squeezed past Phoebe to greet me.

"Hi honey," Dad said, with a kiss on the cheek.

"Robyn, you're not supposed to met anyone pee in your bedding dress." Irene's words made no sense. She tried again, this time enunciating more clearly, "You're not supposed to let anyone see you in your wedding dress!" I don't give a shit about stupid rituals. "It's okay, Irene. I'm not following the rules. It'll be fine." I flashed a fake smile her way.

"Never mind her," Dad said softly. "She's a little upset that you didn't ask her to walk you down the aisle." Poor whiney bitch. She's not Mom. Nobody could replace Mom, and how dare she even suggest it. Mommy, I wish you were here.

"So do I look okay?" Dad, in all these years of seeing you flaunt dramatic Hawaiian print shirts and polyester pants like you were King Cool, you now ask me for wardrobe feedback? And when you show up for my wedding in all black, except for a blindingly bright white tie? "You look fine Dad." The blind mobster look is in this year.

"The meal will be kosher, right?" Irene interrogated.

"A little bit, yeah." I smiled.

They disappeared, presumably to inspect the venue. Nanette applied mascara, and Betty adjusted her belt.

Justin had disappeared. Damnit.

I walked to the corner of the room and picked up my purse, dug up my phone and called Justin. It rang. It rang again. Then again. Then again. It kept ringing. Justin didn't pick up. It didn't even go to his voice mail.

Shit. What happened to him? Everything's going to be fine. Where is he? This is my day. My perfect day. Did he die? It'll be all right. Will he get back on time? My wedding day. Will there be a wedding? No groom. My day.

"Well hello, bride" Rabbi Wyse entered his office. "That's a beautiful dress." You mean that I look beautiful, right? I mean, because I know the dress is beautiful. We all do. But what about me? Am I not beautiful in it? "Thank you."

"Are you about ready to sign the ketubah? Where's the groom?"

"He went to run a quick errand. I can't get ahold of him."

"Okay. Well, I'm sure he'll be here shortly. I'll make sure we're good to go in the sanctuary."

"Thanks, Rabbi."

I walked outside with my purse. Damn. I didn't see Justin anywhere. But I did see Jonathan and Angela pushing a stroller in which slept my baby nephew, Josiah. Angela glimmered with excitement.

We said our "hellos" and gave hugs.

"Josiah just fell asleep," Angela said, giggling. I bent down to behold my first precious glimpse of auntie-dom. He lay soundly, innocently. Josiah's lips were red and full; his cheeks, pinkish, and he was wearing the mini-kippah[15]—a tiny white silk one—I'd sent them a week ago, for this occasion. Soft brown curls peaked out from under it.

"He's so beautiful. Hi my sweet Josiah. It's your Auntie Robyn." I kissed him gently on the forehead.

"Sorry to rush, but I've got some loose ends. Go ahead and put your things down. We'll be signing the ketubah soon." If the groom ever comes back.

"Okay, no worries." Jonathan grabbed. "We'll be inside."

"See you in there." Angela chimed.

I grabbed my phone and pressed the first name on my speed dial. It rang. It rang and rang. It rang and rang and rang. It didn't go to voice mail. He didn't pick up. He can't possibly be opting out. Could he? No. Not possible. Everything's going to be all right. Stay calm. It's your day. My day. Our day. Everyone else's day? Breathe. I looked at my watch. Four thirty. Time to sign the ketubah.

I twisted around to head back in, and Shira took abrupt strides towards me.

"Is everything okay, Robyn?"

"Well, no. I don't have a groom."

"Wait." She peeked over my head and towards the parking lot. "Is that Justin?"

I looked over my shoulder, and a sigh of relief streamed from my mouth.

Justin immediately caught up to us. "Sorry, honey."

"What happened? I kept trying to call you, Justin. You scared me."

"Nothing. Everything's fine. I washed the car but lost my phone. I must've left it on the hood. I drove off without it. It probably got flattened somewhere on the 880."

"Well, everyone's waiting for the ketubah signing," Shira hurried us. "Let's get over there."

In the Rabbi's office, with a beautifully hand-scripted ketubah on display atop the large flat table, it was Justin's turn. My family, and Nanette and Betty, hovered around the table. I had just signed my name in both English and Hebrew, and handed Justin his pen.

"Hm mm?" he said, raising an eyebrow. Justin bent over, with his face nearly touching the document, as if to study its every letter.

"Justin," Nanette interjected, "what are you doing?"

"Looking for loopholes." He grazed it up and down. "Just looking for loopholes."

"Oh, stop, Justin." I playfully swatted his arm. "Sign it already."

"Alright. Here we go." He signed in big letters. "There's my John Hancock."

Shira and Nanette took turns signing as witnesses.

"Mazel Tov," the Rabbi proclaimed, "I'll put this on display by the entrance."

The song, "Lechi lach,"[16] started.

233

The singers' notes flowed harmoniously to one of my favorite Debbie Friedman tunes.

While lined up at the doors for the processional, Irene instructed the group. "Count one, one-thousand, two one-thousand and so on and so on until we are all there."

Dad, standing next to me, conveyed an apologetic expression. He'd so rarely shown any concern for me, but I felt connected with him now, today, my wedding day. This moment of walking down the aisle together was monumental, like a gift of love and forgiveness that we exchanged without words. My eyes welled with tears, as did his.

Irene walked so slowly down the aisle that Dawn and Jonathan looked at me and each other. The three of us shared an Engel sibling eye-roll moment. Pick up the pace, woman. The sun's going down.

I touched the top of my veil, to assure that it was secure. Almost time. I breathed in Mom's grace and love.

Dawn strolled down the aisle, as Jonathan and Angela prepared to go next. Josiah lay cozily in Angela's arms. His kippah looked so darn cute.

A profound silence emphasized the moment. Then, "Sunrise, Sunset" began.

Justin took a mindful stride forward.

Dad shifted his elbow sideways. I threaded my arm through his, and took a deep breath. We looked at each other and slowly stepped forward.

We reached the start of the "aisle"—a lengthy stretch of butcher paper that led to the bimah.[17]

Just don't fall. Don't fall. You'll be fine. Enjoy the moment. This is it. I'm getting married. I'm actually doing it—marrying the love of my life! Don't fall. They're all here for me. Don't trip. Smile. Don't fall.

Nobody's standing. What the fuck? Keep smiling. Be gracious. Stand-up, people! I'm here. Maybe they can't see me yet. We strolled further down the aisle. Stand up. My smile widened.

This is it. I did everything to make this day easy for you. You can't stand up for a few seconds?

They didn't budge. I was more than halfway down the aisle.

Dad and I dropped arms. He stood still, as I approached Justin.

Don't fall. You're doing fine. Don't trip. They didn't stand. What the hell? Don't fall. See Justin. Smile. Don't fall. It's my day. My wonderful day.

Hand in hand, Justin and I ascended two steps and stood under the chuppah.[18] Sunlight emanated through the stained glass window behind us. I sensed the eyes of everyone I loved, all focused on me.

Circling Justin, I felt like royalty. We'd practiced this ritual—symbolic of our creation of a sacred space—several times. Keep it slow. Don't trip. Enjoy the moment. Don't trip. You're doing fine. Don't fall. His turn. Keep smiling. It's my day.

Justin walked around me once.

And then a second time.

And a third.

We held hands and slowly spun around in a seventh circle together.

Rabbi Wyse welcomed the guests and introduced the Jewish wedding ceremony, which is very brief. He said some words about how the kids loved me when I taught Sunday school there. He talked about us as a couple, how lovey-dovey we were during services. "I wish they'd paid more attention to my sermons than to each other." He said my "Cheshire cat smile" hasn't left my face since I met Justin.

To follow were a few quick prayers in Hebrew and then English.

Dawn stepped forward and handed me the page on which I wrote my vows. I glanced down at it. Overwhelming emotions choked my vocal chords.

I couldn't speak.

Several seconds passed.

You can do this. You can do this. I pushed the words out. A quivering sincerity emerged, one that captured my deep love for the groom.

> Justin,
> Our relationship has been so different, in so many wonderful ways, from anything I could have imagined experiencing in this lifetime. There's a perennial and dreamlike quality to your love. You love me with such a relentlessly generous and tender heart, without pride or pretense, and without being stifled by fear. You love me with a full commitment to conquer any and all challenges that we face, whatever the cost.

Before you came into my life, I was a hopeless cynic—on a good day. Your love has somehow transformed me into a woman of faith. I promise to do my best to carry us through life with this faith that you have unknowingly given me. I promise to do my best to keep faith in us, that together we can successfully navigate whatever lies ahead. I promise to do my best to keep faith in your pure intensions, rather than clinging to any shortsighted notions of how I think things *should* be. I promise to do my best to remind you of the faith I have in you as the sincere, competent, sweet, generous, witty, handsome and all-around wonderful man that you are. I promise to do my best to keep sight of our loving union, knowing that we are, and always will be, each other's beshert.

In sum, I promise to do my best to express and embody true, loving faith for the rest of our lives.

"Do you, Robyn, take Justin to be your husband, promising to cherish and protect him, whether in good fortunate or in adversity, and to seek together with him a life hallowed by the faith of Israel?"

As I said, "I do," Justin's eyes watered and his face glowed of pure joy.

He removed his vows from his jacket pocket and began.

Robyn,

This ring is to me not a symbol of obligation, but of desire and my heart's fulfillment. It is a reminder to me that if I do not always agree, I promise always to listen, that if we do not always see eye-to-eye, we can know that we are always looking in the same direction.

It is a physical reminder that we have been brought together not by pre-destination, but by the fulfillment of our own singular, successful searches for happiness and for the true mate for our souls—our beshert.

It will always remind me that today, I become not only a husband, but a son-in-law to Gerald, a brother-in-law to

Jonathan, Dawn and Angela, and an uncle to our dear little nephew, Josiah.

I joyfully glanced at Angela, holding Josiah, now squirrely, in the first row.

> I will do my best to honor all of these roles, as your family has so generously, without   reservation, welcomed me into their hearts and lives, as have you.

Justin turned towards the guests and continued.

> Everyone here knows that I am the lucky one; they're too polite to say it, but they know. The Rabbi knows. The congregation knows. My dentist knows. Heck, the judges I usually appear before all know. But it is only important that I know it.
> You are my beacon, my harbor, the refuge for my soul in troubled times, and the light of my life in good ones, as I will be all of these things for you. You are the love of my life.

A few more prayers and rituals concluded, and it was time for the Jewish wedding's iconic gesture: the breaking of the glass. The Rabbi wrapped a small glass cup in white cloth, explaining that this ritual has a number of meanings. It reminds us of the destruction of the Holy Temple; of the fragility of humanity; and that even in joyful moments, there is the potential for great sorrow. (Justin had told me that the ritual would afford him one last opportunity to put his foot down.)

Rabbi Wyse placed the packaged glass inches from Justin's right foot. Justin stomped. No noise; he missed. The audience chortled. He stomped again, with forcefulness this time, creating a high piercing noise that defined successful shattering.

Our mouths powered forward and we were locked in a kiss.

"Mazel Tov!" They shouted. Justin leaned further in, passionately, lowering me with his arms, as our lips continued to coast along each other's. I had a quick flash of that famous sailor-nurse post-wartime kiss.

"Well, you may kiss the bride now," the Rabbi joshed. There was a burst of laughter, Justin eased me up, and we grabbed hands. Guests applauded. Justin and I skipped down the aisle, frenzied with exuberance, like two kids who'd just been let loose in Willy Wonka's Chocolate Factory.

Siman Tov —they sang, clapping—*V'mazal tov[19]*
V'siman tov u'mazal tov...

Justin and I attacked the buffet fixings: a rainbow-colored assortment of juice-drenched fruits; cheesy, buttery string-beans blended with crisp slivers of mushrooms and almonds; freshly baked rolls of bread; and—the main entrée—moist, lightly peppered slices of turkey, which I'd drown in gravy. For vegetarians: a rich spinach lasagna awaited.

But where are the latkes[20]? I want my latkes. Keep smiling. I requested the latkes when we first met with Phoebe. She said that'd be fine, even wrote it down. It was part of the agreement. My day. Best day of my life. I want my latkes. I was looking forward to latkes, lots and lots of latkes. But there aren't any latkes. Not a single damn latke. My day. Keep smiling. David's snapping pictures. Keep smiling. No latkes. Everyone's looking at me. Smile. I want latkes. It's my day. Where are my latkes?

"And now," the DJ announced, "the wedding dance."

Justin, who had his arm around me, dashed towards the end of the head table, extending an outstretched arm—as if to longingly desire a dance from afar. What the hell? That's not how we practiced! And practiced, and practiced. "And now, the Pee Wee Herman" he joked.

Our song, Etta James' "At Last," filled the hall.

I strolled towards him, beaming. Bet he's gonna blame me when he slips up.

We started, behind the music. Not how we practiced. Smile. Step. Step. Keep smiling.

We made it to the middle of the floor. We had the stance right, but I felt rigid, off-kilter. Step. Step. Touch. Step. Step. One. Two.

"Quit back-leading," he whispered in my ear. Quit changing things up and throwing me off. I'll never marry you again.

I held a smile, and held it, and held it through an elegant twirl.

"Good job," I whispered in his ear. I felt my muscles loosen, as I relaxed into the dance. Step. Step. Raise arm. Fingers up. Step. Step. Don't fall. Start the turn. Smile.

When I turned, I caught a priceless glimpse of Leah's five year old daughter, Sasha. Mesmerized, she stood alone, about equidistant from us and the table at which she and Leah had been sitting. She'd leaned her head to one side, propped by her hands—with fingers interlocked. Little Sasha gazed at us throughout the dance. Her stance proclaimed, "How romantic."

Step. Step. Smile. Don't fall. My day. Doing fine. Step.

Step. Step. We neared the big finale. Don't blow it, Justin. Keep smiling. Almost there. We practiced the dip so many times.

Step. Step. Turn.

Lean back. Let go. Too stiff. Drop. Relax. Not far enough. Relax more. Extend arm. Smile. Smile. No, really, relax. They're cheering. Stand up. Smile. Wish I'd been more relaxed. I didn't fall far enough. It's my day.

At last.

We kissed and hugged. They're clapping. They're impressed. Smile. Don't fall.

We walked back to the head table, arm in arm.

"Robyn, how'd you get him to dance like that?" Nanette asked. "Very elegant."

"Lots of lessons, Nanette. Lots."

"And lots of back-leading," Justin said. "My Robby likes to be in charge."

I smiled. "Okay, that too." No shit. Someone has to do it right. And I'm not the one who started arguments during dance lessons because, what? It was hard to find parking. Smile. It's our wedding day. Or because I back-led after you stepped on my foot? Keep smiling. My day. He's a keeper. We're in love. That's why we did all this. I am happy. I really am and don't need to convince myself. I'm so well loved. It's my day.

Nanette looked at Justin. "That's why she's the best thing that ever happened to you, Justin."

"Aw, thanks Nanette."

She gave me a nod.

Something was missing, in terms of the music and dancing. Marco, our DJ, hadn't said anything before playing this song. I'd listed dedications for all of our song requests, gave him the list over one month ago, and he said "no problem." Marco was supposed to announce that this song, "She Works Hard for the Money," was for all the teachers and social workers.

"Hey, baby," I said quietly to Justin, "they're not announcing our song dedications."

Just then I saw Dawn a few seats away, head down as if to analyze the white table linen.

I approached. "Are you okay?"

"Oh yeah, just missing Mom." Well damn, me too. But it's my wedding day. Get over it for my sake, would ya? Maid of Honor. "Okay, I understand," I said.

Justin extended his arm towards Dawn. "May I have this dance?"

"Sure." She stood up, and they walked out to the dance floor.

Justin had been very sensitive and gracious when others were in need of a boost. I remembered, months earlier, when we learned that a neighbor's husband had died. We visited with her, shared fond memories of John, let her cry in our presence.

She served us tea and explained that John was the breadwinner; she was at a total loss as to how she'd go on without him.

When I placed my tea cup by the kitchen sink, as we were about to leave, I saw a $100 bill that Justin had slipped onto the kitchen counter. (He'd cashed a paycheck that morning.) I couldn't help but fall deeper in love.

I grabbed for my plate, to enjoy a few more nibbles—God, I wanted latkes—when I saw Phoebe excuse herself with Dawn to take Justin aside. She had a piece of paper in her hands and was explaining something. The bill, maybe? He nodded a few times, looked unhappy, and went to join Dawn back on the dance floor.

Shira popped up. "Come on, Robyn, let's go boogie."

"Let's do it!"

We hopped close to Justin and Dawn. I placed my hand on his arm. "Honey, what happened with Phoebe?"

"I'll tell you later. Don't worry about it."

"Justin, what? What happened?"

"Later, sweetie."

Resigned, I refocused on boogieing with Shira.

I launched into some John Travolta gestures: finger-pointing-out-then-down, hips thrusting from side-to-side.

Judy ran across the floor chasing her two year old boy. "He can't sit still!" Judy told me, laughing.

"I love it!" I responded.

I hadn't seen Judy in years. She's a treasured friend. Her little family flew from Portland for my wedding. I sat her with Kathryn and Susan. We were all close in high school and college, though I'd rarely had contact with Judy since then. In fact, the four of us girlfriends hadn't been together since graduation. It was great to see them giggling, gossiping, catching up.

I was suddenly struck, literally struck, by yellow fabric. What the hell? I looked around to see Irene's wide tuchas[21] jiggling as she pranced around the room sashaying her scarf. Good Lord. Looks like someone had a bit too much of J&R's finest.

Where was Dad? Oh, holding his grandbaby. Sweet.

Jonathan filmed Dad and Josiah. Then Angela and Josiah. Irene snuggling Josiah. Josiah asleep in Dawn's arms. Josiah with open eyes. Josiah. Josiah. Our precious Josiah. My day.

Angela chatted with Nanette. Betty sat with arms crossed, studying a wine bottle.

David kept his camera on the dance floor. By now, Irene was in the middle of the floor spinning around and forming figure eights with her yellow scarf. "Everyone around the earth, come on!" she shouted.

The bride-father dance, "I Hope You Dance," went on for a few eternities. Keep smiling. This is a once in a life-time moment with Dad. He's proud. Don't fall. All is forgiven. Be graceful. Step. Step. Smile. Pride. Happiness. My Day. Song's too long.

Step. It's dark out now. Step. Sway.

Keep smiling. Is it over yet? Keep smiling.

We *are* dancing. No hope necessary. We've been dancing for like a year and a half.

I thought of the John Mayer song, "Say What You Need to Say," and how he keeps singing that song title but never gets to the point. The irony drives me bonkers.

The song finally ended. "Thank you, dad."

"My pleasure."

We hugged.

Irene jetted towards Dad, giddily. "Now it's my turn with you, sailor," she winked.

Justin and I made visits to all the guest tables, posed for a few more pictures, and I noticed Sasha was still staring at me, wide-eyed.

"Honey, Sasha's looking at me so sweetly. I think she wants my dress."

"No, baby. She wants to *be* you."

He was right. I had it all: the gorgeous dress, the love of my life, wonderful friends—many of whom traveled across state-lines to be here—a family that cared deeply about me (albeit not demonstratively), and a precious new nephew. I never thought I'd have this day, this romantic, fairytale moment that every girl is conditioned to pine for. My day.

"What did Phoebe say to you earlier, babe? Please tell me."

Exasperated, he sighed. "I guess you'll find out sooner or later."

"Hey you two, don't mind me," David said, snapping shots of us. I held a smile.

"Start spreading some news!" Irene belted out a mish-mash medley of Broadway musicals, despite the fact that Marco had attempted to slow things down with John Coltrane.

"Don't worry." Justin quieted his voice. "She gave me the bill," he said, grinning for the camera.

"The invoice we've been waiting for since February? It's July now. We're sticking with the initial quote." And where were the potato latkes she promised?

"Ssh, sshh. Yeah. She said not to tell you about the bill until after the honeymoon."

Sasha, Leah's five year old daughter, and Rafael, Adam's six year old boy, ran by, giggling. It looked as though they were flirting. How cute.

David kept snapping photos. Keep smiling. Nothing can take away from your day. My day. Everyone else's day. "What about the bill, Justin? Tell me." Smile. I insisted.

He sighed heavily again. "It's higher than the initial quote."

You're kidding. I didn't even get latkes. I want latkes! Smile for the camera. "How much higher?"

"Don't worry about it. We'll take care of it later. It's our day, babe."

"How much higher, Justin? Five-hundred?" Smile.

"No."

Jonathan came by with the video camera. "So how is the newly married couple?"

"Great," we said in unison, smiling.

"What do you think of your new nephew?" Jonathan prodded.

"He's a precious angel. I think you did good," I said.

"That kippah fits just right. He's adorable," Justin added.

"Yeah, I got plenty of footage of my boy," he laughed. "You can't really tell this is a wedding reception. Josiah's the star." Great. Smile. My day. Good work, Josiah.

Keep smiling. "How much higher, Justin? A thousand dollars?"

"No baby."

"Ladies and gentlemen"— Marco cleared his throat—"It's time to toast to the bride and groom."

"Let me get this straight," —I held a smile—"she doesn't give us the final bill until the middle of our wedding reception and it's more than $1,000 the original quote?"

He smiled and warned, "Everyone's looking at us. Yes, more than that."

Still grinning, I ask, "Over 2,000?"

Yes. We lifted our glasses, half-full of champagne. Shira grabbed mine from my hands. What was that about? She wanted to give a toast. Didn't she have a champagne glass? I scanned all of the champagne glasses on the tables, each one nice and shiny and void of a drop of champagne. It seemed only the head table got champagne. But now Shira had mine.

"May your years ahead be full of playful laughter," she continued, with my glass of champagne held high. Some guests sat dumbfounded. Some held up their glasses with cheer, as if they didn't notice their glasses were empty.

Irene grabbed a bottle of J 'n R's finest from the head table and topped off her glass.

Dawn, now verging on despondent tearfulness, held an empty glass in one hand and used the other hand to dab her eyes with the linen napkin.

I nudged Justin. Smile. Keep smiling. "She forgot latkes and champagne and she's trying to milk us for over 2,000 dollars?"

"Yes, my dear," —he held a grin—"about 2,500 more."

Fuckin bitch. Smile. What a cun- cun- cunning thing of her to do. Keep smiling. Good luck wrestling me for another penny, Phoebe. I'll kick your ass. Bring it on, sister! Right here and now! Smile. It's your day, my day. Breathe. Smile. What the hell? Happiness abounds. How can she do this? Be happy. It's my day. Beautiful dress. Dress is beautiful. That it is. Beautiful I look. No try, only do. Smile. Be happy, Yoda say. My day it is. Smile.

Shira handed me the microphone and put my champagne glass by my plate. I didn't lift it, didn't want to draw more attention to the fact that only the bride and groom were served champagne. I stood up.

"I can't say how much this day means to me and," —looking at Justin, I added, "how much you mean to me. And to all my girlfriends, 13 of you came. It means so much that you're all here. Some of you crossed the state, and others crossed stateliness. I love you all, Shira, Kathryn, Becca, Susan, Judy, Leah, Joanne, Barbara, Nicole, Felicia, Lara, Elizabeth, Genice, and I hope I'm not missing anyone. Thanks so much for being here. And to my family, we've been dealt more than our fair share of tragedy. So I'm very grateful that, with Justin, we're moving things in a more positive direction.

And with our new, adorable nephew Josiah"—I looked over at him, boastfully— "we deserve these blessings, and I'm glad to contribute to happier family moments."

I concluded, "I'll end by saying," —turning to Justin—"I can't wait to share married life with you, my love, love of my life." I felt so filled with, and surrounded by, love that none of my smiling was fake or forced. All of the mishaps were, simply, irritants that I wouldn't be touched by. None of it would ruin our day. My day. The best day of my life.

Everyone gathered around the wedding cake. Bubbles floated by; by now all the kids and a few of the teens were blowing them.

Phoebe handed me the knife. Smile. What an idiot. She's handing me a knife. Don't do anything stupid. Not until later. The couples nuzzled together, except Dad and Irene. She was too busy giving the DJ kisses on the cheek, no doubt wishing him a happy birthday.

With mouth wide open, and eyebrows raised to the top of his forehead, Justin pretended to bite down onto his clenched fist. I laughed as I sliced the cake. We agreed we wouldn't smash cake into each other's faces, and we kept our word. Instead, our sharing of cake unfolded with gentle care.

Phoebe stood by and retrieved the cake cutter from me. "Robyn, you can keep this when we're done," she offered. Oh yeah, thanks, bitch. I bet it's worth, what? Twenty-five hundred dollars? "Thank you. That's nice of you." Bitch.

Becca and Samuel approached me and Justin as the last song ended. "We're going to leave," she said. "Mazel Tov. It was a great party, Robyn."

"Yeah," Samuel added, "Thanks for inviting me too. And your dress is beautiful." Me too, right? I look beautiful in it, right?

"Everything was so nice," Becca said. "You did a wonderful job."

"Thanks so much, and it was great meeting you, Samuel."

They departed after brief hugs.

"Oh," Becca said, turning back around—Yes? I'm a beautiful bride, right? Wait for it. Wait for it. Wayyy— "That little kippah on Josiah was the perfect touch. He stole the show."

Smile. Smile. "Thanks!" I guess. Go away now. It's my day.

Guests had been trickling out the doors, and a few tables were barren. Phoebe cleared out and packaged the food, leaving one piece of foil-wrapped cake for us, a big one, at least; and five cases of champagne—the champagne she'd forgotten to set out on the tables. Great. Just what this newly married couple needed all to ourselves, a shitload of champagne.

One by one, and in small clusters, family and friends wished us well, imparting hugs and kisses. Wait. Who's helping us with clean-up? Smile. Don't leave yet, everyone! It's my day. Somebody stay to help, please!

"Robyn, toss me the bouquet. You didn't do that part." Nicole needed to take advantage of a sudden lack of competition for the bouquet toss.

"Oh yeah, not my favorite ritual. I was going to just hang onto it, but we have enough left over flowers to take home. Okay." We positioned ourselves less than a half foot from each other. I looked directly at Nicole. "Here we go." I basically dropped the bouquet into her hands.

"Yay!" She jumped for joy and chuckled. "Thanks, Robyn! This was a really fun party. And your dress is beautiful. But can you do it once more?"

Seriously? "Okay, here." I tossed it again. She caught it.

A giggly Nicole said, "That was fun. Can you do it again?"

I tossed it yet again, from two feet away. She caught it yet again, from two feet away. "Yay! I'm going to get married next!"

"Silly lady. Congratulations." My day. I look beautiful too. Right? "So I should really get to cleaning up the rest of this mess."

"Oh, do you need help, Robyn? I can stay and help, but I'll need a ride home."

"Yeah, we could use the help. Thank you. I'll take you home, or we'll take you. We'll figure it out."

Is it over yet? My feet are killing me. My day. Smile. I'm exhausted. Grin. What a magical day. Blissful sigh. Ouch. I'm tired.

It took a solid hour to clean up. By the time we made our last run to pack the car, it was dark out. There were no lights near Justin's car. I carried his big vase out and placed it by the car door. Nicole headed back inside to collect the disposable cameras from the tables.

Justin shoved the last case of champagne into the backseat. As he pulled his arm back, Justin pushed the car door further opened and it tapped the vase. It didn't fall but we heard a dim, high pitched spark of impact.

"Why'd you do that?" he asked, accusatorily.

"What? You did it, honey."

I knelt down and eyed the vase. "It's just a little crack, babe. You can hardly notice it. Come on, we just had the most phenomenal wedding. We just got married!"

I wouldn't let him taint our day. My day. I'd be happy. I was happy. Despite the lack of latkes, $2,500 padded catering bill, and empty champagne glasses for the wedding toast. Despite having to clean up after our own wedding. Despite missing Mom and having to deal with, instead, a drunken high-society snob insisting on kosher meals, a video starring my precious, sleeping three-month old nephew, a somber Maid of Honor, a Dad dressed to kill – literally; DJs who ignored our instructions. Despite the Guestzilla Factor, I had it all. I'd forever treasure this day, the best day of my life.

"You put it there," he said.

"Yes I did, my love, and it's not my fault that it's dark outside and that you hit it with the car door. Baby we just got married!" I jumped gleefully. "I love you so, so much, Mr. Case! It was the best day of my life."

He let out an audible breath and wrapped his arms around me. "You're right. I love you, my darling wife."

"I love you, my sweet husband." We kissed.

Nicole appeared with the disposable cameras and a handful of miscellaneous party favors. "Can I keep these wind-up monkeys, Robyn?"

"Sure."

After I opened the passenger's side door to my car for Nicole, I watched Justin drive away. Pastel colored messages on the back window of his car read, "Just Married!" and "Down with Bush!"

"I'm exhausted, but it was really fun, Robyn."

"Yeah, I'm still floating, Nicole. Let's get you home."

My day.

Chapter Fourteen: After the Happily Ever After

When considering the fairytale, most of us scoff at the Fairy Godmother's magical powers, and that Cinderella traveled to the ball in a pumpkin-turned-stagecoach. Nonsense; it's only a fairytale. Yet we don't tend to question the story's ending. Cinderella and Prince Charming lived happily ever after. Of this, we have little doubt, even though it's a fairytale.

My head propped against a pillow on the loveseat's arm, as my feet took respite on Justin's lap. His eyes drifted quietly towards mine, while Justin set aside the Oakland Tribune. A bemused tingle pranced through my body. The same vibe had clearly infiltrated my new husband.

"I can't believe we're married," Justin said, massaging my feet.

"I was just thinking the same thing, sweet-love. I can't believe we're married!" I'd finally arrived. Paradise.

It was a restful Sunday, mostly. Justin and I proceeded to amble by the Piedmont Avenue stores, share Chinese food, peruse used books, and admire a variety of miscellany. We happened upon a miniature pair of cowboy boots in a consignment store—reminiscent of the ones that brought us together and perfect for Josiah, maybe in a year or so, should he decide to jump on a horse or join the junior cavalry. Amused as we were by them, I took them to the register. "I love that you're always thinking about our nephew, Justin. You're a good uncle."

"I can't help it. He's so little," he held up his hands, palms facing each other, five or so inches apart.

"Yeah, he's adorable."

"You're adorable, my Robby." Justin leaned in and kissed me.

I dug into my purse for cash.

"We should get going," Justin said as sundown neared. "I hate Sundays, knowing I have to go back to work tomorrow. I hate it."

"Okay, sweetie," I took his hand and brushed against him. "You still have me. And guess what? We got married." I swooped up our arms, our fingers still interlocked, as a sign of victory. "Woohoo!"

Justin drew out a huff. "Yes we did," his voice sharpened, "but I still hate Sundays."

I didn't know what to say, permitting a pregnant silence, as we headed back to the car. I felt hurt. Here we were, newly married. We'd recently hung the ketubah in our bedroom. Marriage to the love of our lives: what we've wanted all along. Justin had a good job now too, so financial stress had decreased dramatically. Wasn't all of this enough for him? Wasn't I enough for him?

At home, I kicked off my shoes and entered the kitchen. Determined to make his Monday less stressful, I'd pull together a lunch for Justin. What first stood out, though, was Justin's regular contribution to the kitchen ambience: an ever growing pile of dirty dishes. We had no dishwasher; I was it. So I got to work—running the water, splashing a bit of soap on an aging yellow dish pad, scrubbing off the main chunks of gunk, rinsing, and storing each item on the dish rack.

"Dar-ling,"— Justin's voice was loaded with a double-bind message: I love you. I hate you when you do that.—"What are you doing?"

"Honey, I'm doing the dishes. I know you're better at it than me, but it needs to get done."

"I'll take care of it later, dear."

No you won't. You never do. "No worries. I got it."

Justin's irritation permeated his silent alliance with the television screen. As obsessed as he was about clean dishes, he seemed more intent on filling the sink with dirty ones. I was incensed at being unable to rinse my hands because infested kitchenware blocked the sink nozzle.

Admittedly, dishwashing isn't my strength. I recalled Noah. His greatest, and perhaps only, talent was his absolute mastery of the art of washing dishes by hand. Yeah, well, give Justin Ivory liquid, a Brillo pad, and an ounce of motivation, I bet he'd out-shine that dude in one scrub.

I wonder what ever happened to Noah, how clean his dishes are these days. Regardless, he's probably getting more sex than I am—if only with dead bodies. Gross. I suppose that'd be even worse than celibacy.

I thought my sex life would've taken flight after marriage. Shit, we had some fun on our honeymoon, but spent more time seeing the beautiful sights of Vancouver Island. Tea-time is good and all, but I didn't expect to get out of the hotel room that much.

I put the last plate in the dish-rack, washed my hands, and remembered what I'd come into the kitchen for. So I made a whopping turkey sandwich on sourdough for Justin, then slipped it into a lunch bag. I added a green apple (his favorite fruit), and a

Ziploc baggie full of pretzels. He wasn't a pretzel fan, but I was trying to help him lose weight, without being obvious about it. Justin had started gaining before our wedding. I'd guess he'd put on close to forty pounds since we met. I was starting to gain too, but not nearly to that extent. I kept exercising at the Oakland Athletic Club, and jogging around the Lake, while Justin honed his fine-motor skills with the remote.

Next, I took a post-it from the office and wrote a note: My love, I'm thinking of you. I love you beyond the stars, my wonderful husband. Forever and always and always and forever yours- xoxoxRobby.

I dropped the note into the lunch bag and put his lunch in the refrigerator.

Popping into the living room, I announced, "Babe, I packed a lunch for you to take to work tomorrow."

"Oh, you didn't have to do that." He remained zoned in on his show—something with cops, guns and fast-paced violence, something I hated.

"I know," I said cheerily. "I wanted to because I love you and we're married and stuff."

Justin's response shielded an exasperated sigh. "Alright, thanks."

"You're welcome, babe."

"Honey, it's 10 o'clock. Ready for bed?"

"No, it's too early." He stayed glued to the screen. "I'll go when this show's over."

"That's okay. I'll wait up with you babe."

"No, Robby. Go ahead. I'll be there as soon as it's over."

"I'd rather wait up, sweetie. I don't want to go to bed without you."

He didn't respond.

I caught myself falling asleep on the couch, sedated by Andy Rooney's voice.

After 11pm, I awoke to late night news and Justin's snoring. I fumbled for the remote and shut off the television. "Honey, time for bed," I tapped his shoulder lightly.

Justin's snoring halted. "Huh?" he grunted.

"It's after 11, babe. Let's go to bed."

"Okay," his head separated slightly from the couch pillow. "I'll be right behind you."

"Okay, hon." I sifted to the bedroom, and wrapped myself under the sheets, aware of little else but the fact that Justin didn't join me at all that night.

I awoke as I'd gone to bed: alone.

Justin came in, already dressed in his usual business attire —a suit and tie—and carrying the brief-case I'd given him last Hanukah. He generally left the house for work 20 minutes before me.

"Bye," he said. Justin imparted a curt kiss, as I merged out of bed.

"Bye, Justin. Have a good day. And don't forget the lunch—"

The door slammed shut.

I opened the fridge. The lunch bag I'd packed for Justin dominated my view.

I plucked another blade of green grass, tossed it aside and rested my face in my hands. What do I do? Why am I feeling this way? Nothing made sense.

I dropped my hands from my teary face and looked out at Lake Merritt for answers, for solace, something. My God, I just got married 6 weeks ago. Six weeks. What's happening? Why am I so miserable? The sun chafed my hair. This can't be happening. I've been successful at everything I've set out to do, very successful. A duck floated slowly along the water. I'm trying so hard. Why am I feeling so fucked up? Marriage is supposed to be happy.

A word popped into mind, and it scared the hell out of me. We just got married six weeks ago. I can't live without him. We're so in love. Go away, "divorce"! You're not an option! I married for life. I married Justin for a lifetime. Whatever the cost. Keep faith. I promised.

A big black Labrador led its owner on a jog along the lake.

It'll get better. It has to. You'll make it better. You'll feel better. Everything's going to be alright. Think of all the love, how deeply you love each other.

I plucked a few more blades of grass, pushed myself up and faced the apartment building, prepared to go back home yet more unsettled than before.

At the intersection of Grand and Harrison, the light turned red. The words: "Don't Walk."

Justin was still at work when I walked in. Six or seven-day work-weeks weren't uncommon for him. So goes the lawyer's life. Further, it wasn't uncommon for Justin to arrive home reeling from stress. So goes a man's life when he's too proud to express the full spectrum of emotions.

I routinely tried to interject fun. "Honey, there's a dance class at the Veteran's Hall down the street. I heard it's really fun. We should take a class. Would you consider it?"

"No. I don't want to go dancing," was his response.

"Well, do you mind if I go by myself?"

He paused, considering it. "No, that's just not right. I don't want you going alone."

Trapped. I'm trapped. I can't have sex, I thought, because my new groom won't even share a bed with me. I can't go dancing, one of my favorite things, because he doesn't want me to. I can't go dancing with him, because he'd rather watch TV. If I rebel, I'd create further tension between us.

I thought about how tempted I was to cheat on him. I craved a night out on the town, salsa dancing or the bar scene, some place where I could get lost in the sexy excitement of hopes for a connection and sexual intimacy.

I fantasized about going out to a local pub and hooking up with a stranger. Yet I did nothing about this fantasy, except to look at my wedding ring. I married for a lifetime, until death do we part. A lifetime of celibacy defined my future. What a dismal thought.

I don't remember when it started, but I couldn't comfortably make phone-calls when Justin was home.

"Who were you talking to?" he'd ask, whenever I ended the call.

"My friend, Shira," I'd say, for example.

"What were you talking about?"

"Nothing, honey. Her Mom's sick, and we caught up on other things. Why?"

"I'm your husband, that's why."

By this time in my life, I was very well versed in domestic violence—the cycle of violence, the control issues, the way that the abuser attempts to isolate their partner. I'd done training sessions on this, counseled women who'd been battered, worked at a shelter that housed abused women and children.

Yet in my marriage, I wasn't clearly aware of the abusive dynamic. There wasn't physical violence, so it took a more subtle form. Not unlike my childhood, I wasn't conscious of the fact that I was a victim of emotional abuse.

When drowning in mess, we can't see the mess for what it is. Mess is messy like that. It skews our sense of reality and blocks out healthy comparisons. We have to swim above and beyond it, before we can take in the full perspective with new lenses.

One afternoon I sat on the loveseat across from Justin.

He was sprawled across the sofa—an old, fat man with graying hair. Justin's snores drowned out the television. A screeching awareness entered my otherwise clouded brain: I married a miserable pain in the ass.

Fights became routine. Justin insisted that I watch CSI with him, for example. I declined, telling him that murder shows scare me. "Don't call it a murder show!" he snapped.

"Are you kidding? It is a murder show, Justin. It's a television show in which at least one person is murdered per episode and the plot is wrapped around solving the murder. You know I hate watching these shows."

"It's the best show on the air. I refuse to watch Dancing with the Has-beens."

"Okay, well I'll be in the bedroom. I'm not going to watch it with you."

"I want you here with me." He'd raised his voice.

Quietly, I told him "No thanks," and walked to the bedroom.

Fear and anxiety broiled within. I found myself crying uncontrollably. "You're overly sensitive," I told myself. "Marriage is hard, and divorce isn't an option." Plus, Justin always returned with warm hugs and the promise to do whatever it takes to make things work.

Six months or so into our marriage, Justin came home chewing on his lower lip and breathing loudly.

"Hi, honey." I approached him, and we briefly kissed on the lips.

"Hi," Justin grunted, while putting his briefcase down by the door.

"What's wrong, babe?"

"Forty-five minutes! Forty-five God damned minutes to park in this neighborhood. I'm so fuckin' sick of this!"

262

"I'm sorry honey. I should've moved my car out of the garage earlier. I didn't think to do that."

"No, Robby. I told you I don't want you parking outside."

"Why? It's no problem, sweet-love. Spaces free up before dark."

"Do NOT park outside. It's not safe. You could get mugged or worse. I'm sick of repeating myself."

"It's fine, Justin. I can take care of myself. The neighborhood isn't that bad and I'm home before dark most every night."

"Why do you always have to argue with me?"

"I don't, sweetie. But I love you and don't want you to be so stressed. There's an easy solution to the problem, that's all."

"If you don't have to argue with me, then why are you arguing with me, Suzanne?"

Whoa. I was suddenly both angry and enlightened. "I'm not Suzanne. I'm your new wife, the better one, the love of your life. Remember? Don't treat me like I'm Suzanne!"

"Well then don't act like Suzanne!"

I threw my head back against the sofa cushion. Silent tears flushed my face.

"Oh, what's wrong now?" Justin softened.

"Everything's wrong, Justin. We should be happy. We're newlyweds. I mean, nothing's perfect, but I'm not happy. And you're not either if this feels like your first marriage." I pressed my hand against my tears. "I love you, baby, but I don't understand why this is so hard."

Justin opened his arms. "Come here."

I fell against his chest, still sobbing.

"Robyn, it just slipped out. We were married for twelve years. I said her name out of habit, that's all. You're nothing like Suzanne. I love you more than anything, okay? I'll do anything to make it work."

"Justin I'm really scared, scared that if we don't get help…we're headed for a divorce."

"What?" Justin let go of me and asked, sharply, "Are you threatening me with divorce?"

"No, Justin. I'm not threatening you. I want our marriage to work. I don't want to keep fighting. I never want to fight with you. We need help, that's all."

"I'm not going to some damn shrink. It'll be okay. We'll keep working on it. I'll do whatever it takes, but I'm not going to a damn therapist."

"What's wrong with counseling, Justin? Nanette's been through it, and Nicole and almost all our friends, and I'm pretty much a lifer. Dawn's a couples' therapist. She suggested it too."

"Wait. You talk to your sister, Dawn, about us?"

I downplayed my communications with Dawn. I'd told her practically everything—how miserable I was, how he refused to fall asleep with me, much less have sex with me; but that divorce wasn't an option. I'd make it work. "No, not in any detail, honey. Dawn just wants the best for us. Sometimes couples need professional support. There are tons of therapists around here. I'm sure we can find a good one. Please, honey."

"Okay, okay." He walked into the kitchen, dismissively. "I'll think about it."

I followed him to the refrigerator. "Thank you, honey." I extended my neck preparing to kiss him. Justin leaned over but stopped me with his words, "I won't forget that you threatened me with divorce, and that you're being a pain in the ass."

I pulled back and retreated to the bedroom, where I slept.

Alone.

In tears.

Again.

The next day, Justin walked in with a gorgeous bouquet of red and pink roses, and a card. Inside, a handwritten note provided the reassurance I needed.

Dearest, Darling, Cutieosity of the most Cuteiciousness of the Most Cute,

Everything is going to be all right. In fact, everything is far more alright than we really had any expectation of, or any right to expect. We love each other; we're married, and we always will be. We're going to adopt and expand our loving family.

I'm sorry about last night, and I really, honestly don't know why I said such a dismissive, disrespectful thing when you were about to kiss me. I will never do that again. There's no excuse for treating the love, and light, of my life with anything other than warm appreciation, and to realize how lucky I am to have you in my life.

I left a message with a couples' therapist that my colleague, Julie, recommended. I realize I need to work on my lack of communication skills—the missing brick in the wall of love that surrounds us. I know we'll be, and are, wonderful together. You are the only part of my past that counts and the only part of my future that matters.

I love you very, very much, dearest darling Ms. Ware.

Yours until the ocean wears diapers to keep its bottom dry.

-Justin Case

I finished reading and I set the card on the coffee table. "I love you so much, Justin."

We embraced soundly.

"I know how lucky I am," he emphasized. "I just want to do right by you, and I feel responsible for you. But that's not your fault, my Robby."

"Thank you, baby. It means a lot. But you're not responsible for me."

"I need to be the husband you deserve."

"You are, sweetie. We'll be okay."

For the next four months, Justin and I attended couples' therapy on a sporadic basis. I was glad to see a male therapist, Daniel, assuming it would ease Justin's comfort level to talk with a man.

We'd scheduled weekly evening sessions. Sometimes, Justin had to be in court and couldn't make it. Other weeks, he had to work extra late and couldn't make it. When we did go, therapy didn't fix our problems.

"She put a gun to my head to come here," Justin told Daniel during the first session.

"I feel like he'll never let go of the fact that I mentioned divorce." I looked at Justin. "I was only saying it, honey, because that's where we're headed if we don't make things better."

Daniel sat silently, mostly.

Once or twice during therapy, Justin referred to me as Suzanne.

"That's a very telling slip of the tongue, Justin," Daniel remarked.

Okay, what does it reveal? I anxiously awaited Daniel's words of wisdom, how Justin was clearly bringing his former marital problems into our marriage, add to that Justin's lifelong interpersonal issues with an abusive father and a mother he was enmeshed with, all of which stifled Justin's healthy ego development.

But Daniel just sat there. Damn him. I wanted a better therapist. I wouldn't dare suggest it, though, because at least Justin was going once in a while.

After sessions, Justin sometimes hugged me lovingly. Other times, he maintained an angry distance between us. Still other times, he acted as though nothing had happened and re-focused on the television when home.

March 4, 2007: Dear Diary, It's only eight months into our marriage. I'm so fuckin scared! I can't lose him. I don't want life without him. I love him too much. He loves me too much. What would I do? What do I do? I'm full of so much fuckin pain. I have to make this work. What choice do I have? Divorce isn't an option.

When grocery shopping one evening, I perused greeting cards and picked up one for Justin. It depicted a tranquil beach scene: a sailboat in the vast ocean, the sun setting in the distance and birds flying overhead; somewhat reminiscent of our spot in Bodega Bay. The front read "I just want," and the inside message, "to love you until the end of time."

I'd signed the card "with all my love forever and always and always and forever, your Robby."

I was excited to give it to Justin when he arrived home. "I have something for you, baby. Don't get too excited. It's just a card."

"Thanks," Justin said, taking the card and placing it on the coffee table.

"You're not going to open it?"

"I'll get to it later. I'm hungry now."

Ten months into our marriage, I decided that I'd finally put an end to our sleeping separately.

"It's all that I ask," Justin. "I'm not asking you to have sex with me. I just want us to go to sleep and wake up together like we used to."

He grabbed the remote and amped up the volume.

"Justin, I'm talking to you. Don't ignore me!"

With a hot huff, he turned down the volume. "What now?"

"Honey, it's 10 o'clock. I'd like us to go to bed together. What time do you want to go to sleep, babe?"

"I don't know. I'm not tired yet. It's too early."

"Okay. I'll stay here and wait up for you."

"No. Stop it, Robyn! I told you I'll be there when I'm ready."

"I'm not okay with this, Justin. I won't have a husband who doesn't sleep with me."

"Then maybe you should've married someone else!"

"Yeah, maybe I should have!" I retorted.

Moments passed. Justin murmured, "All right. I shouldn't have said that."

"Well,"—I crossed my arms as I sat on the loveseat, facing Justin on the couch that he'd made his bed for the duration of our marriage—"I'm going to sit here until you join me."

"Suit yourself."

I sat and sat. Neither of us was going to budge. We were a good match in terms of tenacity.

Justin began snoring. I watched as his head snapped back, tossing the pillow out from under him and onto the floor.

"Justin wake up!"

"Huh?" he mumbled.

"Honey, how's your neck? Your head snapped back. The pillow's on the floor."

"That's what you woke me up for? Damnit, let me sleep! Pain in the ass." He turned around to sleep on his side, with his back to me.

"Don't curse at me!"

"Well quit pissing me off. Leave me alone and back the fuck off!"

"I won't be abused, Justin. I don't deserve this."

"Oh, Christ. I'm not abusing you. Just leave me alone!"

I went to bed alone again.

What happened to the man I fell madly in love with? How'd he turn into such a demon?

As unrecognizable as my husband was, I recognized him all too well. The fear and angst that dominated my young life had returned.

Dad never abused me, never even spanked me. The unpredictability of not knowing from one moment to the next if he'd either love or despise me, however, had clearly seeped its way into my relationships with men. My fight for love partnered with it.

Yet I was so sure of Justin's love.

Somehow we're moved to the places we most deliberately strive to avoid—the places that taunted us as children. They stifled our growth and any semblance of worthiness. We land back in the thick of it all, as we're striving desperately to find the opposite. I was certain I'd found it. Instead, I was back in that father-daughter relationship. It was a struggle I'd never win, no matter how hard I tried.

Mental health issues are too monstrous to alter, especially when the troubled person doesn't admit to having problems. I'd thought my marital struggles were about my deficits as a wife and person, but these things didn't even factor into the equation.

Surprisingly, Justin wanted to continue sessions with Daniel, but only in my absence. I agreed, glad he was getting help. It seemed as though Daniel was biased in Justin's favor. Daniel had said things to me during sessions like, "You need to lend him money, because that's what couples do for each other." I believe Justin saw in Daniel a male ally, one who agreed that his wife was a nuisance.

Though I enjoyed a reprieve from tense therapy sessions, I was apprehensive when Justin would come home on Monday nights – after therapy sessions – in an even worse mood than usual.

The summer of 2008 set the stage for some of the worst wildfires in California's history. Justin and I watched the news, when we heard that Paradise had been badly hit.

"Honey, where's Paradise?" I asked. "My family used to go there on vacation, but I don't remember where it is."

"It's a few hours north of us...Oh, no!"

"What's wrong?"

"I just remembered my friend, Ruthie. She lives in Paradise. At least, I think she still does."

"Who's Ruthie?" And why have I never heard about her?

"We used to date, but we decided we're better off as friends. I have to find her number."

"Do you know her last name or if she got married?"

"Yeah, it's Graham. I went to her wedding."

Justin retrieved his laptop and searched.

"Here she is!" He took out his phone and dialed.

"Ruthie! You recognize my voice?" He laughed and continued. "Long time, stranger. You okay over there? We're watching the news, me and my adorable new wife, that is. Just needed to make sure you're okay."

He listened for a while, then continued, "I'm glad to hear it. I haven't seen you since your wedding. How's it going?"

He paused, then chortled, "So the wedding was the highlight, huh? Sorry to hear it."

Justin motioned to me to sit next to him. Looking at me, he said, "My new wife is here with me. Let me have you say 'hello' to her."

I nodded at Justin. "I don't need to"—the phone was in my hand. "Hi, Ruthie. We're glad you're okay."

"Thank you," she said. I didn't detect a trace of personality. Was she jealous? This was just weird. "Well, I'll give the phone back to Justin now."

"Okay," Ruthie replied.

Goodness, lady, I thought. Get an emotion.

When he hung up, Justin said that Ruthie told him she refused to lose track of him again. Did they want each other back? Why did he want me to talk to her? The whole thing was weird.

On Sunday, August 3, 2008, Justin finally started to work on the adoptions application we'd set aside months earlier. I'd started my part long before, and we both knew I'd follow through in a timely manner. His procrastination would likely be our biggest obstacle. Thus I was excited and hopeful upon seeing him start to type responses. Nanette and Betty had agreed to provide references for us.

When Justin finished some of the basic questions, he said we'd go through the rest of the application in the upcoming weekend. I readily agreed, thrilled that he'd finally made an effort to grow our family.

"We're going to have a little one! We're going to have a little one!" I cheered, jumping up and down with my arms raised in a victory V.

Justin chuckled and reached for the remote.

The next day, I wandered around the Alameda Town Centre after work. My body flooded with nervous energy. I realized I was scared,

scared of my husband. I didn't want to go home to Justin. He treated me with incredible sweetness one moment and was a piss-ass the next. It scared me. What would happen when I actually make a mistake where he's concerned, I wondered. I hadn't yet. I gave him and our marriage the best of me, but I was bound to slip up at some point. How would he react then?

On the other hand, things were looking up. Justin had started the adoptions process. He was still in counseling and would meet with Daniel this evening. It'd get better.

I decided to treat myself to a visit at Color Me Mine, one of those ceramics places wherein you paint a figurine. I chose a rose, my and my Mom's favorite flower.

As I focused on each paintbrush stroke of each rose petal, layering soft pinks and reds and highlighting spots with an orange-yellow, I'd entered a new realm. The process elevated my entire being to a more focused, relaxed state than I'd known for a very long time.

My God, I realized, I hadn't done anything at all for myself, just for me, since I'd been with Justin. I'd ignored all of my fun, creative energy. But this hour was for only me. My time.

The rose turned out beautifully. I'd treasure it, my only gift to myself in the past three years.

Much calmer now, I made my way home.

As I drove up Montecito, I noticed the prime parking spot directly in front of the entrance was open. My lucky day. I pulled over and called Justin. "Honey it's me. I know you're in counseling now but I just wanted to tell you that I parked right in front. Don't worry. It's a few feet from the door. I'll be inside in two seconds. Park in the garage. Love you. See you soon."

I sat contently on the couch and considered making a monthly ritual of trips to Color Me Mine. Maybe I'd paint an item of Judaica next, like a Passover plate or Shabbat candlestick holders.

Slam! A savagery flared from Justin's being when he shut the front door. "I told you not to ever park on the street, God damnit!" His tight reddened face spewed words of rage and betrayal. Justin dropped his briefcase and stomped towards me.

I stood up, in defensive mode, no time to think.

"You never listen to me, Robyn! I keep telling you not to park on the street! You could get mugged or killed but you're too God-damned stubborn to listen to me. I'm so sick and tired—"

His rant was interrupted by a beastly screeching hysteria, such an unfamiliar noise that I could scarcely believe it was mine.

"I'm sick of this! I'd much rather get mugged than deal with your angry temper every day! I'm sick of walking on eggshells. I'm sick of you yelling at me, for what? For not a God-damned thing! I don't do anything wrong, except to love you and try to make you happy! It never works!" My limbs shivered with a forceful surge of adrenaline. "I don't deserve any of this!"

Justin darted out the door and slammed it shut.

All I could think to do was take a warm bath, to settle my body and regain composure.

I watched my legs floating on the water and realized I was terrified. I needed help. Where did he go? Would he come back? What do I do now? I can't believe I screamed like that. I felt horrible for it. I'll apologize when I get a chance, I reasoned. I hope I get a chance.

I dried off, tossed on a t-shirt and sweats, and called Dawn from the bedroom. I told her everything that had transpired. As I was talking, I heard the door close. My breathing eased a bit; Justin had come home. "We're finally really moving on adopting a child," I continued. "Maybe that's what put him over the edge. Well, he's home now, so I better go try to talk to him. He'll be pissed that I'm talking to you, though."

"Well, tell him that I support you both," my sister said, "but you shouldn't bring a child into the picture until he gets his temper under control."

"Yeah, definitely not. I won't. Anyway, thanks for listening. I'll keep you posted."

"Okay. Good luck, and call me back."

"Okay, thanks. Bye."

"Bye."

Stifled by rage-infested air, I timidly entered the living room.

Justin laid on his back on the couch, his burly arms across his chest. His face burned with stone-cold frigidity. His eyes glared with a monstrous venom that I'd never seen him exude before. It was perhaps the scariest sight I'd ever seen and one beyond description.

I believe without doubt that Justin had broken that night. By this, I mean, I believe he had a psychotic break.

Had Justin admitted to having mental health problems, rather than denying this and assaulting me with his rage, I would've maintained compassion. Then again, had he acknowledged and worked on his mental health, he wouldn't have been harboring a lifetime's worth of chaotic emotions that built-up to the night's vicious explosion.

"Honey—"

"Don't call me that!" He stared vapidly and didn't turn towards me.

"Justin, I'm sorry I screamed at you."

"Who were you talking to just now?" he interrogated.

"My sister."

"What did you tell her?"

"Nothing. I just told her we were having problems, and she said we shouldn't bring a child into our lives yet. She supports us both."

"You're lying. I heard every word. You told her secrets about me. You've betrayed me! We're through."

I raised my right hand—which shook with nerves—to look at my wedding ring. "But I still love you."

"Well, you're not acting like it."

"I'm sorry, Justin. I'm sorry I yelled. Dawn supports us. She just said we shouldn't bring a child into our home until you control your temper."

"God damnit, Robyn! How many times do I have to repeat myself? You keep betraying me. We're through!"

"What do you mean? We're getting…a divorce?"

"You brought it up in the first place, so yes, we'll be divorced in six months!"

Oh my God. "Oh my God." It's all I could say and keep saying for the moment: "Oh my God."

And then I asked, "Who stays here?"

"You can stay until I pay you the rest of the money I owe you. Then I want you out!"

By that time, Justin had owed me close to eight thousand dollars. By that time, too, I knew he'd fail to repay me, or it would take years. Until now, I'd do anything to save our marriage.

But in that moment, I knew I had to save myself. I needed to leave and never return. This I knew without a doubt.

Not for a second, not upon receiving a lengthy letter of apology from Justin shortly before the divorce would go through, nor upon reading a compassionate email that he forwarded via my attorney begging me to "come home," nor for any moment on any day thereafter, would I consider returning to Justin.

That night, I entered the kitchen. There, I started clearing the shelves of my dishware.

"What are you doing?" Justin shouted.

"I'm collecting my things," I responded. "You said we're getting divorced, so I'm packing."

"You're being passive-aggressive."

Passive-aggressive? Me? We're not getting a divorce? You didn't mean it? This is some type of sick, twisted control game? Fuck that.

I stood atop a step ladder and looked at our china set. "Who gets the china?"

"I don't know." He paused. "I guess you do."

"Great," I said quietly and matter-of-factly. "I get the china."

Tears hit the ivory white, silver trimmed Royal Doulton plates that I pulled, one by one, from the upper cabinet and stacked on the counter. "I get the fuckin china."

"Our love reduced to a mediocre set of porcelain dishes," I announced, sarcastically, bitterly, in shock.

Justin served me with divorce papers at work the next day, August 4, 2008—thirteen months after we married.

Thirteen.

I got the fuckin china.

Chapter Fifteen: Glimpses of Paradise

It's said that the average cost of divorce in this country is $15,000. It's sad to consider the scores of couples living unhappily together, because divorce is unaffordable. On the other hand, freedom from a toxic marriage? Priceless.

A consistent, gentle trickling of water lulled me to sleep three weeks post-marital breakdown. I'd re-claimed residence in Alameda, this time at Ballena Village. My spacious studio apartment in the front courtyard overlooked a serene pool of water that swerved through plush gardens, under foot bridges, and into miniature waterfalls. In the middle of the pond out front, a fountain proudly sprayed streaks of bright, wet droplets that arched onto a green blanket of knee-deep water. Its soft, rhythmic splattering eased me to sleep. For a while, sleep was all I knew to do in order to avoid reality.

September 25, 2008: I met Prince Charming. I had him for 3 years. Or was it 2 or 1? Or did I even have him at all? He was there, here, to hold me and kiss me, to tell me we'd be together forever. Our love was limitless, I was sure. What the hell happened? I don't know how to exist. God damn you, Justin! Damn you for not being willing to do whatever it takes, for beating me down with your rage, for getting so sick and stressed that you destroyed us. But I know you weren't in the right mind, honey. I know you didn't want to lose me. I never wanted to lose you. I'll never stop loving you, 'til the end of time, my beshert. Always and forever and forever and always. But I won't go back to you, not ever. I'm sorry, Justin. I can't.

Sometimes, the concepts that ground us in quiescent certainty are the same ones that cast us into pelting hailstorms of insurmountable disbelief.

Can my happily-ever-after start now? I asked, looking up at my eggshell-colored stucco ceiling. No response, so I crashed stomach-first onto my mattress and buried my head in the pillow. A river of tears spilled out of me. Damnit. Why this pain? Why do I keep losing everything and everyone? How do I get through—a revelation instantly curbed my stream of helpless conjecture, only a few seconds into it, like a shot of whiskey at the brink of an Icelandic winter. Sensing the thrill of a radiant smile that had spontaneously spanned my face, I popped up. One freeing reality dominated my mindset: I can have sex again! Thank God!

I mean, I wasn't ready for sex, but the simple knowing that I wasn't doomed to a celibate existence boosted me. I figured I'd give myself time, say six months from marital separation, to start dating again. For now, I scrawled out a To-do list:

1) Have sex.
2) Send writing samples to publishers.
3) Start blog.
4) Get divorced.
5) Have sex.

What seemed easiest was jumping to the middle of the list, so I did. I'd written a few creative pieces about my misfortunate encounters with men. I chose a few of my favorites, typed and printed them.

December 2, 2008
Dear —name of publisher or editor—,
Please accept this writing for publication.
Sincerely,
Robyn Alana Engel

That's it. That's all I typed, five or six times. I'd never heard of a "query" letter: the all-important document that says "Pick me!" The query expels with elegance and impeccable veracity (I'm doubtful this phrase makes sense; I'm using four-syllable words to sound as though I've grown as a writer since then, like having learned that the insertion of parenthesized information, while perhaps mildly entertaining, is grammatically obscene and only serves to baffle the reader) how I'm more special than the millions of other writers in the world who fantasize about being interviewed by Oprah and landing the #1 spot on the NY Times bestseller list, or simply being able to afford a new pair of socks or really cool stash of paperclips.

I figured I was being professional enough by placing my letters, unfolded, in manila envelopes and dropping them in the mailbox. All the others would lazily email their documents.

A few hours after writing my To-Do list, I checked off number three and drew myself a small smiley face.

Regarding number four, I'd taken step one and hired a seemingly reasonable, nice attorney. Once I did, the twisted ugliness of a legal battle I never thought I'd embark upon pained me for what seemed a perennial purgatory.

"I asked my colleagues if they knew Justin," my attorney told me. "They said he has a reputation for being very contentious."

"Really? I'm not surprised." I chuckled, uneasily. "Well, I can vouch for that."

At one point, Justin demanded that I come in for a deposition to address my betrayal. Presumably, I'd unlawfully disclosed marital secrets. My lawyer explained the deposition process, adding that it was a ridiculous request on Justin's part; he had no grounds for doing so.

"You mean he wants to interrogate me for telling my sister that he has a bad temper and wouldn't sleep with me?"

"Well"—he paused—"Yes, that's a fair estimation of what it amounts to. Don't worry. It's not going to happen."

Yet these types of shenanigans would continue, and they'd continue to cost me money, fear, anxiety, tears, and bewilderment. For a lengthy stint of time, I thought I'd never be able to checkmark number four.

My greatest fear, on a much more austere note, was that Justin was suicidal. He'd become someone I never knew before, and was clearly bent on self-sabotage. I saw all the signs, now that I had some breathing room. Even more, I feared he'd die by suicide before the divorce went through. I couldn't fathom the ensuing grief or the "widow" label. It sounds so horribly depressing, definitive, and old. Who would date a widow? I still loved Justin, too. That love wouldn't simply disappear.

One morning, in March of 2009, I awoke to notice my pillow case was wet from saliva. I'd just had the most extraordinarily lascivious dream. I was at a buffet, a chocolate buffet, gawking at homemade crepes bulging with generous amounts of Nutella; shiny pink and brown scoops of ice-cream in large bowls that housed volumes of hot fudge, topped with whipped cream and maraschino cherries; mocha almond fudge cake embellished by white chocolate frosting and dark chocolate roses; and double chocolate cheesecake on a chocolate graham cracker crust. I stood close to the crepes, so close I could almost taste them.

In that moment, life was all about chocolate. Life was sweet. I was so happy. Then I woke up. That's it—a name for my blog, I thought. "Life by Chocolate" was born that morning.

Perfect, I said, as I looked at my new blog page and wiped off a smudge of saliva that had found its way to my collar bone.

Chocolate didn't quite cut it, though. I burned for sex. They say that's normal for a newly separated or divorced woman in her forties. Well, I don't know if anyone but me says this. I so desperately wanted to feel desired again. I was also desperately determined to shield myself from further pain.

So there I was, back at the all-too-familiar venue of on-line dating. This time I sought sex with no strings. Naturally, this wouldn't take long.

On Match dot com, Thomas advertised "Free massages!" I knew what that meant: "Foreplay, but I'm too respectful to say it." If he wants foreplay, I figured, he probably wants the sex to which it comes 'fore.

When he saw that I visited his profile, Thomas messaged me. I responded, and a connection had begun. Our emails were friendly, so we advanced to phone-calls. During a brief, cordial chat, I told Thomas that I didn't want anything serious or even exclusive.

We met at a Starbucks for our first date. Thomas appeared fit, with a dark complexion and warm smile.

We sat with our respective cups of coffee. I watched his mouth move as words came out. Thomas said some things about work and the military, I think. Wait, was he in the army? I've never gone for a military man. Regardless, I basked in thoughts about his moist lips, and his soft, smooth skin.

"I guess she had it planned for a year, before she dropped it on me," he said. I scolded myself for not paying attention and was pleased to note that Thomas wasn't a bundle of self-pity about his impending divorce. He was simply trying to navigate through the shocking end of a fifteen year marriage.

"That's strange, but I hear that happens a lot, where one person had it planned for ages," I added. "In my case, it just came out in mad fury. I don't even know if he meant it. But I'm not going to be with someone who manipulates that way. Plus he scared the hell out of me."

I didn't process his response, though he did respond. I wrapped my fingers around my cup of a mocha something-chino-or-other, admiring Thomas's brown eyes.

Thomas walked me to my car and leaned in, as I'd hoped he would. In the next moment, I was listlessly lost in a deliciously heated episode of kissing.

"Mm, I forgot how good this feels," I broke away briefly. It's amazingly fun, I realized.

As he navigated his palm along my back, I suggested we move into my car for privacy.

We continued for another half-hour or so.

Thomas nibbled my ear lobe, sifted his fingers through my hair and whispered, "Come home with me."

"It's too soon," I responded. "I mean, I want to, but not so fast."

"Okay, it's okay."

We finally said "good night" and made plans for another date.

Thomas and I picked up sandwiches and sodas for a day-hike in Berkeley's Tilden Park. I learned that I liked a lot of things about him. Not only did we relate to each other's marital plight, Thomas was five years my junior, active and athletic, intelligent, affectionate, and pleasant. We partook in a lot of kissing and wandering hands, but I still would be unable to checkmark numbers one and five.

It felt exhilarating to be dating again. When I told Dawn about Thomas, she said, "Sounds like he's just what the doctor ordered." I agreed.

On date three, I showed up—as invited—at Thomas's place in El Cerrito with an overnight bag. After a pasta dinner and red Merlot, we found ourselves perusing his music collection. Thomas pulled out a favorite, Plain White T's Delilah, and played it.

"I love this song too," I told him.

He reached towards me with both arms. "Would you like to dance?"

I rested against Thomas' chest, swaying to the music.

I felt both of our hearts racing, as we were kissing, touching, and moving towards the bed. Clothes came off, slowly at first, and then quickly—tossed on the carpet, on the bed, shirts, shoes, panties, boxers.

Thomas's bare skin rushed against mine. His plush, king-sized bed seemed a glamorous place for my first post-Justin liaison.

But as he pressed his body against mine, moving up and down, lowering his hand to do some work with it, he sighed. "Sorry," he said. "Let me keep trying."

Shit. Just my luck. Guy can't get it up!

I was hot, wet, and impatient. "It's all right, Thomas." Damnit!

"It's not you. I really want you, Robyn."

Why would it be my fault? It's not my penis. "I know. It's okay. We can try again tomorrow."

Despite frustrations, we fell asleep shortly thereafter.

"I know what it was!"

Thomas's exclamation woke me from a sound sleep.

"Huh?" I opened my eyes and saw him smiling. "What is it?"

"I know why it didn't work. I went on a 10-mile bike ride yesterday morning. I remember hearing on the radio that bicyclists sometimes have problems getting an erection."

"Oh, okay. That's good, honey." I closed my eyes and rested my head on the pillow. I popped them open. "Thomas—"

"Yeah?"

"Will you stop riding your bike, please?"

"Definitely."

Fortunately, Thomas's suggested correlation between bike-riding and impotence proved helpful.

The next night, after he hadn't ridden a bike in over twenty hours, we tried again. This time, everything worked. Thankfully.

"We'll have to keep testing the theory," he joshed, "just to make sure."

"I agree," I said, planting kisses along his chest.

Thomas slid his hands up along my waist, and began fondling my breasts.

"Dang! Your breasts are huge," he announced, in a tone of thorough disgust. "They're humungous!" Okay? I didn't know what to say. I thought men like big boobs. But if not, I can't help it. I wasn't born with these. They grew out of me when I was a late teen. It's not my fault they didn't stop growing on command. Or ever.

The next week, when I was on my period, I mentioned it to Thomas as things heated between us.

"Oh. Well," he said awkwardly, "I'm not really used to that. I'm used to women who don't have to worry about that anymore."

It seemed I wasn't Thomas's type: the flat-chested menopausal or post-menopausal cougar.

Still, we liked each other. He was attentive too. Thomas gave me compact discs with his favorite romantic music. He listened to stories about my work, and we shared divorce woes.

Meanwhile, I reminded him occasionally that we wouldn't get serious.

Around six weeks into our romance, Thomas called to tell me about a hiking date he had with another woman.

That would've been perfectly fine with me. After-all, I set the rules, and we weren't monogamous. But it wasn't fine with me, because he liked this other woman.

"We didn't do anything," Thomas assured. "You don't want to be exclusive, so I'd like to see her again, and I thought I should be honest with you."

I went ballistic. "You fuck me last night and you're suddenly wanting to date someone else!"

"I, I, I'm sorry."

We concluded that this wasn't working out. At least I concluded that he concluded that after I hung up on him.

When debriefing with Shira, she pointed out that Thomas was simply protecting himself and following the rules I'd set.

"I guess so, Shira. But I'm the only one who was supposed to be dating other people." We laughed in unison.

Several months later, I emailed Thomas to apologize. He readily accepted and appreciated my apology. Amiable closure was had.

Best of all, I'd checked off numbers one and five on my To-Do list. And I'd added big (really big) smiley faces.

In the greater scheme of things, the economy crumbled. In my work life, we were seeing salary freezes and hearing rumors of program closure. I was hopeful that, should my department fold, I'd be placed elsewhere in the agency, since I did well to bring in dollars by hosting training sessions on topics like stress-management, heartfelt parenting, and childhood depression.

But my extra efforts afforded no assurance.

Working in social services inevitably creates nervousness regarding job stability. Three categories of people are hardest hit by economic downturns: the poor, the sick, and those who help them.

On a nippy winter evening in 2009, I found myself scrolling through ads on my computer screen. Most of the men were seeking "a real women" and "NO DRAMA!!" (It's ironic that so many men who are anti-drama are highly pro-caps and exclamation marks.) As I scrolled down, a Michael Bublé lyric caught my eye.

I like Bublé. I also like a man who likes Bublé and is willing to admit it. Upon further perusal, I discovered that he likes dancing, so I sent a "wink."

Carlos wrote me. His English was a bit choppy. It being his first and only language, and me still ready to add checkmarks to numbers one and five, I forgave this.

Our first date was at Burmese Superstar in Alameda. Carlos drove from San Mateo, where he lived.

"It's my favorite place to eat in Alameda," I told him, as we waited for our food to arrive. "I mean, next to Tucker's Ice-Cream, which is just next door." I grinned.

He grinned in response.

Silence. Guy doesn't talk. Okay…"So, not much traffic driving here?"

"No," he said. Carlos seemed relaxed, just a man of very few words, I guessed.

Thankfully, the food arrived when I considered commenting on the weather.

Between bites, there was meager discourse. He's pleasant enough, I thought. Not a dark, dashing, head-turning man, but a calm, balding, brown-mustached decent one.

When I took my last bite, Carlos picked up the bill. Points for that.

"Okay, w, well," I sputtered as we stood by my car door, "Thank you."

He said, "Okay, go." Excuse me? You're telling me to leave? I didn't mean to inconvenience you, rude ass. I was merely giving you half a second to make a move, ask for a second date or something. I placed my hand on the car door handle.

"Wait," he said. Thank goodness! Carlos reached out and conferred a robotic hug in combination with a sibling-like pat on the back. Great, just what I'd been craving.

"Bye." I smiled and opened my car door.

He'd already turned to walk away.

I drove home feeling confused, sad and rejected. Even though I wasn't excited about him, and he seemed devoid of substance, Carlos was supposed to be totally into me. Damn.

But it seemed I'd misinterpreted things. Through email the next day, he suggested we go to Allegro Ballroom for salsa dancing the following Sunday. Carlos did like me, and he was coming to my domain again. Better yet, he was coming to my salsa dancing domain.

We danced well together, and for several hours—doing salsa, meringue and cha cha. He spun me in triple-spins, dipped me gracefully, and displayed good stamina. I hoped it was a sign of things to come.

Again, though, the "goodbye" was lukewarm at best. He hugged me, this time a bit warmer and more relaxed.

He must be gay, I told myself on the way home. Come on, Robyn. You should have thought of it sooner. The dude likes Bublé. Hello. It's nice to have a good dance partner, though. Right? I don't know. I suppose. Yeah, no. No, yeah. Oy, this dating thing is frustrating as hell.

Over the next few weeks, we exchanged friendly, non-romantic messages. Carlos even called, but he failed to ask for another date. That's it. He plays for the other team. I'm sure of it.

By now, it had been close to a year since Justin filed for divorce. My attorney had informed me that I'd done my part. I just had to wait and have faith. "I'll believe it's over when I see my maiden name again," I told him.

Finally, Carlos suggested we explore his neck of the woods. "Yes, but I can't go this weekend," I told him. "I'm taking a friend out for her birthday on Saturday night. How about the weekend after that?"

Carlos had planned a full-month long vacation to Mexico with his family during what was left of the summer. We agreed to take a rain-check, with a promise for a night on the town in early September.

"If I don't get a chance to talk to you before you leave, have a great trip," I told him. "I'll see you when you get back."

"Thank you, Robyn. Have fun with your family. I'll think of you."

He'll think of me? That's sweet, another good sign. I'm not sure if absence will make the heart grow fonder, but it will keep my hormones in pre-heat mode.

Time could not move more slowly at work. Then I got a phone-call from my attorney. "Robyn, I think it's over," he informed.

"Really? I really hope so."

He said, "Let me get back to you when I confirm."

"Okay. Thank you. I'll keep my fingers crossed."

He called back ten minutes later and said the divorce had in fact gone through. "Congratulations!"

"Thank you! Thank you! Thank you!"

I dashed to Myra's office. Myra, the administrative assistant, and I had become friends. When I told her the news, Myra cheered with me and gave me a smothering hug. In that moment, I was reminded of the grandmotherly woman at Negri's who was so excited to see Justin, I could barely breathe when she embraced me.

"Congratulations, Robyn! Let's go for a Frappuccino, my treat."

I felt so free and so giddy. "This is the best-tasting drink ever, Myra. Woohoo!" I giggled. "I just realized I dropped the 'f' word. Justin's last name was Feldman. I'm an Engel again!"

Myra guffawed. "I'm tickled for you, Robyn."

Back at my desk, I did some calculations. Justin filed for divorce in September of 2008. It's October, 2009. Thirteen months. Married 13 months. Divorce took 13 months.

Thirteen.

Thirteen.

Thirteen.

Meanwhile, I'd reconnected with Carlos. He had a good, busy vacation, he said, and was glad to be home. We confirmed a plan for me to go from work to his place in San Mateo that night. He wrote: "We eat here. If you need change to your close, there is a extra room." Reminding myself that writing is not his specialty, I excitedly pulled together my travel hygiene packet, extra undies, and black rayon dress with a low neckline, dance shoes, red lingerie, and black lacey Victoria's Secret bra.

I sat with Carlos in his living room. His place was subdued with earth-toned furnishings and silver-framed ocean scenes on the walls.

"Did you take those photos?"

"Yes, you like?"

He casually took my jacket off and hung it on a coat rack. Carlos placed his hand on my back, walked me around to view his pictures and his home. His bedroom door was open, but we didn't enter. I noted a luxurious bed enveloped by a thick cream comforter and a series of fluffy tan and blue pillows.

While Carlos put dinner—burritos and chips—on plates for us, I picked up my bag and excused myself. In the restroom, I wriggled into my little black dress.

He imparted a quick direct glance, one that says "I like how you look," when I walked back into the living room, then gestured towards the coffee table. "Dinner is served."

"Thank you. That's nice." I sat on the sofa next to him, and brought the plate to my lap. "So, I got some good news."

"Yeah. What's that?"

"My divorce went through. Finally." I smiled. "For a while there, I never thought it would."

"Well then we have to celebrate." Carlos put his plate back on the coffee table. He walked into the kitchen, and returned with a bottle of Pinot, a corkscrew, and two wine glasses. He lowered the items onto the coffee table in front of me.

"Yes. We need to celebrate," I agreed, my insides jumping up and down gleefully. I could hardly believe that I had a date— one with immediate potential for romance (i.e., sex)—just as my divorce finalized. Then again, I couldn't be too hopeful. He likes Bublé.

We toasted to my divorce, chewed dinner and drank wine. I had one and a half glasses to his two or three. Even with alcohol to loosen him up, Carlos remained a man of few words.

At one point, he looked contemplatively towards a photo that hung on the wall in front of us. "What are you thinking?" I asked.

He twitched his head, as if I'd just brought him back to reality.

"I'm thinking you should have more wine."

"I'm good," I smiled.

A few moments of silence passed, and he said, "We should get going."

"Yeah, sure. I'll just get my things."

The Underground Pub in Redwood City was dark and dingy, in a sketchy neighborhood, and had a fairly small dance floor. With some wine in me, under the circumstances, I loved it. Carlos impressed with his dance moves, in spite of the added alcohol. He grabbed a beer or two between stints of dancing. The music was fun and fast, and our chemistry felt right. Romance seemed assured, but I still didn't know.

Several hours later, we sat and watched the few dancing couples that kept at it. Carlos put his hand on my thigh. I covered his hand with mine. His face lit up with the look of a child who was about to steal a chocolate-chip cookie. He quickly planted a brief, moist kiss on my lips.

Next thing I remember, we were on Carlos' sofa, wrestling my dress off and unbuttoning his shirt.

"Mm, mmm."

Sigh. "Mm, mmm."

"I'd like you to spend the night," he told me.

"Yes. I want to." We kept kissing, arms and legs entangled.

295

This is going well. I think I'll get romance (i.e., sex) tonight.

Carlos abruptly stopped. "Do you have condoms?"

"Me, um. No." You're supposed to have condoms. See, I decided not to get them because that would mean I'm expecting sex. And if I expect sex, it won't happen. It's like when I wash my car it rains. I want to have sex with you, and I won't have sex without a condom, so I didn't buy any. You're supposed to have them, buddy. "You don't have any?" I asked.

"Why would I have condoms? I'm divorced." Are you kidding me? That makes as much sense as —well, my condom argument.

I would soon learn that few places in which a person might find condoms are open on a Friday night at 1:30 a.m. in his neighborhood. We drove several miles to find a little gas station. I waited in the car, slightly embarrassed. It was a pre-sex drive of shame.

Thankfully, he got some and we were back at his place, this time in the bedroom. Carlos was, well, making me feel really good. The sex was really nice, and it happened easily. He didn't have to work at it. There was nothing awkward about it. It wasn't orgasmic, but I was thrilled. Romance (i.e., sex) and a divorce! My lucky streak had started. Or so I decided.

The sexiest part about that night was waking up mid-sleep. We both awoke at the same moment. Carlos instinctively lunged onto me, and we enjoyed another round. Then, as I readied myself for more, he said "I can't." Damn.

"It's alright," I responded. I guess I was trying to push my luck. We faded back to sleep.

In the morning, Carlos offered me breakfast. I wanted to get home and wash up, so I politely declined. We kissed "goodbye," and I left.

I remember walking along Webster, perusing women's shirts on a clothing rack, and feeling off. I didn't feel sad or bad, necessarily. In fact, I wanted to announce to the world that I had a sexy date and sex last night with a man I hardly know and don't particularly like all that much.

It felt good and naughty, but it also felt strange. Maybe I had a smidge of regret that I'd had casual sex. My other few experiences weren't quite as casual in that, at least, I knew and liked the guys better. This was more like a one-night stand.

My phone rang. It was Carlos. "I feel kind of weird," I told him. "I mean, it was great. Thank you for a wonderful night. I just feel kind of strange. I don't usually do that."

"Why don't we just take it one day at a time. How does that sound?"

"That sounds perfect."

Carlos came to visit me in Alameda the next weekend. We found ourselves having sex before getting out the door.

I liked how effortless the sex was, vastly different from the discourse. I assumed Carlos enjoyed it too, until I noticed him staring blankly at the ceiling as we lay side-by-side on my bed.

"What's wrong, Carlos?"

"Nothing. Just…we don't have an emotional connection." Are you kidding me?

"Well, that takes time," I told him. "Carlos, I don't want casual sex. I mean, I don't want to jump back into marriage, but I'm not the kind of person to sleep around. We'll get to know each other better. Give it time."

He didn't respond.

Over the next few days, Carlos and I exchanged non-substantial emails and agreed to meet again the following Saturday. This time, I would drive to him.

By Saturday, I was really looking forward to another romantic (i.e., sexual) night with Carlos. I'd be there at 6pm. We'd get some dinner and go dancing.

Shortly after 5pm, Carlos called. "I don't want to see you every weekend, so tonight doesn't work" he declared.

"It's Saturday evening, and you're canceling on me!" You don't want sex?

"Robyn, we don't have an emotional connection."

"Carlos, it takes time. That builds when people spend time together."

"I want to date you, but not every week."

"Once a week is too much of a commitment for you? That's crazy. You're confused." And maybe you do play for the other team.

Adios, Carlos.

Two weeks later, he called. I hadn't expected to hear from Carlos ever again. We'd said "goodbye" as if that was it.

"To tell you the truth," Carlos confessed, "I miss you." He wanted me to come over right then, on a Saturday night. Clearly, horny.

"I have plans for tonight, but are you saying you want to date again?"

"Yeah, but not every single weekend," he reiterated.

"I don't know, Carlos. You've already hurt me."

"Okay, well, if you're not interested in me then, never mind."

There was a silence, our respective egos engaged in a face-off.

"Okay, bye," I said casually, taking my ego to the finish line.

"Bye."

That was the last I heard from Carlos, though I saw him again. Months later, I went out dancing with Shira. We were at Café Cocomo in San Francisco.

"Oh my God," I nudged her, as we stood by the bar. "That guy with the black leather jacket, the one talking to the bartender, is Carlos."

She stretched out her neck to get a better look. "I can't see him well, but it looks like you're not missing much, Robyn."

"Nah."

Carlos happened to walk right by us with his drink, and his eyes happened to catch mine.

"Hello," I said with a smile.

He didn't say anything but rudely glared and kept walking.

Shira saw it all. "Well, fuck him," she told me.

"Yeah, fuck him. Well, no. Never again." We laughed.

Things were quiet at the office on a Thursday afternoon. I'd just revised a program manual and signed into AOL to check my email. This awaited me:

Jan 7, 2010, 2:25pm From Bonita Bennett
Subject: You!
Hi Robyn,
This serves to inform you that I finally got around to reading your submissions and though the word count is low (see the attached writers' guidelines) I was quite impressed. So much so, that I wish to print two of your pieces in an upcoming issue: The Kiss That Saved My Life and the Unforgettable Dating Moment. This would be subject to editing and pulled together as one piece for an article called...Two Days In The Life Of A Single.

"Woohoo!" I pushed my chair back, and bounced up and down madly, like a yo-yo on crack. "Yay! Woohoo! Awesome-sauce!"

Myra rushed over, eyes glowing with excitement. "What's going on Robyn?"

"Myra, I got published! I'm going to be in Being Single Magazine!" Being Single, hmm. Had I found my niche as a West Coast Carrie Bradshaw, minus the sex, sexy men, and 5,000 square foot closet?

I wasn't sure, but I started thinking that the more I date and fail at romance, the more I stand the chance of making people laugh about my unromantic romantic life and non-sexy sex life. It's a lose-win-win.

A few weeks later, I received three hard copies of Being Single in the mail. My heart pumped feverishly as I flipped open the magazine to find an incredibly exotic, dark, sexy woman's face looking up with subtly flirtatious deep brown eyes. Below her, my name in bold black font. I announced aloud and to myself, "If this doesn't help my dating life, nothing will."

It wouldn't help my dating life; nobody contacted me because they'd seen how incredibly sexy I looked in that photo. My friends wanted to know which tanning salon I used, and who did the phenomenal photography. I told them that photo-shopping had made great strides.

In July of 2010, Jonathan and Angela brought Josiah to visit me.

Josiah and I were already in love. I was there when he took his first steps, to take pictures and cheer him on. With his Mommy holding one hand and his Daddy, the other; Josiah had stepped forward, one little foot at a time—showcasing a precious mixture of trepidation and gusto. One step, two…turned to twenty, forty, fifty, and eventually over 100 steps. He's been darting full-speed ahead ever since.

When he was two and a half, Josiah and I invented the game, Tickle and Tackle, which is played as its name implies. This amounted to my laying face-up on the couch, laughing hysterically, while Josiah giddily stood on one arm of the couch and then lunged onto me with a ruthlessly loving body-slam. Needless to say, he declared himself the winner every time.

I thoroughly enjoyed my time when the Engel threesome visited me at Ballena Village that summer. Josiah splashed around in the swimming pool with us, built sandcastles on the beach, and played with my old wedding favors in the apartment.

"Where's your TV, Auntie Robyn?" he inquired.

"I don't have one, sweetie."

"Huh? No. Where is your TV? Really."

I laughed. "I know it's strange, but I don't have one here, love." I'd given up television after marital breakdown. Fights over CSI and TV-time turned me off. "I do other things like read and write."

Josiah giggled. "No, Auntie Robyn. Where is the TV?!"

We put a DVD, Toy Story III, into my computer drive, and Josiah was thrilled. He watched silently, attentively. When it finished, Josiah had one question, "Are we going to buy Auntie Robyn a TV now?"

They'd only been gone an hour when one lone tear trickled down my face. I didn't expect or quite understand my emotional state. We had such a great, fun-loving time. I couldn't get enough of my nephew, but I'd see him again soon.

Why am I feeling this way? I wondered. It was as if I'd said "goodbye" to someone I loved dearly. That's why; I had.

But this was different than having said "goodbye" to Justin when I went away for a weekend, or having to continue to say "goodbye" to Justin every day for perhaps the rest of my life. It was a softer, warmer, much sweeter "goodbye."

It struck me that I had just said "goodbye" to the love of my life, the new one. Being Josiah's Auntie is pure heaven. His beautiful beaming smile, flavored with a heaping teaspoon of mischief, tickles my heart. He adores me too. I can tell by the way he body-slams me with an elbow to my rib cage, a choke-hold taxing my windpipe, and a stinky foot pressed leisurely against my nostrils—all accompanied by ferocious laughter.

Sure, I would've been a great mom some of the time. I'm equally convinced I'd have been a lousy mom at other times. I'd have made so many shameful parenting mistakes.

Once at work, I shouted "Cool it!" to my young clients. Dad used to always yell at us to "cool it!" How did Dad's voice possess me? Scary. I never wanted to be like him. It became painfully obvious that I'd have to work hard every hour of every day to combat my upbringing.

Add to this, all that healthy parenting involves. I'd have had to virtually create myself anew.

And how can so many people afford to be parents, or can they?

It would've been worth it, I'm sure. That parent-child connection is a bond like no other. Yet it didn't happen for me. Yet again, I was starting to feel okay, maybe even good, with that.

Not that this path is better, necessarily. It's both better and worse. Maybe it's the better road for me. It offers what parenting doesn't: time and energy to pursue my own interests, to write, to nurture me, and to be a proud, loving auntie to my Josiah and whatever little ones might join the family.

October 5, 2010: Good things are happening, Dear Di. But I'll never get over losing the love of my life. I can't just go on like the world expects me to, or like everyone thinks I am. It's like I'm secretly carrying around this ugly ball of pain. But since I keep smiling, they

303

all think I'm fine. I loved him with all my being, Di. He shattered it all. And between you and me, I doubt I'll ever be able to trust a man again. How can I? And how could I ever trust myself to choose a good one? I can't.

Meanwhile, friends provided sound-bites on Justin. The consensus, based on sightings of him at Java Rama in Alameda, or walking near the courthouse in downtown Oakland, was that he looked miserable, grossly overweight, and disheveled.

Nicole called me after seeing Justin one day when she jogged around Lake Merritt.

"It was scary, Robyn," she reported. "He was in his car and then stopped suddenly behind the car in front of him, and then," Nicole paused—attempting to recall the details—"he got out and then was at the driver's window of the car in front of him, screaming. He looked really, really pissed off. I didn't hear any of it, but he was like shaking and raising his fists and it looked like he was about to punch the guy out or something."

"Oh my God. Did anything happen? I hope there wasn't a fight."

"No, nothing like that. I didn't see what happened before it. But there wasn't a fight or accident or anything. He went back to his car, and they both just took off."

"Scary! Justin's a ticking time-bomb. Imagine living with that for any amount of time."

"Robyn. I'm just glad you're not with him anymore."

"Me too, Nicole. I guess I down-played how bad it was when we were together. Mostly to myself. Then again, sounds like he's spiraling downhill really fast."

I hung up concerned about Justin, while relieved that the divorce was over and he wasn't my concern anymore—in theory. I also worried about the other driver, knowing how frightening it is to be on the other side of Justin's rage.

Patterns repeat themselves. Thus the word, "patterns." In the early fall of 2010, I again faced job loss due to agency fiscal woes. I soon found myself, though, in the running for other local management positions. When I considered those near-offers, like supervising a program for young women who'd survived the horrors of sex-trafficking, I cringed. I didn't have the strength or desire to take on such a crucial, intense role, not now, maybe not ever. The mere thought of returning to social work, in fact, caused trepidation. I needed a break.

I closed Craigslist job listings to sift through pieces of mail on my desk one afternoon, I set my bills aside and perused a flier from the California Writer's Club. A retreat in the Santa Cruz Mountains enticed me, but it was only one week away.

"Is it too late to sign up?" I emailed Fran, the coordinator.

She responded immediately. "We just had a cancellation, so one last space opened up. Jump on it, while you can."

"I'm in. Thanks! Will put a check out asap." I wrote back.

I arrived at the retreat center, exhausted from the long drive through rainy weather and mud-seethed clusters of mountain road. The welcoming ambience impressed with grassy fields, towering redwoods; a large swimming pool; clean, comfortably furnished houses and meeting rooms. There was even a full kitchen in the Orchard House, where I unloaded my things.

Amber, a young hipster writer, roomed with me.

"Wow, can I stay longer than the weekend?" I joked.

"Totally," Amber chanted. "It's like so cool here. I'm couch surfing these days and I could dig this for a while. I'd get a shitload of writing done too."

I smiled and gawked over my shoulder into the main room. "How nice. We even get a fire-place."

Amber and I meandered towards the dining hall.

"So do you write books?" she asked. The question scared me.

"Oh no. Well, maybe someday down the road." I looked towards a lengthy blanket of deep green grass set against the evening sky. "I mostly just write silly stuff about my romantic life. Which isn't at all romantic."

She giggled. "That's cool. Yeah. Dating gives you a lot of good material. I'm gonna write a book about my ex someday too. I still love him, I mean, as a friend. I always will. We've got this incredible vibe between us. We're totally in sync, like across all realms. But I finally decided I couldn't live with him anymore. We just couldn't work it out. You know? He's bipolar and he lost his stepdad when he was like seven so he has abandonment issues and when he's off his meds he like can't manage to get anything done. He never worked, so I had the burden of being the breadwinner. I mean, I really love him. He's a sweetheart, but I realized I had to summon up so much energy for like a simple conversation about taking out the trash or putting his socks away. It's ridiculous. You know? And when something bigger happened, forget it. It was like—"

My mind drifted as we approached the dining hall. Maybe I wanted to block out Amber's ramblings; it touched a nerve. Her ex sounded like Justin. Maybe everyone has a Justin in their past. I guess my story isn't that unique.

Amber was still talking about her ex, I think, when we arrived at the hall.

I managed to dodge Amber when in line for the buffet. She started babbling with everyone she met. I made brief and friendly hand-shake introductions with several men and women, mostly older than me; with strikingly white or graying hair, receding hairlines, or no hair. That's when I first surmised that it takes a very long time to write a book.

We served ourselves heaping servings of spaghetti; Caesar salad; and toasty garlic bread, right out of the oven. I was glad to see that hot chocolate was available too. That always makes me happy.

As I looked for a seat, Fran summoned our attention for introductory words. I sat between two middle-aged women, both of whom relayed quick smiles.

"Emma will be a day late," Fran announced. "Her assistant Patricia left the job, and she's pretty taken aback. I talked her into coming anyway. We love her and always value what she has to offer to the group. So you'll all be able to meet her tomorrow."

I wasn't sure about the significance of that information. A keynote speaker was flustered by her assistant's sudden departure? I didn't know writers have assistants. Cool. They must make good money. At least, this Emma woman must do okay.

My first workshop the next day was on the *pitch*. Having grown up a Dodger fan in the 70s, my brain jumps to Fernando Valenzuela when I hear "pitch".

But writers have their unique way of twisting definitions or coining new-old terms to fit our needs. Like when we want to feel popular and worldly, which is all the time, we call the crap we're writing a WIP for "work in progress" or MS for "manuscript." And when we want a dedicated, sharp self-sacrificing sucker to edit our manuscript for free, we post on our blogs, Twitter and Facebook an "opportunity to be a beta reader." And the catchall phrase for any aspect of writing is "meme." Inside scoop: There's no consensus within the writing community on the definition of "meme," but it's been wildly used for years. Drives me bonkers.

Anyway, today's cause was the need to advertise our (real or imagined) book in a brief enticing blurb that will make it stand out amongst a million competitors. We were to write a pitch in less than fifty words.

I grabbed a pencil and index card, sat contemplatively, did a lot of erasing, kept moving phrases and changing words. Finally, I counted only forty-four. I was golden, but it's silly and needs work.

"Let's see how this worked out," the presenter said. It was time to read our pitches to the group. Crap. My heartbeat hastened. I didn't know we'd have to read them aloud.

One by one, people sounded so professional. I thought about how I don't fit in with all these real writers. I don't know what the hell I'm doing.

But some of them gave long speeches. Really people? She said fifty not five-hundred words. Don't ask a writer to keep it brief.

My turn arrived. "Robyn, you're up next."

I breathed in nervously and pushed my chair back, then stepped over to face the audience.

"This is like the shitty first draft that Anne Lamott talks about," I said, excusing myself in advance. I read:

She's 4'8" of heartfelt ferocity, and nothing can stop this middle-aged livewire from achieving her fairytale—not jolting tragedy, not countless dating disasters, not even the sudden death of a new marriage. Not until Robyn Alana Engel finds her happily-ever-after…alone.

They clapped.

"It's really good," the presenter said.

She said it was really good!? Maybe I could actually write this someday.

Emma puffed out air, took off her black raincoat, and talked about her long, crazy drive. When folks were taking seats with food in hand, I approached, floating on a newfound boost of confidence.

"May I sit with you?" I asked.

"Sure. Have a seat."

I was immediately drawn in by Emma's warm, sincere manner. I liked her spunk too. Emma said she lived in Paradise, a small town several hours north, nestled in pine trees and close to beautiful mountain ranges.

"It sounds wonderful," I said. "I went there with my family when I was a little girl. I have pictures of me feeding chickens in some couple's backyard."

"Yeah, that sounds about right. Do you like small towns, or are you more a big city girl?"

"I think I'd welcome the change of pace. I grew up in LA, and I've been in the Bay Area for almost twenty years. I'm getting tired of the daily frenzy."

I remembered the random coincidence that Justin's ex-girlfriend, Ruthie, the one with no personality, lives in Paradise. But surely she's an anomaly. Paradise sounds like its name.

We were interrupted by a ring-tone. Emma dug her cell phone out of her pocket and looked at its face. "Oh leave me alone already," she said, dropping it back into her pocket. She smirked. "Sheesh. The boy's thirty-two years old and still needs me for everything."

She's at least in her later fifties, I'd say. Clearly she was talking about her son. "Yeah, they never really grow up," I chuckled.

"They sure don't. So do you have kids, Robyn?"

"No. I wanted them, but now I'm starting to feel relieved that it didn't happen." I paused. "I'm just out of a divorce. The kid-window is closed." It's cemented shut, I thought, and then embellished in my head. Electrical barbed-wiring and a highly sensitive alarm system surround the premises, in fact, with glow-in-the-dark "No trespassing if you value your life" signs every few inches. It's tighter than White House security down there.

Fran put her food-filled plate on the other side of Emma. While pulling a chair out, she told Emma, "I'm so glad you're here. Is it a definite that Patricia's gone and not coming back?" It seemed Fran knew, and thought highly of, Emma's former assistant.

"It's 99% likely," Emma answered. "She got some high-level job. I can't compete with the salary they're offering her. She's about to start training." Fran nodded emphatically.

Then, without an ounce of forethought and in nothing but a lackadaisical, mechanical manner, I vocalized these words as they popped into my head: "If you lived closer, I'd sell myself on you. I think you'd be great to work for, and I need a job."

Indifferent to this verbiage that flowed without inhibition, we turned our heads to refocus on the food on our respective plates.

Gulp. What did I just say? Since when am I so opportunistic or confident?

The seed was planted, though. There'd be no turning back.

"Uh, well, but you need someone good with computers. Right?" I challenged. "I stink at that."

"Yes, I really do," she affirmed.

Phew.

"There's something about you, though," she chimed. "And I train my people really good. Really good. You'd be fine."

Gulp.

We realigned our eyeballs on the pasta. Or was it pizza? Wait, was it even lunch? It might have been breakfast or dinner. Maybe chicken? Oh, I don't know. I just remember every fraction of a millisecond of that conversation.

Our faces snapped back to spy each other.

"Well, just *how* bad are you with computers?"

We shared a laugh, knowing my answer didn't matter.

As I walked back to the Orchard House, Dr. Phil visited my head. "This could be a changing moment in your life, he said. Then he repeated, clearly enunciating each syllable, as he is wont to do, "a changing moment in your life." I stopped in my tracks. "A changing—"

"I heard you, Doctor Phil! Quit repeating yourself. I got it!"

Alas, I caught clear and beautiful glimpses of Paradise.

Chapter Sixteen: Oz

"Oh, I" —fumbling, sputtering, stuttering—"pay no...attention to that man behind the curtain. Go, before I lose my temper! The Great and Powerful...Oz...has spoken!"
– The Wizard of Oz, when exposed as a fraud by Dorothy and her friends

---

Before making the move, I checked in with Emma a handful of times. During one of these calls, I spoke with her former assistant.

"Patricia stopped by to visit," Emma said. "I thought I'd put you on the phone with her, to talk about the job."

"Sure, great," I replied.

Patricia's voice projected confidence and encouragement. "You'll learn so much. You'll soak it all up, and it'll be great for your writing."

"Great. Yeah, I'm really looking forward to it." I replied. "Can you tell me a little about the area, the social scene and all? Like would you recommend living in Chico or Paradise? I'm trying to decide."

"Definitely, Chico. There's a lot more to do, and it's a younger population too. But even though there's more to do, we don't really have a shopping mall or—"

"Oh yes we do! Don't scare her away now!" Emma interjected.

"No we don't," Patricia corrected Emma. "Robyn needs to know that there isn't any *real* shopping here. The Chico Mall doesn't count."

Girlie giggles ensued.

"That's alright," I countered. "Is there a Ross?"

"Yes, we have Ross," Patricia informed.

"Then I'm good. That's all I need," I said cheerfully.

Before ending the call, Emma offered Sarah's number. This long-time friend of Emma's had been attempting to rent out her spare room. Sarah would be happy to rent the space to me, while I secured a more permanent housing situation.

A new year, 2011, had ventured into its early stages as I lowered my car window to taste the crisp pine-spiced air. Sarah's house appeared a cozy, woodsy abode, and I parked between trashcans and a majestic oak tree.

Dropping my bright pink duffel bag near the door, I knocked.

Within seconds, I was met by an attractive man, average height, about my age, donning a full mustache, almond eyes, and a cordial grin. God bless Paradise! I liked it already.

"You must be Robyn. Welcome."

"That's me," we shook on it. "Thank you."

"I'll go get mom." He vanished.

Sarah, a stubby woman with red-gray curly hair, appeared and hugged me. "Good to meet you. Come on in. So you met my son, Norman."

"Yeah, it's great to meet you both. Thanks so much for letting me camp out for a few days."

"Oh no problem. I've been trying to rent the space out for a while. Had a few renters, but they come and go so fast, I can't keep track. Let me show ya around."

We walked through the main house to a door that led to a separate space. This side unit was equipped with a mini-kitchen, bedroom, bathroom, and bulky electric wheelchair.

She pointed at the chair. "I'll get that thing out of the way for ya. I only paid $150 for it at an estate sale down the road. Otherwise, these things cost a fortune, and ya never know when ya might become handicapped." True. I supposed, wondering where she'd stored supplies for the already anticipated Apocalypse of 12/12/12.

"Is it pretty safe around here?" I asked, simultaneously shifting gears and setting my bag down.

"Yeah, it's pretty safe, though my purse got stolen from my car one night. And, well," she mumbled, "there are some other more violent crimes."

Note to self: Don't leave purse in car overnight. Note in response to note to self: Why would I do that? Second note to self: This is a hush-hush town. Proceed with caution.

"Mom, I'm going to that health lecture at the church," Norman entered and announced. There's something about the way he said it. I can't put my finger on it, but his emphasis on "health" was eerie. It's as if he's had arguments with her about the validity of church sponsored health lectures, or as if he's got some embarrassing medical condition that they don't discuss openly, or as if she has simply been wanting him—a middle-aged man who's living with his mother—to get out of the house from time to time. At any rate, my attraction died that moment. I'd also lock my bedroom door, just in case.

The next day, as I reviewed housing listings in Sarah's living room, Norman stampeded through shouting, "Draconian measures!

Draconian measures!" He's not talking to me, is he? I spun the chair around, and yes, he was.

"This is outrageous! A 12-hundred dollar ticket for driving without my lights on, and it was daytime! It's that stretch of freeway between here and Sacramento. Watch out over there. They get you every time. Take another route, or keep your car lights on for the whole drive. They're looking to steal from as many drivers as they can."

"Twelve hundred? That is outrageous." I was puzzled and slightly amused. He uttered something about not having his insurance card, or not having insurance, so they hiked up the fees.

"Draconians!" Norman scoffed.

I had no idea who these Draconians were, and why they stalk interstate 80. It didn't seem the proper time to ask about this, though. "That sounds criminal!" I agreed, with all the sympathy I could muster.

"You bet it is. If you can't drive, you can't travel. You can't travel, you don't have the right to peaceful assembly. The government is robbing us of our freedoms. I'm going to fight this thing to the full extent possible."

The man knows his constitutional rights. I envisioned him handing me a sturdy, colonial style rifle and commanding, "March with me, woman!" We'd go parading down the streets of Paradise, armed with finely polished weaponry, shouting "Freedom from Draconian measures! Down with Draconia!" I'd do the beauty pageant wave and become very popular in my new stomping ground.

Instead, Norman cooled down and left the room.

If those Draconians have anything to do with Dracula, I thought, I'm definitely on his side. Dracula's side, that is.

I scrolled through listings and ruled out the many renters seeking someone who's "420 friendly." I also ruled out a "newly remolded" apartment unit, and one described as "close to cancer." Good Lord, could they possibly have meant "close to campus"? What a horrifying misspell.

A few prospects presented themselves, and I soon found myself touring a phlebotomist's house. While I wasn't keen on cohabitation with someone who draws blood for a living, I'd have my own bedroom and bathroom.

But Phlebby's windows were covered in plastic wrap. Weird.

"It keeps the heat in," Phlebby explained. "And we won't put the temperature any higher than 58 degrees Fahrenheit, to save on heating costs." Fifty-eight? I'll freeze to death.

That was the first time I'd ever seen windows insulated by plastic wrap. Now, having lived in this area for several years, it's the last time I'd seen saran-wrapped windows. And Phlebby.

Jason offered my next best hope. He showed me his family's third property: an expansive, new house that I would eventually share with three others. At that time, he informed, I was the only prospective renter. We chatted for a good hour, during which Jason provided tips on the neighborhood, social scene and eateries.

"Go to El Patron," he said. "Their nachos are the best. My son and I love them."

I thanked Jason for all the pointers and asked for a housing application. Jason hesitated before handing me one. "I do need to call my wife," he clarified. "She takes care of all the details in the lease."

Jason stepped into the kitchen to make the call. I admired the clean, cream colored walls and white brick fireplace.

He walked back in, phone in hand. "She said if you're interested, you can bring the completed application by our place this evening at six." I agreed.

I located their house at 5:59pm that evening, then found myself in a family meeting, mafia style. "Sit there," Jason's wife commanded, pointing at a very high stool at the very high kitchen table. Climbing onto it, I was watched by mother, Jason and son, already seated quietly.

"We want to answer all of your questions," Sergeant Mother began, "but there are lots of people interested in the house. I'm showing it to a family this Friday. Our son might move back in too."

I smiled at the son, who looked about twenty. He didn't flinch, maintaining a serious focus on me and his mom.

"I'll make my decision by Saturday," Sergeant said. I expected some knuckle cracking. Instead, Jason and the guy maintained a stern silence as Sergeant Mother studied my application.

"So you'll be working for Emma Munney?" she stated.

"Yes. That's why I'm moving here." She's heard of Emma—good sign.

"I'm publishing my third book now," she nodded, as if she knows all the ins-and-outs of the publishing business. "Uh mm, so you'll be sending emails and little tasks of that nature?"

"Yes. Things like that." I grinned. Come to think of it, I didn't know what I'd be doing. In fact, I didn't know what Emma did. I just wanted to work for a writer, as a writer. Fame and fortune would ensue.

A swelling tension filled the room. I felt the others' eyes on me. Was I—a responsible, quiet, professional, single, non-420 friendly woman in her 40s—good enough to even submit my application for one bedroom in their third property?

The clock ticked loudly.

"Just to inform you," Sergeant continued, "we reserve the right to request a co-signer if, say, the renter is beginning a new job. Here's a copy of the lease." Sergeant pushed a small stapled packet of papers at me. "If we chose you, you'd be required to sign on for six months." She paused. "I can't think of anything else. Any questions?"

Before I had a chance to respond, she concluded our meeting: "It was a rough day at work, and I'm hungry. Nice meeting you." Sergeant extended her hand and relayed a firm shake.

Thankfully, she let go. I was relieved to make my escape.

As I traversed to my car, I flipped through the seven page lease, fraught with enough legal minutiae to keep our nation's healthcare plan at a stalemate. "Renter must take garbage cans to the curb by 0700AM on Thursdays or will be subject to execution." Talk about draconian! Oh, maybe it read "eviction". Either way, I ripped the packet apart and tossed the shreds on the passenger's seat of my car.

Back at Sarah's house, I collected the lease scraps and dumped them into her big green recycling bin.

The next day, I reconnected with Stephen. I'd emailed him about his house before I left town, but when I realized he's a he, I cancelled our appointment.

Note to you, dear reader: As you probably gathered by now, I don't have good luck with men. So I could only envision myself living cooperatively with a female.

But female prospects weren't boding well, and Stephen graciously agreed to reschedule.

When I arrived at his house, I was greeted by Stephen and his black tabby.

He swooped up the cat. "This is Mojo." He smiled. "He's usually a good boy, and he doesn't spray, so you don't have to worry about that."

I reached out to stroke Mojo's head. He stared at me suspiciously, while welcoming the attention. "Hi, Mojo," I said. "I love his name, and he seems sweet."

"Yeah, he's rambunctious too, but he's usually a sweetie."

Stephen snuggled Mojo and kissed his head, then lowered the cat to the floor. "Go ahead, boy." Mojo raced through the kitchen and out the cat door.

Stephen and I proceeded to have a friendly exchange in a nice, comfortable home that would allow sufficient privacy and room for my furniture.

I'd found my home in Chico, eight miles from Paradise, Stephen and Mojo as my two male housemates.

Life by Chocolate blog post, 2/9/11: With both housing and the job secured up North, I shall awake to bid farewell to the San Francisco Bay in twenty days. I'll miss its bold beauty and flavorful culture: the taquerias every few feet in San Francisco's mission district, the bridges spanning broad stretches of shimmering water, the diverse communities that have offered my heart and brain entry into more tranquil enlightenment. I'll miss having 12,000 choices for everything – be it a yoga class, movie venue, ice-cream parlor, or underwater co-ed rollerblading midget sumo wrestling clothing optional, smoke-free match. You can find it all here.

Life by Chocolate blog post, 2/27/11: As I was having discourse with myself about leaving the Bay Area, I also told me, "You can't leave your blog community." Then, I said to me, "Okay now you are being way too silly" - with a gentle dope-slap to the forehead. "They're a virtual community. Hello! That means, they live all over. You'll actually be closer to your Canadian blog friends like Marnie and Kal, and your Northern blog buddies like IT and Pearl. Yeah, you'll be a little further away from some others, but they will stick around. (Fingers crossed.) In fact, they'll come along for the journey." And so I hope you will. Your support means so much.

A cool breeze rustled my hair as I sat on the front porch of Emma's office (or so I thought), anxiously anticipating my first day of work. Ten minutes into waiting nervously, a lively, slender woman bounced over to me. She adorned stringy golden brown hair, bright pink lipstick, a turquoise turtleneck sweater, and otherwise all black (pants, boots and jacket).

"Oh, there you are. You must be Robyn. It's great to meet you" she said, offering a hug. "I'm Heidi. You're in the wrong place," she giggled and flapped her hand down as if to say "No biggie." "It's a little confusing. This one's Emma and George's house. Emma's office is over there." Heidi pointed out a rustic cabin on the same lot about fifty yards away. "Come, I'll show you."

We stepped into the office, where Emma sat with a man I'd never seen before. A small table centered the space. Emma and I hugged briefly. "Our fantastic newest team member made it! Woohoo!"

"Thank you, Emma," I beamed. I'm so glad to be here!"

"So you met Heidi."

"Yes, I did." I looked towards Heidi, who nodded officially, and then took a seat.

Turning to the man, who looked about 40, Emma said, "And this is Darryl." As I shook hands with Darryl, I noticed a fully tattooed arm leading down to a shiny brass wedding band.

"Great. Great to meet you." I felt more elated than nervous at this point.

Emma motioned to the four chairs that squared-off a small card-table. "So we're going to have a meeting to start us off." It was like the pre-game huddle. Go team, go! "Why don't you say a little bit about yourselves, and then we'll talk business strategies. Heidi, you start."

"Sure," Heidi replied. It took no time to realize that Heidi's a fast and furious talker. Unlike most talkers, however, Heidi's babble fascinates. I hung onto her every word.

"Well, I've been helping Emma for three years since I started having back problems from the trapeze," she started. "I was with Barnum and Bailey for seven years. It was so much fun, I have to tell you. But I'll talk more about that some other time. Oh, the stories. Anyway, before that, I played electric guitar and sang with a rock band called the Raisers." She smirked. "It's short for Hell Raisers. Oh yeah, we had a blast, but now I'm way too old for that. My guitar's so rusty." She guffawed. "I don't even know where it is. I think it's in our two-car garage, or maybe my bedroom closet—"

"Okay, Heidi," Emma joked, pulling her watch to her face.

"Oh, sorry," Heidi continued. "Long story short, carpel tunnel took the best of me and, though I used to have 20/20 vision, I have progressed astigmatism in both eyes now and can barely see without very thick bifocals. So Robyn, I never learned computers. I'm really glad you're here. I can't sit in front of a computer. It hurts my eyes too much. My husband—"

The door cracked open. "Speaking of husbands," Emma said. A heavy-set, red-bearded man entered, carrying a few small logs. "Sorry," he whispered, headed towards the furnace against the far wall.

"It's okay, Honey. Come over and meet Robyn."

With his head drooping downward, the man timidly approached me. "I'm George." I could barely hear him.

"Nice to meet you. I'm Robyn." I offered a firm handshake. He didn't respond, turned towards the door and left briskly.

Emma gave the floor to Darryl, as if nothing had just happened. I gathered George is the quiet, anti-social type.

Everyone else around Paradise seemed to enjoy the act of discourse, perhaps too much.

Darryl was a babbler. He shared that he's married to Emma's hairdresser's sister, Peggy. Darryl started datin' Peggy after breaking up with Dyanna. By the way, Dyanna is spelt with a "y." It's "d,y,a,n,n,a." An' Peggy's been waitin' tables at the Cozy Diner on Skyway. They have good pies. Darryl and Peggy live four houses away. Dyanna and her new husband, William, live next-door to them. Will's a good guy. He manages an auto shop down in Chico.

Darryl finally got to the point: "I started working for Emma last week and I'm doing, I think advertising stuff, right?" He looked at Emma, uncertain.

She nodded in confirmation.

"I'll also be doing some gardening. There are lots of weeds that I need to pull up."

Emma nodded again.

My turn. I gave a brief intro, mentioning my publication in Being Single Magazine and expressing eagerness to help in any way possible.

That day, I started a newsletter and familiarized myself with Emma's computer and paper files. Heidi showed me where I could find miscellaneous office supplies, and did some dusting. Darryl took a lot of cigarette breaks outside.

Emma sent us home at four o'clock that day. That was nice.

When she handed me my first paycheck, I realized it amounted to pay for thirty-five, not forty, hours.

As happy as I was to be there, I couldn't let this go. My salary was already too dismal.

I turned to her. "Emma, I see that I'm being paid for thirty-five, not forty hours. Is that right?"

"Hm, mm. I've let you go early several times this week, haven't I?" She sat at her desk, reading a document.

"Well, yeah, but I stayed until six on Wednesday, and yesterday we ended early because we didn't get a computer signal." I never asked to leave early either; you told me to.

"Okay, then don't stay later. Leave at four every day." Wow. You're not so warm and nice anymore.

"But you agreed to pay me hourly for a forty hour work-week."

She kept focused on her reading. "I don't remember that," Emma remarked sharply.

"Well I do," I asserted.

No response.

My mind flashed back to the phone conversation in which I confirmed my hourly rate and specifically inquired as to whether I'd be paid for a 40 hour work-week. I wouldn't have moved my life before factoring in my prospective salary. She had said "Yes, I'll pay you for forty," and, "Get here quickly. I need your help."

Crap. Now, I had to make this work. It meant too much, so I dropped the issue.

The next day, I plugged away at a newsletter. My main article addressed time-management. "Time, life's most precious commodity," I started, and proceeded to expel tips for writers to most effectively maximize their writing time. I wrote a solid article and newsletter.

In fact, I felt pretty good about my overall progress. I'd been busily networking, reviewing manuscripts, and keeping her social media forums current.

As anxious as I was about learning new computer programs, I dipped my toes in immediately—not that I didn't completely flounder and lose a file or two along the way, but I did alright. Meanwhile, I continued to wait for that "really good" training Emma had initially promised.

When I finished the newsletter, I asked if I should put my name on it. "No, my name's fine," Emma responded curtly.

Thus my writing was distributed with full credit to Emma. While flattered, I also felt cheated and wondered about professional ethics —hers, in particular.

On my third week, Darryl was gone. Heidi whispered to me, "It just wasn't working out with Darryl."

"I'm not too surprised," I said. "But I hope things don't get awkward between everyone involved."

"Oh no, it's like one big happy, boundary-less family," she chided, giving me an elbow nudge.

"Good morning!" Emma came into the office, briefcase in hand.

We said our hellos. I glanced at the clock: 11:03 a.m. It seemed Emma's mornings were starting later and later.

Further, Emma was often not around. I fielded phone-calls: "I never got the book I paid for" and "I went to her workshop at the scheduled time and correct location, but nobody was there."

I was beginning to realize that what I changed my life for, *who* I changed my life for, wasn't as appeared.

But I had to make it work. There was too much at stake.

There were fun moments, and I chose to focus on those. "My new job is great," I told friends and family. "I'm doing well, and it's a beautiful area."

As Emma, Heidi and I wrapped up week four at the office, Emma said she had yet to see my blog.

"Oh, it's just silly humorous stuff like my series 'On Why I Choose Celibacy.' I post men's on-line dating ads to mock them. I just gave an award to a guy I call 'Mr. Cemetery.' He's looking for mutual cemetery in a relationship."

Confused, Emma asked, "You mean someone to share a cemetery plot with?"

"No," I answered. "I think he means 'chemistry.' He wrote, 'If the cemetery's good, everything else can fail.'"

Emma and I guffawed.

"Well, I've gotta say," Heidi proclaimed in a didactic manner, "sexual chemistry in the cemetery can be significantly profound."

Emma and I gasped.

"Well, he was my husband," Heidi added.

Emma and I shared an almost forced giggle, eyes glazed over.

"And it was during the winter!"

We sat reticent. Heidi clearly wanted to elaborate but stopped short. The conversation died with this revelation about sex in the cemetery. To this day, I can't help but revere Heidi for that story. God bless her.

Emma arrived close to noon, telling me that Heidi would no longer be working there. "I have you now, so I don't need her anymore," she said.

"Oh, okay. Well, I'll miss her, but I'll get more done."

"Yes, she is a talker." Emma joked.

"Yeah," I laughed, hiding my disappointment. It felt tense without Heidi there, and she'd become a friend.

Then Emma took a call on her cellphone.

"Hi, Patricia. How are you?...Good. It's alright. How's your job going?...Oh. That's not good. Say listen, I'm thinking about something..." Her voice trailed off as she stepped out the door.

Emma came back ten or so minutes later. "Patricia's having a really hard time in her new job," she told me. "I guess she's on her own to figure out some complicated computer tasks. She's really good with computers, but they're not supporting her at all."

I said, "That's too bad."

"Hm mm." She returned to the writing on her desk. I suddenly feared being replaced by the gal I'd just replaced. But no. I moved my life for this job. I had to make it work. I'd just started. It couldn't come to that.

Meanwhile, I strived to birth a social and dating life. As the new girl in town, I assumed this would be easy. "I'm anxious to explore the area," I wrote in a personal ad. "I'm gladly accepting applications for a nice tour guide. PS I like chocolate."

Matthew responded. He's a writer. Well, relatively speaking. By this I mean that, unlike the others, Matthew writes in complete sentences. In fact, we had a nice telephone conversation on Sunday. I elaborated on my stuck-in-the-mud-on-a-date story; the one wherein I was stranded overnight in the middle of the desert with Kenny. We had no cellphones. It was cold. I thought I'd die. Kenny offered only a stale Oreo cookie—which I gratefully accepted.

"In the end," I concluded, "we made it out okay. I broke up with him shortly after arriving home safely."

Matthew was thrilled to hear it. "So the bar's set pretty low, huh?"

"You got that right." I responded. "Bring me a stale Oreo cookie, and you're the man!"

We agreed to meet at Tea Fusion on Saturday.

I'd finally fallen into a dream-state. Something slammed against my bedroom door, jolting me awake. There was creaking, and then there was my door sliding open, and then there was Mojo on the pillow next to me. "How'd you do that, cat?"

I'd locked and closed the bedroom door. Maybe not hard enough. Though flustered, I admired Mojo's perseverance and resourcefulness. Plus I was too tired to move him. Resigned, I peered at my unexpected bed guest.

"Look, sweetie," I told him, "if any boy's going to be so desperate for my company as to pummel through my locked bedroom door in the middle of the night, I prefer that boy be a man, a nice and smart one with, for example, testosterone. Alright? Go find one for me."

Mojo stared with faux innocent green-yellowish irises that lent credibility to his deep black pupils. He didn't budge. I turned my head away from him and closed my eyes. "Good night, silly boy."

My sleep interrupted by a cat, I had low energy at work the next day.

Come time to leave, I had to pee. One problem with Emma's office is that it lacked a restroom. I'd thus become used to walking to her house, opening the door and trekking through the living-room to use the bathroom.

"I just need to make a quick bathroom run before I leave," I told Emma.

As I hopped towards the house, I enjoyed the crunching sound of leaves under my feet. I don't remember opening the door, but I had. And I stood motionless at the doorstep, numbed by a shocking sight. Slightly to my right was the kitchen. Clearly within view, standing in said kitchen, was George. Naked. Completely, unashamedly naked; fat, round, and pink like a grapefruit but not nearly as pleasant an image.

Naked George didn't hear me or see me. He lackadaisically sliced some greens on a built-in cutting board. Fortunately the cutting board hid from view the worst of it—small enough to be blocked from view by a cutting board.

Gulp. What do I do? I have to pee. I couldn't walk through the house, so I quickly turned back and jetted towards the office.

"Um, Emma, this is kind of embarrassing but I couldn't use the restroom because of George."

"Oh don't mind him. He sometimes gets off early." I hate to think how he gets off.

"No, it's not that. It's that he was standing there in the kitchen—"

"Yeah, what? He was in the kitchen doing what?"

I tossed the words at her in one fast breath. "He was totally naked."

"Oy vey, I told that man not to walk around the house naked," she stated. "You know, a few of my girlfriends drove by the other day and saw him through the windows. They said 'Well that's too much information!' I'll call him."

She dug into her bag for her cellphone. "Honey, Robyn went over there just now to use the restroom...Yeah, well, what are you doing now?...Hm, hmm. Hm, hmm. And what are you wearing? Do you know she just saw you?...Okay, bye."

He said, "I wish you hadn't told me that."

Bizarre response, I thought. He wishes he didn't know that I know that he's standing there at the cutting-board completely naked, and now Emma knows that I know that he knows that I know that he was standing at the cutting-board completely naked? How about wishing to curb his inclinations to stand at the cutting-board completely naked, when his wife's employees might need to use the facilities?

"Go ahead and use the restroom now," Emma directed. "He'll be in the bedroom. You won't see him."

I nervously walked over again. This time, I didn't see him, and the cutting-board had been pushed back into place.

It was Friday, Good Friday in fact, and the end of my seventh week on the job. I awoke in upbeat spirits. I'd go from work to a Passover Seder[22] with the Jewish group that meets for worship interestingly enough, at a Presbyterian Church.

Brandi and I had agreed to meet there. She was the only other single woman in the bunch, as far as I could tell. Brandi exudes a good mixture of compassion and sass, and she's a Bay Area transplant like me.

In a mood to dress-up that morning, I changed into my red-knit sweater and long black skirt that drapes down to my ankles.

When I arrived at work that morning, I shut my car door as George departed the office, fully dressed.

"Good morning," I cheered, as though I hadn't seen him completely naked at the kitchen cutting-board, or as though I was happy to harbor the image.

George said nothing, failing to even look my way. I guessed he was especially embarrassed, though I didn't know why he'd be leaving the office so early in the morning. Something seemed off.

I opened the door to find Emma sitting at the front room table, awaiting my arrival. Something *was* off.

"This isn't working, Robyn," she said, before I could say anything. "You're costing me too much," she continued. "I pay you even more than I paid Patricia."

Many thoughts raced through my brain: It's been breaking me to try to make this work. I can't afford a pair of socks or even a crummy stash of paperclips. Patricia isn't a writer, and she didn't relocate from the Bay Area for you. Come to think of it, are you an author? How many novels have you written? Oh yeah, zero.

Emma brought her elbow up to the table-top and leaned her head against her open palm. Eyebrows raised and in a pitying tone that sliced with derision, she informed, "I'm sure you'll find SOMETHING that you're good at."

She pushed a large white trash-bag across the table. "Here are your things and your final paycheck." I glanced in the bag and saw a business envelope containing my final paycheck, mini-thesaurus, wall calendar, and a handful of ginger-peach teabags. Is that it? What's she keeping?

I walked past her and over to my now former desk. "I'm going to make sure that's everything."

Emma snapped angrily, "It's everything!"

I hovered over the desk and didn't see anything else of mine. I quickly looked through the drawers. Nothing.

I walked back towards Emma and took the bag. Composed, I asserted, "I can't believe you're doing this to me. You're impossible to work for, always forgetting things and making mistakes. I moved here for you, but you didn't even give me a chance."

"Needless to say"—her voice reached a dictatorial tone—"I AM the boss."

I turned to the door. "I hope you find someone you're happy with."

I can still see myself then: clenching a large Glad trash-bag, I stood near the door-frame in a long black skirt and red-knit sweater, back towards Emma. I stepped out, taking with me an all-too familiar mixture of integrity and rejection.

Teardrops moistened my hands as I gripped the wheel. I can't believe this. What do I do now? I asked myself. "You'll be okay," I said. "You've been through worse. Everything's going to be alright." My voice, Mom's voice comforted me.

Mom! Damnit! Emma kept my poem that I'd tacked to the corkboard behind the computer screen. I forgot to look there. I didn't want her to have my poetry, especially not that one. I wouldn't go back, though. I had copies of it at home.

Almost hypnotically, and while seeing my hands gripped in a ten o'clock, two o'clock position on the way downhill to Chico, I recited the poem I'd written recently as a tribute to Mom…

"Kindred spirits, you and I. Fragile souls, enduring ties. Secrets known, never shared. Countless fears, never scared. So much achieved, though never proud. So much lost, though not aloud. My ground, my heart, my love and calm. My kindred spirit. My soul. My Mom." [23]

We never let go.

In Chico, I pulled into a Bank of America parking lot and took out my phone.

"Heidi," I said through tears, "Sorry I didn't call you before now. It felt awkward. Emma did the same thing to me. She just laid me off. I can't believe it."

"Oh sweetie, I'm sorry. I'm surprised. With mine, I expected it. You know, she'd stopped paying me months ago."

"You're kidding!"

"No, but it's alright. I told her it'd be good experience to volunteer. She means well. She's just bad at being organized."

"I moved my whole life here for her. God, I'm naïve."

"Robyn, you have wonderful skills. I know you'll be fine. I know it doesn't help right now to hear that, though. But, really, I've seen you work hard and I've read your writing, and you're so friendly. You'll find a much better place that appreciates you. And who knows? Maybe you'll even meet the man of your dreams. Maybe that's why you moved here."

"I just, I'm just…in shock right now. I can't believe how heartless she is. How did Patricia put up with her?"

"I don't know," Heidi said. "There's really attached, but they fought like cats and dogs."

"That's weird."

It suddenly struck me that this wasn't about me. My angst lightened somewhat. This was about Emma and Patricia's unhealthy attachment. I bet she re-hired Patricia. Those types of toxic connections fester and pull us back in, time and again.

Maybe that's why I was drawn to Emma, and Justin before her, and all the men who weren't good for me. Maybe it all goes back to Dad, my need for love and acceptance from people who have little to offer.

It's not that I've chosen any of this, but I suppose my unconscious has. Damn unconscious. It knows so much more than we do.

I'm so naïve, I thought. I don't notice anyone's potential to take advantage of me until they already have. I thought Emma was a good choice, because she's *not* a man; my issues were only with men. Not true. My issues were with everyone. Then again, I realized, that's not true either. My issues were with only one person: myself.

It was time to stop chasing a dream through others. I needed to give it to myself, to count only on myself to make my life what I want it to be.

I also needed to cancel my date with Matthew.

"I'm sorry," I told him. "I'm in a really bad space right now and need to cancel our plans."

"Are you okay?" he asked, compassionately.

"Yeah, I mean, I guess I will be. I'm shocked and upset right now. Something happened today and, well, I lost my job that I moved here for."

"I'm sorry to hear that, honey. It's tough times."

Matthew's compassion moved me to cancel the cancellation.

"Now call Brandi," I said aloud and to myself.

Her immediate response to my job situation was, "Do you want me to come over?"

"You're sweet, Brandi. No it's okay. I just need to be depressed. I don't know if I'm going to the Seder tonight.

"Well, Robyn, I'm here. If you decide to go, we can go out afterwards, or you can always leave early if you don't feel like staying."

"Thanks, Brandi. I just can't believe she pulled the rug out from under me like that. Maybe I will go tonight. I don't know what else to do with myself…besides cry."

"I'm sorry, Robyn. Are you sure you don't want me to come over?"

"Well…no, but I'll go tonight. Thank you, Brandi."

One positive thing about the Passover Seder is the inclusion of four cups of wine. As I sat next to Brandi, I couldn't help but continuously reach for the Concord Grape Manischevitz staring at me, as if to say, "Come on, Robyn. Be a good Jew. Drink me four times and four more times than four times more than that."

I poured my fourth cup, and Brandi laughed. (Mind you, we're talking about little Dixie cups.) Everyone else appeared focused on the service which hadn't yet taken us to the second cup of wine.

"Are you okay, Robyn?" Brandi joked.

"I think I need another cup of wine, before I can answer that. And I'll probably need a ride home too," I goaded.

The time arrived. I waited at Chico's Tea Fusion Café.

I waited longer.

Fifteen minutes later, Matthew called, lost. I was annoyed. Yet another fifteen minutes later, I headed back to my car.

Then, a fair-skinned brunette ever-so casually steered his car into the parking lot. I recognized him from the photos in his ad. Matthew parked, jumped out and approached me.

"I was about to leave. I don't like waiting," I barked.

He smiled warmly.

"You didn't have a GPS or directions?" I asked. My navigational skills equally challenged, I imagined the pair of us capturing the title of the Biggest Losers on The Amazing Race, then voting each other off the island but being stuck with Gilligan and Mrs. Howell, too inept to find a way out.

"Yeah, waiting isn't fun." He understood. "My Mapquest directions were wrong. Oh, well. Wanna grab a bite?" Matthew held a smile.

Matthew craved the small-town, pseudo-gourmet feasts provided by Applebee's. This would've involved further navigation by motor vehicle, so I suggested Chipotle, an easy walk from there.

"It's my treat," he said upon arrival. With that, I dropped the last of my irritation.

Our lunch discourse was fascinating until it started. Then, I was nearly propelled into R.E.M. sleep by talk of carburetors, generators, alternators, and other four-syllable *ors* and *ers*. All I could do to stay stimulated was think about vibrators.

"Sorry if I'm boring you."

No, it's…it's alright." I can't believe I almost told him his diatribe isn't boring.

I should add that Matthew's patriotic. He'd joined the military during the Reagan era. Proudly, Matthew said, "Reagan is still my President."

Not good. Not good at all. I can't date someone for whom Reagan is President. Never mind that Reaganomics devastated the social service programs that Kennedy spearheaded, and my career field would never fully recover. This aside, Matthew seemed nice. I didn't want to have to inform him that Reagan was dead.

Matthew escorted me to my car at the Tea Fusion parking lot.

That's when it happened. He reached out and blanketed me in his warm, non-threatening arms. I decided I'd earned and needed this nice hug, so I relaxed in Matthew's embrace.

It was just a hug, and we wouldn't see each other again. But it wasn't just a hug. It was a moment on the verge of Paradise that would see me through.

I arrived home to Mojo, running up to greet me, and Stephen, watching TV in the living room.

"Hi, Stephen."

"Hey, Robyn. How's it going?"

"Well, not good, actually. I just lost my job yesterday."

He took the remote and lowered the volume.

"Yeah," I continued, "the job I moved my life for. I plan to say here and everything. I just need a new job. I can't believe I'm in this position so soon after I moved.

Stephen conveyed an expression of empathy. "I've gone through job loss too. I'm sorry, but you'll find something else around here, I'm sure."

"Come by and visit us. We love entertaining writers!" I read this email and shouted, "Fuckin idiots!" It appeared Patricia had sent the message to Emma's distribution list.

After conniving to replace me, that bitch didn't think to remove me from her email contacts? Does she think I'll buy her novels? Did she forget that she didn't write any novels? And what the hell kind of message is this? You love entertaining writers? Does this mean that you only love the writers of the humor genre? Or writers in the zombie or vampire world? Or that you've prepared a song and dance routine for writers' entertainment? Is buttered popcorn available? What's the fee? It might be worth my time and investment.

I wrote back, simply, "REMOVE!!"

Weeks later, I saw Patricia at the local Barnes and Noble Café. I recognized her from her Facebook page. She sat and chatted with a very attractive man. Don't be mad or jealous, I told myself. For one, that's probably her brother. Second, she likely didn't plot against me. Emma's the ruthless one.

But Patricia's gorgeous appearance, lack of a belly, and tight curly golden-brown hair fueled intense envy.

I watched Patricia and her male company stand up. They merely shook hands "goodbye." I felt better instantly; there wasn't a lip-lock.

It got even better when I noted that Patricia's blue jeans dropped straight down her backside; she had no butt. I have something that woman doesn't, I thought proudly. I have a butt, and mine's ever growing, down and out, inch by inch, day by day. Relief and vindication achieved; Patricia has a lousy job with a faux expert, and I have a real ass.

As I pressed my mocha to my lips, I thought, right now, all is right with the world.

Chapter Seventeen: Rebooting

In February, 2014, as I write this chapter, Sunset Magazine reported that Chico, California tied with Bend, Oregon as the best US city in which to "reboot your life."

"You piece of shit!" I screamed madly, glaring at a black tadpole shaped figure spinning in circular frenzy atop my otherwise comatose computer screen. Blood raged through my corpuscles. An hour had passed since I planted myself at my desktop P.C., planning to read job listings and distribute my resume to prospective employers. The angst of not receiving a paycheck, going on two months now, set me afire.

But my damn computer refused to cooperate. I couldn't even re-boot; it wouldn't shut down. What the hell!?

Let me explain my emotional unraveling. Computer problems induce in me feelings of utter incompetence and stupidity. I also tend to liken these glitches to my existence, if only for the sake of silliness. For example:

- Problems with the hard drive mean I'll never find a man who can have an erection.
- Software issues = same as above.
- Problems with memory = Alzheimer's inevitability.
- Viruses= I'll get STDs without having had sex.
- Browser snafus = Vision problems. I'll go blind. Too much masturbation.
- Rebooting issues = Full-proof strategies that work for everyone else in the world won't help me, because I'm incredibly incompetent and unlucky in every way. I'll never connect with anything or anyone worthy for any length of

time before losing everything and everyone worthy of any of my time. To make matters worse, I can't even successfully give-up and shut-down.

"Damn piece of shit!" I punched the keys consecutively. "Control...Alt...Delete!" I tried again. "Control. Alt. Delete. Still nothing!"

I switched up the order. "Alt...Delete...Control...Damn! Delete...Control, Alt."

Growling, I pounded all three keys simultaneously.

Then again. Again. And again, like a starved lab rat madly pressing a lever to get a scrap of food.

I shoved up to a stand, slammed my chair over, and pounced belly-down onto my bed.

Emotions cascaded through me, as I reached for a box of tissue below the nightstand. Aware that Stephen wouldn't be home for hours, I permitted my histrionics to continue in full-force.

"Nothing works! I wailed. "Not one God damned thing!"

My eyes unleashed a gulf of salty water. "I can't even make anything better. It keeps getting more and more fucked up!" I dug into the tissue box and padded my face.

"Damn her! I moved my life for her. She fuckin ruined it." In a snarky, high-pitched toned, I mimicked Emma: 'I'm sure you'll find SOMETHING that you're good at.' Fuckin bitch!" Why do people always treat me like shit? Justin was worst, or best, at it.

"God damnit Justin!" I punched my mattress with both fists. "I gave you everything, and you destroyed me. You fuckin shredded us

343

into pieces. I loved you with every ounce of me. How could you do this to us?" I blew out a glob of mucous. "I never wanted to lose you, especially not like that."

I shifted my head on the pillow and caught a blurry glimpse of my pink, ceramic rose on the nightstand— the rose I'd painted on what unbeknownst to me would be the final night of my marriage. The one and only thing I did just for me, for self-care, during my relationship with Justin. Everything else I did during those three years was for him or for *our* future. The future that he killed.

I took in a wisp of cool bedroom air. Dampness trickled down both sides of my nose.

The door freed open and Mojo rushed in and jumped on my bed. He curled up beside me, as uninvited as he was welcomed.

I stroked Mojo's shiny black fur. He stared at me, a semblance of my smile greeting him.

"How'd you know to burst in right now, silly boy?"

Mojo meowed in response, before sinking into a nap. "Yeah, I know. I'm boring you with this self-pity crap." I rested a hand on his head. "I'm boring me too, sweetie-pie. I mean,"—I blow my nose into a wad of tissue—"I'm a good person, right? Damnit, I *am* good. And I've gotten through much worse than this. I'll be fine. We know this. Don't we, Mojo?" I heard the murmurs of a faint cat-snore. My tears slowed, as I emitted a quiet giggle.

The rose came into clear view. Speckles of light jumped off its petals like crystals of reality, and rationale took hold.

It's ridiculous, I realized, to let others make or break me. A destructive old habit. I couldn't win with Dad; I'd never get his consistent love and approval.

Emma taught me that it's not only men who will crush me. I quickly fell in non-romantic love with a woman who'd bring me a different kind of fairytale. And I'd live happily ever after thanks to her.

"It's bullshit! Right, boy?" Mojo didn't budge, but continued a subtle purr.

I pulled myself up and off of the bed. Leaning over Mojo, I kissed his back. Then I wandered into the bathroom.

Edging my head into the sink, I splattered lukewarm water onto my face and grabbed a pink washcloth from the towel rack. Sighing, I dabbed my face.

I looked wide-eyed at the mirror, as if in a trance. For the first time in my life, as I glanced at the mirror, I saw Mom's face—her kind, calm, loving face. "Pretty lady," I whispered. We've shared so much, I realized…blue eyes; fair, freckled skin; curly hair tinged with auburn streaks. Loss, secrets, and living to please others. We'd both been damn good at that, huh, Mom? Not so good at loving ourselves.

Water dripped from my hair. Drying the ends with the washcloth, I pondered the fact that Mom always had short hair; mine was never so short. She was always tamer and more soft-spoken than me too. I'm the feisty one who lives out loud, whereas Mom played by the rules. "Fake it 'til you feel it," she'd advise. It's not bad advice, just not always a genuine or courageous way to live. I don't settle like Mom did, and that's a good thing.

So many realizations spiraled through me, I trekked into my room and dug up my dear old diary.

<u>May 7, 2011:</u> Dear Di, I need a new angle, to be more positive, you know? Of course you do. You've accepted all my negativity since we met. For starters, I'm going to call you Liv instead of Di. Di is too morbid. It's time I focus on life and the good stuff. I've been doing it all wrong: believing that someone or something else would lift me out of despair and into lifelong happiness. That's bullshit. I don't think Mom was generally unhappy, Liv. But I'm certain she gave up a lot of herself to become a wife and mother. We've seen some of her artwork and writing that she did before she met Dad. It's amazing. She didn't do any of that after they married. I'm not sure what I'm trying to say, Liv. I do know that, like Mom, I've accomplished a lot. Unlike Mom, I haven't secured the traditional fairytale. But maybe this difference between us speaks as much, or more, to my fortune and strengths as it does to my bad luck and deficits. I won't stay with someone who disrespects me. I'm lucky I got out of the marriage when I did, and that Justin didn't physically hurt me. I'm lucky to be in Chico now, even though I don't have the job I moved here for. It felt like home right away. Anyway, I love you and let's face it, you're me. You're my insides. Pouring out my soul to you all these years has gotten me here. Thank you.

I placed Liv back into my desk drawer and walked over to the bathroom door-frame. I studied the image in the mirror. "One more thing, lady," I whispered, almost embarrassed but certain: "I love you." I gave a thumbs-up to the woman looking back at me, now rejuvenated and ready to tackle life.

I strolled into my bedroom towards the chair I'd purposely knocked over earlier.

As I rounded the corner of my bed, I rammed my left knee into the edge of the wooden bedframe. "Ouch!" I shouted, hopping frenetically on my right foot. My yelps and laughter combined in raucous discord. "Ouch! Ooh. God that hurts. Silly klutz!"

In many ways, my housing situation was ideal. Stephen and I were like a married couple: living together, sleeping separately, without a smidgen of sexual tension or romance. Even better, we got along fine. Plus Stephen did his own laundry. He also possessed the one trait I'd desperately needed in a man: computer skills.

I knew if I tried to reboot once more, I'd only aggravate myself all over again. So I approached Stephen for a favor. "When you get a chance, Stephen, do you mind looking at my computer? It's totally frozen. It's not doing anything."

"Sure. Do you have time now, Robyn? I can go look at it."

"Yeah. That'd be great."

He followed me into my bedroom and sat at my desktop. I kept a careful distance and pet Mojo, who laid beside me on my bed.

Stephen ran some computer tests—I think—and said something about the modem. He suggested saving all my files on an external drive or something like that. In fact, he said he had an extra one I could use.

Stephen connected it for me and backed-up my files. That took a while. He worked patiently. Justin was never so helpful with anything technical or really, anything at all.

As files were loading, I asked Stephen, "So, is it basically dying or dead?"

"Um, yeah. I'm afraid so. You really need a new C.P.U."

"What's that?" I giggled, embarrassed that I had no clue what he was talking about.

Stephen grinned. "The C.P.U., computer processing unit. This tower." He pointed at the big black structure, the one that murmured and occasionally flashed beams of light, under my desk.

"Oh, duh." I chuckled. "Yeah, it's pretty old. Crap. I have a lot of writing to do. I can't really function without it working."

"Well, just let me know if you want my help buying a new one. I can go shopping with you."

"That'd be great, Stephen. I don't know what to look for."

A few days later, Stephen drove me to Office Depot, where he helped me pick out a new C.P.U. He asked the young salesman all sorts of questions in tech-lingo, like about memory and gigabytes, I think. As he was doing this, I felt lucky. I'd never had a male friend extend himself that way. When we return home, Stephen took the time to connect it all and assured that I was good to go again.

June of 2011 rolled around, my 45th birthday loomed, and I still faced unemployment. "I just got an idea," Angela said, when we spoke by phone. "Josiah loves you, and he loves to celebrate birthdays. Why don't you come down here for your birthday?"

I couldn't resist the invite, so I didn't.

It was wonderful birthday; I felt very much loved, especially by Josiah. "Auntie Robyn!" he shouted, lunging at me and knocking me off-center every chance he got. Josiah sat in his car-seat in the back of Jonathan's Toyota. I sat next to him and took his hand. With Angela in the passenger seat, Jonathan drove the four of us to parks, Joe's Crab Shack, Redondo Beach, and Josiah's T-ball games.

During one of these commutes, Josiah and I discussed my hometown.

"You live in Paradise, Auntie Robyn?" he asked. Josiah didn't want an answer so much as he wanted to display his smarts.

"Yes, honey. Well, I live in Chico. It's very close to Paradise."

"No," he shook his head. "You live in Paradise. Paradise is far. Is it more than 40 miles?"

"Yeah, sweetie. It's even more than 40 miles."

"Forty miles is far," Josiah asserted, and then, "One-finity is bigger than 40."

I chortled. "You're right, babe. One-finity is very, very big."

Josiah nodded, proud of his intellect. "Auntie Robyn, how old are you?"

"I'm turning 45."

"Forty-five?" He raised his eyebrows. "That's a lot!"

Damn straight. "Yeah, it's kind of a lot, sweetie. But it's not as much as one-finity."

Josiah nodded in agreement. "Auntie Robyn," he said slowly. "Auntie…Robyn." Josiah considered my name. "Robyn is your second name."

I laughed and kissed his cheek. "You're right, sweetheart. Auntie comes first."

Josiah beamed and giggled lovingly. Angela turned around from the passenger's seat, imparting a warm smile.

It had been such a love-filled trip that I arrived home to a contrasting emptiness. The house was quiet; I was alone.

Mojo didn't even greet me; he must've been down the street.

Sadness settled in with each garment I unpacked. I folded a pair of jeans, and lacked the inertia to put them in my dresser.

Instead, I decided to call my close girlfriends. I hadn't told them about my job loss. Now was a good time to glean their support.

"It's hard to talk about, because I'm still embarrassed and feel kind of foolish," I said to Shira. "But I lost my writing job."

I heard her gasp. "Are you coming back to the Bay Area?"

"No. Definitely not. I'm going to make it work here."

She listened empathically and said "Keep your chin up, honey. I know how hard it is. Looking for a job is like looking for a man and there's major anxiety about money and all. It totally sucks."

"It really does." I responded, a bit lifted by her empathy.

"But you'll land on your feet," she added. "You always do."

"Thanks. What's going on with you, Shira? It's been a while."

Shira went on to tell me how well things were going with Ian. "I finally met my match, Robyn," she said, "and it only took fifty years!"

"You inspire me, Shira."

Next, I reconnected with Kathryn.

"Holy shit, Robyn," she said. "Emma sounds like a nutcase. So many of the writers I know, besides you of course, are weirdoes."

"Yeah, true. I just didn't realize it. But I'm screwed," I added. "And I'm really taking this hard, Kathryn, like I'm the one who's messed up."

"Girl, I read your blog and all the stuff you do on-line. You're amazing. She just wanted an excuse to get rid of you."

"You're right." Kathryn always said what I both knew to be true, and needed to hear.

I started feeling better. "Oh, I didn't tell you about what I saw when I went to use the bathroom. It was really disturbing, Kat."

We got a hearty chuckle out of my description of George, the big pink grapefruit. "I've never seen anything like it, and I hope I never do again."

Ever the most grounded of my friends, Susan conveyed thoughtful doses of reality.

Talk about my job-loss furled into my loneliness and seemingly perennial bad luck with men. And then my stupidity over changing my life for Emma, because she seemed like a warm, no-nonsense expert.

Susan interrupted my rant. "Stop it, Rob. Come on. You're smart and strong and you just don't have faith in yourself. Maybe you need to quit chasing the so-called fairytale. You have so much going for you. Maybe you're as close as a person could be to having it all, already."

I never considered that. "Hmm, I don't know."

She chuckled half-heartedly. "Look, Mike is wonderful. I couldn't be luckier. And we're so proud of our children, but it's no fairytale."

351

I smirked, lightheartedly.

"Here's how the happily ever after really goes, Rob. Are you ready?" she asked.

"Sure," I replied.

"So like you and Justin, you first get overwhelmed being married, but it's really happy sometimes. Still, Rob, you don't have time for anything when you have kids. You have to worry about drugs and health and school and their friends and their heartbreaks and money and food and I could go on and on and on. Really, I'm envious of your freedoms. You have time to breathe, Rob. You can even write a book. And believe me it's going to be a more interesting book than one I'd write, if I ever had the time to write one, which I won't." She giggled.

"Yeah, the grass is always greener, Susan. I just still want what you have with Mike."

"I know, and you can still find it. But that's not always easy either. It takes a lot of work."

"I'm sure it does, Susan. I poured so much into Justin and our marriage…And look how things ended!"

She sighed. "I know," Susan softened, "but he wasn't the right one. You fell in love and gave it your all, and there's nothing wrong with that. It's just unfortunate that he was so troubled. But enjoy your freedom while you have it. You'll miss it when you do meet the right one."

I paused. "Susan, thing is, I also want to be okay with myself and my life if I don't ever fall in love like that again."

"So be okay with it, Rob. Choose to be. You deserve to be!"

"Yeah, I guess it's as hard and as easy as that."

"I mean," Susan added, "you can still have hope for it again. I'm sure you'll find it. In the meantime, enjoy your life. Do all the things I can't do because I'm married with children." She laughed. "Have fun for both of us."

"I'll work on it. Thank you, Susan. You know me too well. I guess I just needed a pep talk, and I knew you'd be good for it."

"Anytime, Rob. You're like family."

After that conversation, I sat on my comfy beige sofa and slowly scanned my living room: small-framed photos of Josiah atop my bookshelves propped up a handful of birthday cards from my Chico friends.

My eyes caught the shimmery gold-framed wedding photo of a glowing new bride with her new love, Josiah, on the first day we met. At three months old, he slept through the ceremony. Smart kid—a child prodigy.

Rows of books lined the middle shelves, a number of which were written by my blog friends.

On the bottom shelves resided hefty photo albums spotlighting my travels, family, and friends.

Yearbooks from Orville Wright Junior High and Westchester High School occupied the bottom shelves, several of which I helped design and one of which included my poetry.

Mojo burst through the cat door and zipped towards me. He jumped up to the back edge of the sofa and planted himself firmly for a nap. I threw my arm up above my head to pet him, silently thanking him for being there.

Contentment defined the moment.

In late July of 2011, I met Shantel, supervisor at a local social services agency. I'd been checking their website frequently for job openings, and they finally had one.

Shantel glanced at my resume, when I sat in her office for an interview. "Wow, you've got a ton of great experience."

"Yeah, please don't hold it against me," I replied, smiling but not joking.

"No, it's awesome." She reviewed my resume, skipped a few questions because she thought they might strike me as patronizing, and asked a few questions that I answered with ease. Shantel then asked about my availability.

She called the next morning to offer me the job. "Yes, I'm excited. Thank you!" I told her.

"No, thank YOU. We're lucky to have you."

I drove Lily, a client, to the Chico Transit Center, where she'd catch the bus bound for her job at the Work Training Center. I pulled into a space in the parking lot at Salem and Second Street, and we noticed that her bus had yet to arrive.

Lily nonchalantly took the black pen that rested in my cup-holder and started writing on her left hand. I watched as she meticulously formed each letter. "I luv…" I expected the next word to be Kyle, her beau of the week. Instead, she inscribed an "m", and then a "y." Maybe she'll write "my boyfriend," I thought. Yet she wrote, "myself."

She then enclosed the statement, "I love myself," in a big heart and dropped the pen back into the cup-holder.

"Awesome, Lily!" I cheered. "That's who you should love most. Not enough people love themselves."

Lily glowed and responded, "Well then they're hella stupid!"

"I agree. It's stupid not to love yourself. It can get people into a lot of trouble too. YOU come first."

"I know." She looked up towards Second Street. "There's my bus. See ya!"

I wished Lily a good day.

As I drove off, I thought about the fact that those labeled "oppositional," "disabled," "intellectually challenged" or what have you, are often quicker to learn the lessons that take the rest of us years or a lifetime to learn.

The light turned green, and I realized I'd driven too far. Switch to date mode, I told myself. Meet Luis at Starbucks.

Luis and I had connected through the on-line personals. (Old habits die hard.) We'd had a nice phone conversation. This father of young children had been the victim of marital infidelity. He seemed a nice man who described himself as a "true gentleman."

I pulled into a parking space on Broadway, dug up a few quarters for the meter, and walked in to see his friendly face at a front table at Starbucks. Luis appeared dark and attractive, like his photo.

Conversation flowed easily. He talked about his children; and his obsession with good books, including Anne Lamott's. I'd never met a guy who professed an affinity for her writing. Lamott's work eloquently combines the two main traits I strive for: sass and inspiration. This man scored bonus points for mentioning her.

"She's awesome," I said. "Anne Lamott is my writing role model." He too was excited that we shared a fondness for the same author.

As we sipped Frappuccinos, I told Luis about my newness to Chico, writing ambitions, and former marriage. We covered a lot of terrain, comfortably and easily.

Luis ended the date with an affectionate hug and asked if I'd like to go to dinner next time.

Happily surprised about such a good first date, I readily agreed.

In fact, I entertained thoughts of motherhood as a renewed possibility.

"I would like to have you over for dinner," he told me by phone the next day. Sounds romantic, I thought. "Only thing is," he continued. "The kids will be with us."

My eyebrows shot up. "The kids will be there?" I asked.

"Yeah. You like kids, right? I'm sure they'll like you."

"I do like kids, Luis. But I think it's way too early to meet yours."

"I don't see what the problem is," he countered. "I have women guests over all the time. The kids don't mind. I'll make a nice spaghetti dinner. We can have wine, but they won't have any." He chuckled, thinking himself a cleverly refined parent.

"I don't think that's appropriate, Luis." I proceeded to educate him on positive role modeling, the dangers of alcohol consumption, and basic common sense.

"My kids are the most important part of my life. If you can't accept that then we can't date, I guess."

"Luis, that's not what I'm saying. Your kids should be your first priority. But I don't want to date a family. I want to date a man." I thought to add: for example, one with testosterone. "You've said you're financially stable. If you want to date you could, say, hire a babysitter. But I'm not going to argue. I'll just wish you luck."

"You too, Robyn." He sounded dejected and confused. "Bye."

"Goodbye." I closed my phone, wondering—as usual when it comes to dating—why do I bother?

It seemed I was on a roll (a non-sexual one) with single dads. And dating them would provide vast opportunities for friendship with benefits. Minus the friendship. And the benefits.

Note: I don't mean to offend all single dads, just the ones I've dated. Yet I don't blame them either. They didn't sign on for any of this. They're clueless about romance. These guys' hormones are buried under a life of McDonald's value meals, soccer practice, and trips to the emergency room.

Chris proved my point. Apparently, Chris and I were the only two well-educated democrats within a 200 mile radius. We met on-line. A father of three, he and I enjoyed two pleasant dates: dinner at La Hacienda and a short hike in Bidwell Park.

Both dates were platonic and devoid of sexual undertones, yet he continued to text and call me. Our conversations were friendly. Clearly, though, things weren't leading anywhere.

"Can I call you back? I'm putting the kids to bed. I'll call back in 75 minutes." Those were Chris' last words to me one evening. *Seventy-five minutes.*

As I write this, eighteen months later, Chris still hasn't called. I suppose it's understandable; nobody's more stubborn than a child who refuses to go to sleep, much less three of them.

Bobby and I exchanged fun emails and made tentatively tentative plans for a possible first date. We'd meet at Tea Fusion on Monday evening. "I think I can definitely do that," he kind of confirmed.

"The confluence of events has occurred," Bobby emailed Monday morning. "My dog got sprayed by a skunk, Tammy has soccer practice that I forgot about, family is coming to town Friday and blah blah blah (with no apology…) This is the life of a single parent. Sigh."

Overwhelmed by confluence, Bobby ultimately suggested I date someone "not as busy." I decided to look up "confluence" and avoid anyone who uses the word.

I also realized I need to stop attempting to date dads with young kids.

Then someone entered the scene with full-grown offspring who'd flown the coop. This scenario could work, I thought.

Mr. Salsa was that someone. We met on the dance floor at Studio One. He immediately took it upon himself to teach me how to improve my Latin dance savvy.

This man appeared to comprise the idyllic mix that baited my desires—shortness; youth; and smooth, sultry confidence with every gesture.

After over an hour of dancing with him to salsa, merengue, and cha cha music, I told Mr. Salsa, "I'm beat. I can't keep up with you." Oops. I hadn't meant to open the door for sex talk.

"You'll improve," Mr. Salsa shot back. Not very nice, I thought, but at least he didn't run with the sexual innuendo. Naïve man. Hot dancer.

"Will I see you next week? I hope," he reached out for a hug.

As we hugged, Mr. Salsa kissed my cheek. Nice. "Sure, I'll be back." I flashed a smile.

It wasn't difficult to fantasize about Mr. Salsa. Someone so suave on the dance floor had to be good in bed.

Then again, I envisioned him correcting my every sexual movement: "Don't look down! Chest out! Your rhythm's off! Stop. Watch me...Kick, ball, change. Kick, ball, change. Kick, ball, change." Yuck.

As our attraction grew, Mr. Salsa's lingo left me in a primal state of bewildered arousal.

One week at the studio, he wrapped an arm around my waist and proudly introduced me to his friend, Ruben.

"This is Robyn. She's going to be my new wife."

In your dreams. "I think not, but where's the ring?"

"We'll go to McDonald's, for onion rings." He humored himself, and only himself, with his (lack of) wit.

As dancing wrapped up, I agreed to join Mr. Salsa for a bite to eat. Arsenio's was closed at that hour, but the drive-through was still open. So we picked up tacos.

"We can eat here," he said, "or we can eat at my place. It won't be comfortable in my car."

That was likely his plan in the first place. I did want to eat comfortably, not in a car, so I agreed.

After finishing some carne asada in his dining room, Mr. Salsa walked me into his garage to show-off a few things.

First, he introduced me to his cockatiel, then an Amazon parrot, and, finally, an Asian love bird.

"How you doing? How you doing?" The birds kept repeating, as he kissed their beaks. I felt at once intrigued and nauseous. I stared and chatted a little with the birds, giving one of them a light touch on the head.

"Lemme show you something else."

He then strolled over to some sort of fitness swing trapeze apparatus. "Watch this," he boasted. Mr. Salsa plopped onto the swing, and then abruptly whirled upside down into a backbend.

I had no words.

The man popped back up and hopped off, moving over to an immense black vat in the corner of the garage.

"Do you like hot wax?" he inquired.

The night grew weirder by the second. "Say what?"

"Hot wax. Watch."

He dipped his left hand into the barrel, apparently full of hot wax. "It's good for cuts. See…" He pulled his then zombie-like hand up and proceeded to strip a layer of hot wax off his fingers, one by one.

The door opened behind us and his roommate, clearly half-asleep, stuck his head in. We both gave him a casual "hello," and I took the cue.

"I'm sure it's good stuff," I said quietly. "I should get going now."

To his credit, Mr. Salsa did not dip any part of me into hot wax nor did he pull me onto his trapeze. To my credit, I didn't touch his cockatiel. Well, I had grazed its head, to which Mr. Salsa didn't react. He casually walked me to my car.

Following a hug and a kiss on the cheek, I drove home, stupefied and intrigued.

A few evenings later, Mr. Salsa sent an email invitation to join him at his place for a "stake" dinner. "I have the house to myself," he added.

I turned to Mojo, eyeing me from atop my bed pillows. "The man probably plans to burn me at the stake with hot wax and nobody would witness this but his exotic birds, Mojo. What good are they except to ask 'How you doing?' like a fowl Joey Tribiana?"

Coincidentally, when he inquired, I was about to write a blog post about Mr. Salsa.

"Thanks, but I'm wrapped up in something," I wrote. "How about another bite after dancing this weekend instead?"

We caught each other's eyes the moment I entered the studio.

Mr. Salsa and I danced a lot that night. Our dancing was hot and free flowing. His verbiage, limited. In other words, I got worked up.

As I reclined for a break, he approached. I looked at his deep gray-hazel eyes, and my hormones raced.

"Hey, shorty!" he exclaimed.

"Excuse me! What did you call me?" I couldn't believe it.

Mr. Salsa pulled a chair alongside me.

He extended his arms in my direction, turning his hands palms-up to welcome mine. I placed my hands in his anticipating a sweet, endearing apology.

"I don't mean anything by it. My mother's your height. You remind me of her."

How romantic. I let go of his hands then looked at him, speechless. But our eyes met with twisted passion. Damnit!

I don't think I'd ever wished so hard that my hormones had a brain cell.

Mr. Salsa put his hand on my shoulder. "So, are you hungry?"

"Not really. I could always eat, though. What are you up for?"

"I just want to unwind. Care to join me?" he asked.

I envisioned wine, massage maybe, romance…"Sure."

We walked down the chilly, semi-lit street to his car.

"I'll follow you in my car," I told him.

"Okay. Or you can come with me."

"Um, well, that's okay." I tried not to insult. "This will be easier for us." I might need a quick escape.

I pulled into his driveway. It was dark out, no stars to be seen, and Mr. Salsa awaited my arrival by the front door.

He escorted me in, took my jacket off and hung it on a coat rack by the door.

Behind him, a few bottles of unopened wine stood on the kitchen counter.

"Have a seat," he gestured towards a plush, black sofa that faced a dark wooden coffee table and big screen TV.

"Okay." I walked over and sat at the end of the sofa, wondering if he was going to offer food or a drink. He didn't. Instead, he sat next to me and took the remote.

"Wanna watch TV?"

"Sure," I responded, our legs touching and his hand on my thigh. He turned on the TV, but neither of us noticed what show came on. Mr. Salsa readjusted the sofa pillows, placing two of them against the arm of the couch. He slipped off his shoes and shifted onto his side, his back against the sofa back.

"Let's just relax," he said softly, pulling me down in front of him. I kicked off my shoes.

Mr. Salsa held me, but it was a weird hold. I couldn't feel his arms against any part of my body, but I saw his hands locked just below my chest. It felt verging on romantic, as though he had the right intentions but a clumsy execution.

"I don't like it when you call me 'Shorty'," I asserted, as if to say, "Get your shit together if you want any action tonight."

"You remind me of my mother, I told you." He reiterated, apologetically.

"I know, but a woman doesn't want to hear that she reminds a man of his mother."

Mr. Salsa paused, uncertain. "What do women want to hear?"

"I don't know, maybe that we're beautiful or sexy" or anything excepting reference to the woman from whose uterus you originated.

"You are very sexy," Mr. Salsa responded. "You make me think crazy thoughts."

With those few words, he righted all the wrongs. I turned to him, and we kissed passionately. His hands crept up my back. His fingers unlatched my bra, as he kissed my neck.

Mr. Salsa paused, sat and then stood up.

He held a hand out towards me. "Come with me," he whispered.

I took his hand and found myself in his bedroom. "No sex. It's too soon," I said.

"Okay."

Then in one swift and definitive motion, he pulled my pants and underwear down and off of my body.

Ignited by an intensity between us, I wasn't upset and hadn't resisted. He lifted me onto his bed. We continued kissing, hormones erratically surging but slowing to a pause. Mr. Salsa wasn't touching me, I realized. He was undressing himself and then, I don't know, maybe playing with himself. Truthfully, I couldn't tell what was going on. I recall only that his hands weren't on me at all until he tried to pleasure me. And that was odd. I lost any semblance of desire.

Mr. Salsa rubbed my pelvis with his palm, in circular motion, and then an up-and-down pumping manner, as if he was kneading dough. It felt, well, strange but kind of good I guess. With all the activity, he couldn't help but hit a key spot briefly.

We rolled around a bit, then onto our sides. Mr. Salsa was behind me, in a spooning position.

"Ouch!" Something fairly sharp hit my left calf. I didn't know what it was. It seemed it couldn't have been his penis; that was closer to my back than my calf, and it wasn't that long. It also didn't feel like a limb or a finger. I was confused.

He seemed oblivious.

"Do you want to do me now?" he asked. "You know, tit for tat?"

Are you kidding me? Did you really say *tit* for tat? I looked at him, a childlike expression across his face.

"No. Not tonight…I think you can take care of yourself." I gave him a quick kiss, and slowly moved my feet off the bed to collect my clothes. "I'm going to get going now."

The next day, Mr. Salsa sent an email message: "Hey girl how are you?"

I'm not sure what baffled me more, his grammar or cheer. Either way, I responded that I was fine but didn't want to take things further.

"It didn't feel right," I wrote, with apologies.

In turn, he said he understood and he would be friendly with me whenever we saw each other. I assured the same.

Alas, our connection had begun to feel more normal. Then Mr. Salsa emailed:

CALL ME! I CANT GET A HOLE OF YOU!

This email, a few weeks after that night of our date, erupted with urgency. So I called him immediately.

"Hi, it's Robyn."

"Oh hey girl, yeah, my emails to you keep coming back." But I just got your email message. In fact, that's why I'm calling. "And you're not on my Facebook page." Yeah I prefer you don't have easy access to all the writing I'm doing about you, Mr. Salsa.

"Well, I don't like to spend much time on Facebook," I lied.

"Okay. So what are you doing right now?" he asked.

"Not much, some writing projects. It's a lazy day. I'm still in my pajamas. What about you?"

"I just drove my roommate to the Sacramento Airport." He has the place to himself. "So do you want to come over for pizza? You can come in your pajamas." He giggled.

Admittedly, I was tempted by "pizza." He'd been gentlemanly, and I hadn't had "pizza" in a very long time. I craved it badly. I mean, feed me the basic spread topped with sausage, and I'd be fulfilled.

Unconvinced of his "pizza" delivery skills, though, I came to my senses. "Thanks, but I'm going to stay in. Maybe another time."

"Okay. Can I put your number in my phone?"

"Sure, I have yours now too."

We ended the call.

Crap! Did I just blow my only opportunity for "pizza" in this town?

I went dancing a few days later. As I scoped out prospective partners, I watched Mr. Salsa cross the floor in my direction several times. Instead of approaching me, he went for the svelte blonde and brunette 20-somethingers —perhaps, in hopes of sharing some "pizza" later.

I wasn't very nice to him, and he's a decent guy, so I hope he found someone to share a pizza with.

By now, with 2012 coming into view, I was dabbling in various on-line dating sites. In spite of myself, I'd become fairly addicted to the process.

I explained my internet dating habits by telling myself, and my blog readers, that I needed the writing material. It's true, though I was still lonely and hadn't given up on my hopes of finding love again. This was the real reason.

The next man would leave a lasting impression. I call this story: Mr. Ribald's Epistle.

It started when Mr. Ribald "favorited" me. In the world of internet dating, this is high flattery.

His profile boasted a "ribald" and "trenchant" humor. Note: Upon doing the research, I learned that both words are synonymous with "obscene."

He's intelligent, I thought, and that's refreshing. I thus sent a brief, friendly message to introduce myself.

Mr. Ribald responded: "What an unalloyed pleasure to receive your epistle." Epistle? I didn't know I had one of those. Note: Epistle means letter.

I agreed to a phone chat. Epistle to self: Mistake number one.

Telephone discourse was a tad irritating, as I didn't understand many of the words he flaunted. Yet I thought it might be nice to have a walking Roget by my side. Plus I had a hard time saying "no," except when it really matters. I thus agreed to what he enthusiastically termed a "meet and greet."

We met at Tea Fusion, and Mr. Ribald paid for my Chocolate Chai Tea Frost. He also struck me as fairly nice looking and outgoing.

Mr. Ribald jumped at attempts to impress me, though, with a string of non-humorous, offensive, crude, canned jokes.

I sat in bored irritation watching his lips move, sipping my frost, as he delivered punch-line after punchline with the word "balls."

"That's not funny," I responded. You ribald idiot, I thought.

Mr. Ribald tried again, spewing jokes about peacocks and other creatures that walk into a bar.

"Nope, not funny."… "Not funny either…" "I'm still not laughing."

"Well you tell me a joke," he insisted, befuddled.

"I don't do one-liners. It's not my kind of humor."

Exasperated, Mr. Ribald declared, "I think you don't have a sense of humor, so this isn't going to work. I wouldn't have anything to say on our second date...I feel judged."

In Shakespearean manner, Mr. Ribald abruptly and dramatically stood up and began walking out.

As the people at the next table subtly eyed me with looks of compassion, I casually took time to consume the last of my drink, found a napkin on the floor that needed discarding, and began strolling out behind him.

Mr. Ribald stopped and turned around to apologize. "It was entirely my fault," he admitted.

"Okay?" I said, casually, primed by a combination of annoyance, bewilderment, and the singular goal of finding a trashcan in which to toss my cup.

We shook hands and wished each other well.

I'm left wondering if Mr. Ribald's large, trenchant vocabulary serves as compensation for a small epistle.

Thankfully, I'll never know.

I got home that night and madly deleted my dating profile from three dating sites, outraged that I'd essentially been "stood up" *during* a date by a man who claimed I have no sense of humor because I didn't respond to his crude so-called jokes.

It felt wonderfully freeing to rid myself of internet dating, at least for the time being. As I shut down my computer, I realized I'd likely step back into the world of cyber-dating down the road. If and when I did, though, I'd return refreshed and rebooted.

Because there is no Prince Charming.

There is no fairytale.

And I was alas okay with that.

Chapter Eighteen: To Life!

As I was saying, when describing Mom's necklace that I'd just received from my sister Dawn, we Jews pronounce the *ch* with all the phlegm possible, like we're embarking upon a deathly asthma attack: *chkchckcgoskgogghhhh*!

Then we dance for hours because we're celebrating life and all things good.

It's the same spirit in which we elate when the groom smashes the glass to embark upon married life with his new bride.

While the secular "chai," on the other hand, tastes good, it lacks the spunk of the Hebrew "chai,[24]" or "L'Chaim!": to life!

I tighten my grip on the necklace, still gazing blindly at the houses across the street. And then, I watch my last moments with Mom. There I am, a strong yet fragile girl with golden brown wavy hair. I knelt aside Mom's hospital bed that dominated the den. Our hands interlocked. In that speck of time, I experienced all of the loving force Mom's skeletal frame could command.

I zone in on our interwoven fingers, connected like never before, with steadfast determination. So fierce, the hold could surpass time. And it would.

I know that I let go and left the den, but I can't envision it, nor do I want to. That part of the scene has never replayed itself.

"We never let go," I whisper, as I open my car door.

I lower the driver's seat mirror to see Mom's necklace on me. I push the heart lightly towards the center of my neckline.

Perfect.

My phone rings before I start the car. I scrounge through my purse, which I'd dropped on the passenger's seat, and flip my phone open. "Hello?"

"Hi…Is this Robyn?" I don't recognize the woman's voice.

"Yes, this is Robyn. Who's this?"

"Oh Robyn, it's Colleen. I'm glad you're there. I heard you moved. Paradise, is it?"

Who's Colleen? …Oh yeah, Justin's friend. Sweet lady, sang at our wedding.

"Yeah, good to hear from you." I'm nervous. What happened to Justin? Is he still alive? "I moved to Chico, close to Paradise, gosh, over a year and a half ago."

I guffaw. "I guess I've been too lazy to change our number. I just dropped Justin from my phone plan. Is everything okay, Colleen?"

"Well, for the most part. Don't worry or anything. I just want to give you fair warning."

My muscles stiffen. "Warning about Justin? What's going on?" I added, "I'd heard from friends over the years that he was a mess. I did everything I could for him. You know?"

"I know, Robyn. You really did. He's stubborn as hell. It hasn't been easy staying friends with him."

"You've really been there for him too, Colleen." I pause, relieved that she referenced Justin in present tense, but still anxious. "What's going on?"

"Justin called me over to the apartment in Oakland to give me a few things: a couple of photos of us from law school days and a DVD of To Kill a Mockingbird."

"His favorite movie," I say, flooded by emotion. The potency of her words twists into fear.

"Do you think this is it? Do you think he's going to take his life, Colleen?"

"I don't think so, Robyn." I relax a bit. "I definitely worried about that when he ended your marriage, and for a while afterward."

"Me too, Colleen. It's been almost four years since then, so I guess I stopped worrying. I mean, I still do, of course. But I don't want to. I just want to get on with my life."

"Keep positive, Robyn. I wanted you to know that Justin might actually be moving to Paradise."

What the hell? "WHAT?" My heart rate speeds again. Damn bastard has to ruin things for me, just when I'd begun sealing that chapter.

"Well, he said he got evicted and lost his phone service. So I asked him how I could get ahold of him in the future. Justin reluctantly gave me his friend Ruthie's number. He said she'd offered him a place to live in Paradise, in her trailer or something."

I fume with fury. "I don't know what to make of all this." Shit. Hadn't he ruined my life enough? I don't want to run into him around here, I thought.

"Ruthie? His ex-girlfriend?" The one with no emotion. (Note: I purposely left the "s" off of this word.)? I'd spoken to her briefly after the big fires in 2008, right before he ended our marriage. I guess they stayed connected. Romantically? Ugh. I didn't even want to consider it.

"Yes," Colleen sighed. "It seems Ruthie and I are the only friends he has left. I was going to offer him my couch, but I guess she's got extra space up there."

I touch my necklace and slowly run my finger along the heart. I press my index finger onto the "chai". To life.

You'll be alright, I tell myself. Everything's going to be alright.

A bit calmer now, I say, "I really appreciate you telling me, Colleen. I can't help but resent the hell out of him for it, though. But I should just let it go." Slow breaths. Slow breaths.

"I know, Robyn. Just live your life. You can't do anything about Justin. You have your completely separate life now. No point in worrying about him anymore."

"That's true…Well, thanks again for calling. I hope we stay in touch, Colleen."

"We will, Robyn. Take care of yourself."

"You too. Bye, Colleen."

"Bye, Robyn. Take care."

"You too."

I sit still in my car for a few moments, remembering how much Justin and I loved each other—envisioning us on the rocks of Bodega Bay, in line for the Peter Pan ride at Disneyland, exchanging vows under the chuppah. We had so much in our favor.

Then he turned into someone so coldhearted, so bitter and troubled, I couldn't help him anymore. Actually, I never could. He never wanted help. That would've involved admitting to his problems, and Justin never would.

I had to save myself then, and I have to save myself now. I'm doing it.

"Stay on track," I say, looking in the rearview mirror. "Let go of Justin. Hold onto you."

We dart for Tea Fusion's only vacant outside table. Brandi places her iced ginger peach tea aside my chocolate chai frost and declares, "It's about time we caught up!"

"Yeah. It's been a year in a day, Brandi." I engulf my lips around a bright green straw and begin slurping. Ah, a cool, soft, heavenly blend of chocolate chai lingers blissfully on my tongue. "It's great to be here."

"Yes it is. How's it going, Robyn?"

"I'm good," I nod. "I'm on a new track, and I realize more and more how much I feel at home here. You know?" She smiles, happy for me, as she stirs her drink with a spoon. "But I write about celebrating celibacy and embracing singledom and all that crap. I'm really not completely happy being single. You seem perfectly fine with it. As you should be. I just wish I was."

"Haha!" Brandi cackles. "It's because I've had so many years of experience."

"Well, me too, but I can't let go of the hope of meeting someone, Brandi. Then there's the hormone factor."

"It's the hysterectomy I had about ten years ago, Robyn. No hormones, no urges. I'm good alone."

I break from slurpage. "I'm a little envious. Not of surgery. Sounds horrid. But it would be nice to be good alone without having this itch."

I lean back into the silver metal framed patio chair, the sun's rays freely striking my face. "I mean, Mr. Salsa asked me over for"—I place both sets of index and middle fingers in the air and curl them over as I say—"'pizza'. He made it a point of telling me that he had the place to himself. So he wanted to share his sausage…pizza." We chuckle. "Thing is, Brandi, I was tempted. Damn hormones! If they only had a brain!" We chuckle again. "Maybe it's this summer weather all year long in Chico, but I want *pizza*, really good *pizza*, like now…or at least before I die."

Brandi nods in an "I get it" manner and clasps her glass. Orange-pink liquid surges up her straw, halts mid-stream, and shoots back down. "Hold on! Why didn't I think of this earlier, Robyn? I have a guy co-worker, Jeff, who wants your basic friends with benefits situation. He's nice and normal too, wouldn't give you anything to write about."

"Pizza with no string…cheese? Sign me up." I'm excited and abruptly gulp down the rest of my frost.

"Alright, I'll check in with him soon."

"Thanks, Brandi. I appreciate it."

She looks at her watch. "No problem."

I glance at mine. "I guess we should both get going. How about Round Table next time?" I suggest.

"Sure, Robyn," Brandi smirks. "Pizza, pizza," she teases.

We push back our chairs and hug "goodbye."

As I swing my right arm back, I accidentally knock my glass onto the pavement. It's a sturdy, thick one that remains intact. Nonetheless, everyone around us is staring at me right now. Oh, well.

I pick up the glass and place it back on the table.

I look at Brandi, then at the multiple sets of eyes still scrutinizing me.

I shout, "L'chaim, people!"

Closing Epistle

Dear Reader,

You probably wanted the traditional fairytale ending, or maybe just a dose of good sex. Yeah, me too. But that wouldn't mesh right with erectile dysfunction; hints of necrophilia; a 13-month divorce capping a 13-month marriage and related triskaidekaphobia; a trapeze swinging, hot waxing, cockatiel boasting salsero; or Mr. Ribald's epistle. Thus I can't in good conscience end this book with sap or even soft-core B.D.S.M.[25] Sorry.

I am on the verge, though. I feel it. I'm on the verge of publishing the story of my life; the verge of believing to the depth of my being that I'm worthy. Although I don't have children or a spouse, my life adds importance to this world. It's significant, because I am. I'm on the verge of claiming my own form of "sometimes happily," with full acceptance of the fact that the fairytale is only a fairytale.

Like me, all of the men in this story were simply fumbling through in search of that "something"—be it orgasm, marriage, solace, a friend, an escape—something to provide a "happily."

But it's not about landing at a destination. It's about looking towards one, while savoring each gesture along the path. Like exhilarating foreplay that might or might not lead to orgasm; or the tantalizing first bite of bubbling hot fudge smothered over a creamy, mushy banana split sundae, whether or not you proceed to eat the whole thing (and if you don't, I will.). Or sinking into a potentially life-altering moment of profound enlightenment, wherever it may lead. It's about belief in greater things, whether or not they come to pass in your lifetime.

Ultimately, it's a space built upon one ingredient: self-love. This is where hope is at its most real and life, its most generous. Wherein faith conquers an infinite expanse of unknowns. In this glorious intersect of space, time, and energy, resides the verge.

And on the other side: Paradise.

Thank you for traveling along with me.

Love,

Robyn

Dear Life by Chocolate Readers, I hope my story was worthy of your following. Keep a smile.

Dear Girlfriends, especially Joanne, Judy, Sienne, Felicia, Shari, Betsy, and Lara,
You lifted me through the dark and danced with me in the light. I love you.

Dear Bryan, Elsie, Alex, and Elizabeth,
Your friendships, encouragement, wisdom, and belief in Woman on the Verge propelled me across the finish-line. I'm deeply grateful.

Dear Self: You kept fretting, "I don't know how to write a book," but you did it anyway. And you did good!

Dear Mom, Thank you for being my calm. Our love is eternal.

For fun, Alternative book titles:
1) Dates and Nuts, or Nuts and Dates (original title)
2) Celibacy and Suburbia
3) Dude, Really?
4) Why I Keep Duracell in Business
5) Robyn Engel: A West Coast Carrie Bradshaw Minus the Sex, Glam, Glitz, and 5,000 Square Foot Closet
6) Fifty Shades of Erectile Dysfunction
7) One Hundred and One Shades of Anti-Erotica
8) From Birds to Prince Charming: Did Cinderella Really Get An Upgrade?
9) Prince Charming: Richie Rich With A Foot Fetish or A Woman's Dream?
10) The Oys of Sex
11) Chico and the Woman
12) Auntie Robyn's Anti-Fairytale
13) Thirteen

Endnotes

---

[1] Chai means life and is a very special word in Judaism, akin to a blessing for and celebration of all things good in the world. The *ch* in chai is pronounced with the maximum amount of guttural phlegm a person can muster. A Jewish bubbeh (grandma) does this best.
[2] ORT = Lengthy title incorporating Russian words. This Jewish philanthropic international organization helps impoverished Jews throughout the world with a particular focus on promoting vocational skills.

[3] "Will you go with me?" meant "Will you go out with or go steady with me?" Why "out" or "steady" got dropped, I don't know.

[4] Floods. A 1970's term for pants that were too short, thus deeming the wearer prepared for a flood.

[5] Goy. Term for a non-Jew. "Goyim" is the plural form.

[6] Lo Yisa Goy. This Hebrew song means: Nation shall not lift sword against nation. Neither shall they go to war again.

[7] Mensch. A man of integrity, a gentleman, the one every Jewish mother wants her daughter to marry.

[8] Aliyah. Moving to Israel to establish residency and start a new life in the Jewish homeland. Note that some Bay Area Jews do this once they've exhausted the local dating scene, only to return within two years.

[9] Yenta. Jewish matchmaker.

[10] Beshert. Soulmate, one's destiny.

[11] Gary Coleman. May he rest in peace.

[12] Mogen David. Jewish star; star of David.

[13] Meshugenah. Craziness.

[14] Ketubah. Jewish wedding contract.

[15] Kippah or Yalmulke. Jewish beanie, worn as a sign of respect for God.

[16] Lechi lach. This song by Debbie Friedman references God's message to Abraham "Go forth to a land that I will show you."

[17] Bimah. The stage of the sanctuary. There's an eternal light above, and the Torah lives in the ark on the bimah.

[18] Chuppah. Jewish wedding canopy.

[19] Siman Tov. Traditional song to end the Jewish wedding ceremony. It means "good fortune and good luck."

[20] Latkes. Potato pancakes. They're traditionally eaten during Hanukah but rightfully enjoyed any time of year.

[21] Tuchas. Butt, derriere, tushie, or rear-end. In other words, ass, but I'm trying to be polite.

[22] Seder is Hebrew for order. The Passover Seder includes a service, special meal, and four cups of wine.

[23] The poem Kindred Spirits has been published in Just the Right Time, 2012, Amazon-Createspace.com.

[24] Chai/L'chaim. I didn't number these chapters until I finished writing this book.

Coincidentally, "L'Chaim" is my eighteenth chapter. "Chai" not only means life, it also connotes a meaningful number in Judaism, 18. Eighteen, in turn, represents life and good fortune. I'm thus ending my story with a doubly pronounced message of life, hope and much good fortune to you, dear reader.

[25]BDSM. Ugh. I've had to look this up too. A number of times. It stands for Bondage and Discipline/Dominance, Sadism and Masochism. I regret that this is my final footnote. I really do.

Made in the USA
Columbia, SC
02 June 2017